AF795918

MANAGING DISTRESS

Managing Distress

POSSESSION AND THERAPEUTIC CULTS IN SOUTH ASIA

La prise en charge de l'affliction:
possession et cultes thérapeutiques en Asie du Sud

Edited by

MARINE CARRIN

Published with the assistance of the
Centre National de Recherche Scientifique (CNRS), France
Publié avec le concours du Centre National de Recherche Scientifique

MANOHAR
1999

First published 1999

© Marine Carrin, 1999

All rights reserved. No part of this publication may be reproduced or transmitted, in any form or by any means, without prior permission of the editor and the publisher

ISBN 81-7304-212-0

Published by
Ajay Kumar Jain for
Manohar Publishers & Distributors
2/6 Ansari Road, Daryaganj
New Delhi 110 002

Typeset by
A J Software Publishing Co. Pvt. Ltd.
305 Durga Chambers, 1333 D B Gupta Road
Karol Bagh, New Delhi 110 005

Printed at
Replika Press Pvt. Ltd.
Plot No. A-229, DSIDC Narela Indl. Park
Delhi 110 040

Contents

Illustrations

PLATES

FIGURES

Preface

This volume is based on papers read during a session on 'Therapeutic Cults' at the 13th European Conference of Modern South Asian Studies, Toulouse, France, from 31 August to 3 September 1994. Most of the authors have offered revised versions of their papers for publication; I have also included the contribution of Gisèle Krauskopff, who was unable to attend since she was then doing fieldwork in Nepal.

I want to express my thanks to the CNRS for making this publication possible, to Daniel Fabre, director of our institute at Toulouse, for his constant support, to my husband Harald Tambs-Lyche who assisted editorially and with the English, and finally, the authors for their contributions to what, for me, has been an interesting and worthwhile discussion.

MARINE CARRIN

Inroduction

MARINE CARRIN

How can we describe suffering from the outside? Feelings cannot be observed. The only feelings we have direct experience of are our own. How are we to study relationships that are meaningful, between culture and psyche?

In British social anthropology a distinction is often made between private feelings independent of cultural encoding, and feelings expressed by socially articulated symbols (Leach 1976; Douglas 1970). Myth and ritual have been investigated by Levi-Strauss (1962), Turner (1967), Geertz (1973) and many others but their analyses emphasize, as Scheff (1977:484) puts it, 'cognitive and verbal aspects to the virtual exclusion of emotions'. American cultural anthropology accepted inspiration from Freudian theory; nevertheless psychological anthropologists are mainly concerned with the development of a specific range of emotions from children to adults.

Under the influence of Bateson's concept of ethos (1936), a few anthropologists have tried to describe a 'world of emotions' renewing in such an approach the previous school of Culture and Personality, illustrated by Linton in the fifties.

Lutz (1986) has underlined that much of the anthropology of emotions reflect the mind-body dichotomy. When emotions are thought to be products of the body they are considered as sensations, not as feelings. Leaving out this positivist view, anthropologists have more recently considered emotions as experiences felt by individuals in different contexts (Shweder 1985; Lutz 1987; Wikan 1990). In many cases, emotions became a semantic code with its own intra- and intercultural variations. Even relativist anthropologists accept the idea that emotions are universal; only situations where emotions occur seem to be different, as the language of emotions varies according to the cultural values of a society.

The cross-cultural study of emotions involves problems concerning the potential of universal experience as well as the cognitive effects of different lexical coded systems of categorization. But terms for emotions are not only taxa or paradigmatic categories; in many cultures they seem to be defined with reference to complex scenarios. They are often culturally idiosyncratic thus difficult to translate.

For Shweder (1985) there are three main questions regarding the study of emotions: (1) What is emotional life? (2) With respect to which aspects of emotional functioning are people alike or different? and (3) How are these likenesses and differences to be explained? He wonders whether people are alike or different in the type of feelings they feel (the taxonomic question), and if the situations that elicit those feelings are similar.

Some authors have chosen to isolate a core of emotions in different cultures. How it feels to be angry is not the same for the Llongot who believe that anger can destroy society, and for the Eskimo who consider that only children can experience anger (Rosaldo 1980; Briggs 1970).

The life of emotions themselves takes on a special meaning if one believes that emotions, if unexpressed, are dangerous, or that emotions, if expressed, are dangerous and do not fade away.

While some cultures sanction the open expression of certain emotions, others allow certain feelings to provoke a specific form of action such as the suicide among the Ifaluk (Lutz 1987).

Even if emotions are universal, their development or ontogeny seems particular in each culture. The task of the anthropologist should be to study the way in which these feelings are conveyed, the appropriateness of feelings felt or displayed, and the strategies utilized to deal with the feelings which cannot be expressed.

The semantic approach is often illustrated by referring to feelings of depression. Feeling of emptiness is given meaning by the reference to the idea of 'soul loss' (Shweder 1985; Wikan 1990).

Some aspects of the code of emotions involve prior knowledge from the anthropologist. For example, Wikan (1990) and Connor (1986) show how the language of deference and respect is used in Bali in order to conceal grief from others, preventing them from laughing at one's distress. Language is a powerful means of emotional expression and communication. Developing this line of argument, D'Andrade (1987) demonstrates how feelings are mediators between wishes and intentions and create a causal chain which orders experience. Emotions as such form a semantic code which allows us to understand the expectations of social actors.

The social regulation of emotions implies the idea of society as an arrangement of roles:

In Oriya brahman families the public display of intimacy is not coincidental with the private experience of intimacy. Among Oriya brahman the husband-wife relationship is scripted for mild avoidance. Spouses do not address each other, do not eat together. They never display affection in public. Husband and wife rarely appear in public, as a couple. (Shweder 1985)

As Shweder notes 'bedding down together goes in a realm defined as private. . .'.

The management of emotions which cannot be expressed directly vary from denial to somatization (Kleinman and Good 1985). Myths, rituals, games, and religious beliefs may be considered as projective devices, allowing indirect ways of expressing repressed wishes. Rosaldo (1984) and Spiro (1984) disagree about whether Freudian defense 'mechanisms' are a generic property of the human mind. Rosaldo analyses emotional functioning among Llongot head-hunters in the Philippines, and argues that Llongot anger is not repressed and that defensive processes are the product of a Western way of constructing a Self. Spiro (1984), however, argues for a generic human mind and 'an inherent mental machinery including repression, displacement, and projection'. Defensive processes are not automatic mechanisms but strategies which may very with the construction of the self, itself influenced by the culture in question.

THE RITUAL MANAGEMENT OF DISTRESS

Two-year old children can distinguish the perspective of self from the perspective of others. In some cultures, the emotional expression of young children is more varied than the emotional expression of adults.

Mortuary rituals are centred around the distress of separation caused by death, here the distancing device is the core of beliefs that indicate that the dead person is not dead for ever. The dead person is both absent and present and the ritual is supposed to give relief through catharsis. As Scheff (1977:485) argues, catharsis should allow the individual to re-experience the trauma in such a way that the person can do what was not done in the original event—discharge the emotions of grief, fear, anger, or embarrassment.

Soul loss relates to the subjective experience of depression. When people lose their soul they lose interest in life projects. The cross-cultural literature on depression speaks of its 'somatization' (Kleinman and Good 1985). Some populations do it more than others. In a given culture, a variety of ways exist to express distress. I shall follow here Nichter (1981) who criticizes some ethnopsychiatric approaches to disorder which stress the importance of 'cultural factors' but generally limit their analysis, taking into consideration a single mode of experiencing distress in a given society. Nichter proposes rather to consider

> ethnopsychiatric phenomena as idioms of distress underscored by symbolic and affective associations which take on contextual meaning in relation to particular stressors, the availability of social ramifications of engaging alternative expressive models and the communicative power of these modes given alternative expressive models and the communicative power of these modes given intervening variables and the responsiveness of concerned others.

In India, ontogenetic changes in emotional reactions develop around the ideas of touchability, untouchability and pollution. There are many substances that pollute: faeces, menstrual blood, unclean castes, unclean animals, and many ways in which people try at all costs to avoid polluting substances. The high castes feel particularly concerned to avoid the pollution produced by the proximity or touch of low castes. In case of pollution Brahmans wash, freeing themselves from the effects of any such contact. In Hinduism, the body, like the temple, should be kept free from pollution. When polluted, one must purify oneself, and a Brahman, like any orthodox Hindu, will eagerly apply to himself one of the five products of the sacred cow. Brahmans, especially, are scrupulous about what, where, and with whom they eat. Despite all these efforts, it is noteworthy that many Hindu patients seem to suffer from having internalized psychologically the idea of pollution. Kakar, for example, notes that men often complain to be impure 'inside their body and this impurity becomes such an obsession that it generates neurosis'.

Lynch (1990) defines belief, thought and judgment as necessary elements of a cognitive theory of emotion. The contributors to Lynch's volume, though following the cognitive trend, elaborate a theory of emotions which takes into account the Indian social context. As Lynch and Trawick (1990) argue, the sharing of food implies a different kind of emotion if it occurs in a kin or family context, or between the members of a sect. Here, the main difference is that in the second case, the food which is shared between men has previously been dedicated to the Gods. As Bennett underlines (1990), a food offering expresses the religious message of the devotees, just like the 'love offering' constituted by their devotion.

Lynch (1990) considers emotions to be a product of the mind and aims at showing how the emotions, while essential to the development of the individual, involve the self in relationship with others. Emotions presuppose concepts of social relationships and thus can be subjected to persuasion or criticism. One way of expressing repressed emotions and desire is possession, which can be used mostly by women as a strategic, more or less conscious, way of escaping ill-treatment from in-laws or to postpone an unwanted marriage. In some cases—like Havik Brahman women—possession might express even the fear of being poisoned by jealous sisters-in-law. As Harper (1969) and Nichter (1981) have noted, psychosomatic symptoms are often experienced by women whose position is weak with their in-laws, especially when greater geographic and kinship distance has been preferred in order to negotiate alliances. In Tulu matrilineal society the fear of having one's child poisoned by a sister is a real threat, and illnesses connected with digestive problems might indicate the cast of evil eye.

THE PSYCHOANALYTIC APPROACH

The influence of Western psychology has a long tradition in India. The East India Company operated lunatic asylums, both in India and in England, for employees who were declared insane (Ernst and Kantowsky 1983). Later on, Girindrashekhar Bose, who was to occupy the first chair of psychology at Calcutta University, founded the Indian Psychoanalytic Society in 1922 (Kakar 1990:429). In a letter to Freud, Bose stresses the special orientation of the Oedipus complex in India, which he sees as less focused on castration. As Kakar comments, 'the hegemonic narrative of Hindu culture is neither that of Freud's Oedipus nor of Christianity's Adam, but of Devi, the great goddess, especially in her manifold expressions as mother in the inner world of the Hindu son' (op. cit.:436).

The psychoanalytically oriented anthropologists try to grasp the emotions of individuals in life-crisis (Kakar 1984; Obeyesekere 1970; Crapanzano 1980). While the psychological anthropologists are eager to understand how societies teach children gradually to repress or express certain emotions, social anthropologists try to analyse the way in which certain institutions, such as therapeutic cults for example, function to transform traumatic experience. While the anthropology of emotions deals mainly with the concept of person, psychoanalytically oriented anthropology focuses its analysis on examples of individual life-stories. Thus, Alice Nonna and Juliet, characters described by Obeyesekere in *Medusa's Hair* (1981), introduce us to the psychological troubles that women of low class origin may experience in Sri Lanka. Here, the pathological dimension of the trouble reveals the complexity of the emotional patterns, which may produce depression or anxiety. Physical symptoms, as well as possession or other altered states of consciousness, may be considered as symbolic answers to such suffering.

The study of healing concerns not only medical anthropology but anthropology in general, as it focuses on ritual. It is a feature of ritual that it allows participants to distance themselves from the emotions they suffer in life. Thus, Scheff (1977) offers a typology of different kinds of somatic affect, such as fright or anger, which can be overcome through ritual. While the author relies on Freud and Breuer (1966), he differs from them in his interpretation of catharsis. They thought of it as a recall, by the patient, of a traumatic experience, enabling him to verbalize it. According to Scheff, however, catharsis is produced by the aesthetic order of the world as implied by ritual (cf. also Levi-Strauss 1971; Scheff 1977; etc.).

Ritual harmony, then, may seem more real than reality since it offers a possible denial of what seems to be wrong in social life. In Tulunadu, for example, the mediums possessed by *bhūtas* look at human conflicts from the perspective of another world, breaking into human quarrels, and proselytizing the divine justice of the deities they are supposed to impersonate. In this perspective, ritual, though creating an illusion, gives meaning to human action. In healing rituals, the illusion becomes true as the patient is supposed to go through a series of transformations which have a metonymic value. Becoming the follower of a cult, he heals progressively as well as acquiring another identity. Through this progression, the patient develops a symbiotic relationship to the cult (Crapanzano 1973). Thus a therapeutic cult differs from exorcism, where the main task is to get rid of the harmful spirit—even if exorcism often takes place within therapeutic cults.

Turner (1967, 1968, 1969) has stressed the importance of emotional elements in ritual. He proposes, for the symbol, both an ideational and an emotional pole, but he does not consider the level of the individual, and views the emotions as social representations. His 'Drums of affliction' (1968) show a beautiful example of the functioning of a therapeutic cult, but seen as an institution.

PHYSICAL AND MENTAL ILLNESS

In many cultures, illness and its symptoms are expressed in a religious idiom shared by the community as a whole. Obeyesekere (1970:99) speaks of the psychological conflicts generated by status and role, and considers that 'role learning may require drastic socialization of drives. The psychological consequences of role learning may result in many women having hysterical dispositions.'

In ayurvedic medicine, mental disorders and humoral imbalance go together, as they do for somatic afflictions. While noting the difficulty of translating, accurately, the Sanskrit term *papman*, by either sin or hysteria, Zimmermann stresses the equivalence of divine matters and accumulated *karma* with humoral variations in the discourse on remedies (1989:127). In other words, the moral and the medical, the psychological and the physiological, dimensions merge in a single universe of discourse.

In India, hysterical symptoms are often interpreted as cases of possession. Certain temples or pilgrimage places have the reputation for healing those stricken by a demon (*bhūt*). People often interpret abnormal behaviour in terms of possession. Those who come to such a place generally believe in its religious efficacy and in the divine intercessors, saints, or goddesses attached to the place. Beside the spiritual mediators who are supposed to help possessed persons to drive away demons, there are usually temple or shrine attendants who control the ritual process. They invite the devotees to perform certain ritual acts, such as circumambulation of the shrine. The possessed person does not feel alone because he has usually been taken to the sacred place by his family, who feel concerned by the possession, and stay there for some time (Pfleiderer 1981:68). When a family suffering from this kind of symptom comes to the therapeutic shrine, they are offered a theory of illness which is generally based on a magic concept. For example, somebody explains that his neighbour has sent him some black magic substance which has provoked his child's delirium. In other cases, the final stage of the therapy implies that the demon causing the illness has been named, and can therefore be driven out.

Sometimes, the healer questions the patient about his dreams and is progressively brought to understand what kind of pressures might have provoked the trauma. For the Nambudiri Brahmans of Kerala which Tarabout describes, in this volume, a mental illness is basically a shelter of somebody who cannot face reality. According to Father George, Tarabout's second example, the patient is possessed by a 'second personality' who has already accomplished the secret wishes of the subject. This dimension of the subject seems less important for the Tharus of Nepal, where, as Krauskopff shows clearly how a single nosologic category *dabāu* encompasses other disease categories and is cured through very specific exorcisms. Krauskopff stresses that the healer's interpretation deals with the environmental and historical dimensions of the disease, as social memory is involved in establishing the etiology of the disease. Thus, *dabāu* appears as a social disease which reflects how the past might be rooted in the wild environment.

Bourdier (this volume) shows how two medical healing systems, traditional and modern, interact in rural Tamilnadu. The author concentrates his attention on the place and influence of shamanism in a pluralist context. The shaman portrayed here, is often a low caste hindu, though his ideas seem influenced by Irula culture. His career might start by a possession independent of his will that he will then slowly master, a pattern similar to what Opler (1958) describes for north India. In any case the shaman receives a religious call and undertakes a long training marked by different initiation steps. At one point, he should withdraw in the forest and his life here evokes the vows of the renouncer. The Hindu exorcist officiates in the temple of a minor divinity. Bourdier shows that the conflicting intellectual implications of the two medical systems do not create confusion in the mind of the patients. Similarly, Tarabout holds that the logic of the system is irrelevant to the patient, who largely assimilates both healers to the larger class of exorcists. My own experience confirms this: clients judge their healers more on their efficacy than on their religious or intellectual presumptions. The brahmanic healers are fighting the patient's loss of the proper functioning of his sense organs—he no more experiences the *rasa* to the full. Both Hindus and Muslims consult Father George as they feel attracted by the combination of exorcism and psychology he proposes, when he allows the patient to break free from his secondary personality.

SHRINES

The devotees who attend the shrines enjoy a marginal but recognized status (Rollier, Assayag, Shobha Devi and Bidarakoppa). The duration of their stay varies. The devotee learns unconsciously what is expected from him: he must turn, he must dream, while his family must give food and money. Often, a dream concludes the stay.

The contribution of Shobha Devi and Bidarakoppa focuses on three main points: first, they note the historical background of the shrine of Jod Gomaz, the 'twin tombs' situated in Bijapur. This shrine was built to commemorate the saint Syed Shah Abdul Raza Kadri and his disciple Kawas Khan. The sick and the distressed visit the tombs to seek relief but the authors do not offer a real appreciation of the value of the therapy. Here, as in the pilgrimage described by Assayag, Hindus, and Muslims as well, frequent the shrine to find relief from their ailments and misfortunes. From a sociological point of view, it is interesting to know that Sufis often established their hermitage near the low caste quarters. In Jod Gomaz the devotees share the idea that it is the miraculous power of the saint which heals their suffering. Similarly, the saint, buried in his tomb exudes *baraka* (Assayag), and guides his devotees towards paradise. In the different studies dedicated in this volume to Muslim shrines, one notices that the time/space dimension is essential. As Shobha Devi and Bidarakoppa note: 'the devotee should stay forty days inside the premises of the *dargāh* unless his problem is solved earlier'. In all these Muslim *dargāhs*, the patients circumambulate the tomb of the saint. During their stay different symbolic devices are used as metonymical tools of therapy, such as the stone carried by the patients at Jod Gomaz Dargah, which symbolizes the burden of the disease. At Mira Datar Dargah (Pfleiderer 1981), horses made of cloth and cotton are sent out to persecute the *bhūt* in order to prevent him from returning to the patient's body.

Assayag stresses how physical illness and mental affliction are linked in the local conception of misfortune, where 'the disease is considered as an active agent around a person'; he also remarks that people in Karnataka never talk about the causal agent of the illness near the person afflicted. In all situations described in his volume it seems better to be possessed by a deity (*dēvaru*) than by a demon (*jinn*) or (*bhūta*).

THE CONCEPT OF POSSESSION

In South Asia, spirit possession may solve serious psychological conflicts. The patient frees himself from guilt as his hostile feelings are professed by the demons. The psychological problems are expressed in a demonological idiom shared by a whole culture. Rollier distinguishes two kinds of possessed patients: the case of the possessed who recognizes himself as such, and the case where the patient is seen as possessed by his family or by the *mullāh*. Rollier as a psychiatrist (inspired by the Lacanian trend of psychoanalysis) chooses to deal with the psychic economy of the patients who come regularly to Murugmalla, a shrine located on the border of Karnataka, Andhra Pradesh and Tamilnadu. The trauma felt by the possessed persons he describes sometimes relates to aggression experienced by the patients. In some cases the memory of the aggression may conceal a feeling of guilt, often described as feeling dirty or polluted inside (Kakar 1984:51).

Assayag does not want to consider possession in psychological terms, which he finds ethnocentric, but as mechanisms which pervade mind and body into a psychodynamic which possess its own mechanisms such as hyperventilation for women. The body of the devotee has to obey certain rules: for example, the gyrodevotion which implies that devotees go around the *dargāh*, but they are allowed to show socially wild behavior and to express their grievances through the ritual idiom of the *ṭawāf*. For Krauskopff, negative possession is attributed to the Seven Sisters who represent non-localized virgin feminine forces. During the cure, the spirits held responsible for illness are symbolized by objects which contain intoxicating plants. In many cases, and especially in the possession of women, we find instances of women who use their symptoms as a coping mechanism in order to distance themselves from family oppression.

SAINTS, GODDESSES AND DEMONS

In Murugmalla, the saint and his wife form a parental couple. In fact, in each contribution to this volume, the duality of the possession, demon opposed to saint or Devi, is interpreted in terms of a binary process. There are two phases to this process:

1. *Dissociation*: The patient swings or is chained. He suffers from convulsions and incoherent speech, in order to free himself from a malevolent possessing spirit.

2. *Restructuration*: Possessed by the saint or the Goddess, the patient is appeased as the last trances often imply a kind of salvation. While some authors disagree with a psychoanalytical approach they all seem to agree that the possessed person obtains secondary gains from his possession. For Assayag, possession may represent a conscious strategy followed by the victim.

In every case, the persons who profess to be possessed demonstrate at will a behavior corresponding to the ritual set-up associated with that particular deity. The authors agree that the shrine and the presence of a religious intercessor allow the possessed person to build, on a religious model, an idiom of their suffering. But I wonder, with Assayag, how the conjunction of myth, ritual and symbols succeeds in bringing together in one place pathologies which are heterogeneous. In my article, possession implies sexual conversion and thus changes the personality of the possessed person. In case of women this change implies the loss of femininity as the woman ceases to have procreative powers. The therapeutic value of the possession—the positive trance—is acknowledged by all the contributors. Nevertheless, Tarabout, Shobha Devi and myself share the idea that symbolic efficacity is more important than the system of thought which pervades the cure. In the case of the Tharus, however, Krauskopff argues that possession has a collective dimension as the Seven Sisters threaten the social space which prevails over the individual.

WHO ARE THE PATIENTS?

Demoniac possession is often linked to sexuality and reproduction. Victims of demoniac possession are placed in a liminal state (Van Gennep 1969). As an example, young brides who leave their parents' home in order to stay with their in-laws are exposed to the attacks of demons who are often of the opposite sex. As Deliège (1992) notes: 'demons are attracted by menstrual blood, pregnancy, virginity, women's beauty, strength of young men'. In a similar way, in Vietnam, the souls of those who die without having experienced love, try to appropriate the strength and beauty of young and beautiful victims. Among the boatmen of the River of Perfumes the possessed medium speaks the language of the Mon Khmer mountain people as the boatmen claim to have protectors from the mountains. As in my own article, the hierarchy of the pantheon is displayed by the relationships at stake between different kinds of deities, spirits and genii. For Rollier, the dispossession trance does not inform us about the patient only, but also reveals the desire (see here Rollier's explanation of the term) attributed to a deceased person. Consequently, for Rollier the possessed person goes through a depersonalization as he becomes the object of the desire of the other, the deceased. This interpretation gives meaning to the dimension of family history which is often at stake in the formation of neurosis. While many anthropologists have underlined the sexual overtone of possession (Obeyeskere 1970, Freed and Freed 1985), Rollier is more radical as he considers possession as a 'jouissance' or fulfillment which is to be situated beyond sexuality and represents a quest for identity.

Bourdier's contribution, following Beals (1976) studies the interaction of practitioners in a pluralist system, where people seem to have a choice. One may ask here what it means to choose when one is confronted with unexplained misfortune. It is interesting to note that modern doctors think that shamans are efficient in the case of innocent villagers. Nevertheless, the religious symbols present in the physician's office may demonstrate that doctors themselves unconsciously yearn for symbolic efficacy. Bourdier shows how a clinic becomes more popular with out-patients when a shrine dedicated to a local god is erected on its premises, and he concludes that the medical systems intermingle with each other. For him, modern medicine reduces the social pressures endured by the patients.

Bertrand's article concerns the healing practices of mediums descending from isolated Cham ethnic groups in Vietnam. Moreover, the speech of the boatmen is influenced by Mon Khmer languages. The author underlines the influence of India on Vietnamese culture. The medium heals and protects, but he cannot act only to the goods, as the powerful genius he serves, and who regularly reactivates him, is somewhat ambivalent. In Vietnam the healers who are mediums also know herbalism and traditional medicine. They depend on a complex pantheon of divinities, derived not only from Taoism and Confucianism, but also from local cults. In this rich tradition, the etiology of medicine seems to obey a binary logic: one may oppose the interior illnesses, provoked by exposure to heat and cold, to the exterior illnesses, considered as sanctions administered by supernatural powers such as ancestors, genii and, even more dreadful different categories of restless dead. Even more ambiguous is the loss of soul which strike adults after, for example, an emotional shock. For interior illness, such as epilepsy, the therapy combines the use of acupuncture with Western medicine, while exterior illness have to be diagnosed by a medium. Through vision and possession the medium organizes series of transactions with the superior genii, and tries by their assistance to appease the malevolent spirits.

Some of the contributions emphasize the passivity of the patients; in the *dargāh* they circle the tomb, following custom but perhaps also responding to an obsessive urge. Very different is the behavior of the persons who consult mediums in Karnataka as they have to formulate their problems themselves, or even narrate their suffering. As Kakar (1984:49) notes 'a dream regarded as significant by the dreamer is accordingly often taken to an expert—usually a *pīr*—for an interpretation'.

THE PERSONALITIES OF THE HEALERS

Tarabout compares two religious healers, who both combine elements of traditional and modern world. For the Poonkutil Nambudiri Brahmans, treating mental illness is the hereditary right of the house. In this tradition, the cure does not aim at elucidating the inner conflicts of the patient but at offering him peace of mind through reintegration in social life. In my own article, I show how depressed persons, who have transgressed a taboo and are, in principle, excluded from their own society, try to survive by embracing the hindu idiom of devotion. This in turn allows them to start a career as priestess on the condition of following the Goddess' orders. In a similar way, the healers in Karnataka are faced with a cultural dilemma: the medium in Puttur follows the astrologer's suggestions of founding a temple to the Goddess.

As described by Tarabout, Father George seems to establish a parallel between a hypnotic state and the unconscious of the patient. When he hypnotizes his patient, the latter is enabled to liberate his second personality. This evokes what Obeyesekere states about the therapeutic value of possession: 'We think that the state of "possession", "fits", "trance" into which the patient gets when he has his fits of illness permits regression, abreactions, and the release of primary process material' (1970:106). The healer of the Tharus differs from most of the other cases in that he does not develop a very symbiotic relationship with the individual patient. Rather, he becomes 'the master of the site' by controlling the evil spirits through his ancestor energy. The cloistering ritual of the village emphasizes the need to protect the village boundaries which embody a power struggle between men, represented by the priest, and the spirits and malevolent Goddesses of the area.

THE CONCEPTION OF THE PERSON AND THE CULTURAL TRAUMA

Among the boatmen of Veitnam, the body contains a transcendental spirit which possesses the medium. In other words the different souls attached to the person should live in harmony, as they determine the qualities of the person. As Bertrand underlines, an illness is an event which is part of a mythical or a family history, a situation which evokes the family histories of some patients who frequent therapeutic shrines.

Are certain trauma specific to Indian Culture? For Rollier, the experience of separation, experienced at marriage by the young Indian bride or more generally at mourning, may provoke possession. Trances are a symbolical answer to loss or grief, which cannot be expressed directly, or which are persistent and may require the treatment of healers. Kakar (1984) underlines the lack of paternal authority in India and stresses the son's unconscious anger at the father. It seems true, that the women who participate in Siri rituals experience a kind of trauma which relates to the matrilineal kinship system in Tulunadu.

Therapy is a way to work out ideas as practices and ideals. Tarabout shows that when somebody is possessed by a *bhūta* or a *preta*, 'departed soul', he takes into consideration the family Goddess who grants the success of the cure. In Bengal, the importance of the Goddess Kali, who expects her female devotees to renounce their ordinary life in order to become priestesses, represents a much greater price to pay. As devotees' stories suggest, suffering in Bengal implies renouncement in order to become the child of the Goddess.

Far from being rigid the healing rituals allow communication between cultural codes. Shobha Devi and Bidarakoppa explain that both Hindus and Muslims frequent the *dargāh*, but they do not state how the Hindus who have become disciples of the saint deal with this new dimension of their spirituality. The case is very different for a Santal woman who becomes the devotee of Kali, as she will fear the wrath of the *boṅga*, the 'tribal deities'.

THE THERAPEUTIC MEANING OF THE RITUAL

The ritual initiates the patient's interaction with the saint and with the possessing spirit (*bhūt*). Spirits are obstinate: As Kakar (1984) and Pfleiderer (1981) suggest, this obstinacy may reflect the patient's reluctance towards the cure, as he gets secondary gains from monopolizing his family's attention. In some cases, this reluctance is manifested by the behavior of the patient, who, for example, will avoid approaching the interior of the tomb or the inner sanctum of the shrine at the first stage of therapy.

These rituals attract thousands of people but still seem to concern the individual. Does it mean that there are no therapeutic cults in India in the sense of Turner (1968)? Some authors (Shobha Devi and Bidarakoppa in this volume; Pfleiderer 1981) report that group rituals are held on particular evenings at the *dargāh*.

In this respect, the Siri ritual seems closer to the definition of a therapeutic cult since women who participate in Siri are more or less permanently involved in it. But, contrary to some other cults, the Siri ritual conveys a strong regional identity, as it is associated with the prestigious Bunt caste, dominant in south Kanara. Possession by Siri is not considered polluting. As Claus (1975:47) remarks 'the Siri cultists have little in common aside from a personal history of supernatural possession and participation in the annual cult rituals'. This last remark seems to imply that the patient who attends an Indian shrine remains trapped, alone is his own life-story. If we now ask with Kapferer (1979:1): 'how does the performance of an healing ritual facilitate the transition of a patient from an agreed state of illness to a public recognition of health?' we cannot answer that this recognition is definitive.

A healing ritual does not derive its efficacity only from the manipulation of symbols. The logic of therapy which underpins the ritual has to become an intimate truth symbol: it has to become an intimate truth for the patient. In order that the patient should feel cured, it is necessary that something changes in his life after performing the healing ritual. This change can be perceived by those surrounding the patient, and interpreted in such a way that they become convinced that the oppressive power has been driven away. This is what happened to a Brahman family I knew in Bengal. Their son had broken his arm by falling from a tree. According to the boy's father the madness which attacked the son was provoked by a muslim neighbour, who spat several times under the tree whenever the boy was going to school. After attending the shrine of a female muslim medium who diagnosed the bad influence of a *jinn*, the child recovered completely. By finding a muslim therapist, our Brahman wanted to treat the source of evil itself, otherwise the boy could only be temporarily released. Curing, then, may imply questioning radically one's traditions and faith, in order to affront the origin of the problem, often attributed to a 'distant other'.

In other cases, efficient therapy may imply thorough changes in the patient's family life. Ultimately, the surest way to get cured is to become a healer and to replace the natural by a spiritual lineage.

Madness confronts the patient with fragmented experiences of the self which are often attributed to demons or sorcery. Whenever the patient seems to recover he succeeds in reintegrating his lost identities around the gratifying figures of the saint or the goddess. When the Indian urban patient suffers from depression, and consults a therapist, it seems rather that his whole experience becomes unified under the influence of the trauma. Kakar (1984) describes the case of a young salesman who is oppressed by the authoritarian figure of his father, whom he does not dare to oppose. Whenever his therapist suggests to him that this might be the source of his trouble, he answers by going to a traditional healer who, he says, will be better able to deal with the problem. Kakar, he himself tells us, nods affirmatively. As the anecdote shows, the patient's strategy may be to turn back, in defense, to a conscious management of his own problems—preferring demons to the alternative father-figure of the analyst.

The contributions of this book offer examples of multiple therapy systems including allopathy, astrology, exorcism, spirit possession and eclectic combinations. In most of the cases, psycho-social disorders result from conflicts with kin and affines which are translated into idioms of illness. In some cases (Carrin, Bourdier), illness is attributed to ritual pollution, while in others, violence directed against relatives, as in Tarabout's article, indicate mental imbalance. Curiously enough, acculturation often plays a crucial role both as a source of disorder and as an effective way of restoring harmony, using the cultural symbols of another community as a prestigious or more efficient way of healing: the cross in the case of Father George, the Shaivite trident for tribal women, Chinese ideograms for boatmen of the River of Perfumes. Is possession therapeutic in itself? If Rollier, as a freudian psychiatrist, considers that the ritual aims at reconciliating the Id with the Superego, he questions the value of re-establishing a social harmony at the cost of the patient's Ego. Assayag criticizes any psychological approach to therapy but appreciates the gyro-devotion as an efficient way to reduce anxiety. For Assayag, devotion cannot be reduced to a therapeutic device, as ritual action has its own goals. Thus, cults also perpetuate themselves: as my data on Bengal show, the cure is really successful only when previous patients succeed in becoming healers.

On the other hand, Krauskopff stresses that in the Tharu community, the healing ritual is only a platform on which the process of healing is based. In all the cases, the healer has to identify the social tensions at work. The ritual, then, is only marking a step in a therapeutic process, which in the last resort is a matter for society at large.

REFERENCES

Bateson, G. 1936 *Naven. A Survey of the Problems Suggested by a Composite Picture of the Culture of a New Guinea Tribe from Three Points of View.* London: Cambridge University Press.

Beals, A.R. 1976 Strategies of Resort to Curers in South India. In Ch. Leslie (ed.), *Asian Medical Systems: A Comparative Study.* Berkeley: University of California Press.

Bennett, P. 1990 In Nanda Baba's House: The Devotional Experience in Pushti Marg Temples. In O.W. Lynch (ed.), *Divine Pasions*, q.v.

Briggs, J. 1970 *Never in Anger: Portrait of an Eskimo Family.* Cambridge: Harvard University Press.

Connor, L. 1986 Balinese Healing. In *Jero Tapakan: Balinese Healer*, L. Connor, P. Ash and T. Ash (eds.), Cambridge: Cambridge University Press: 21-36.

Claus, P. 1975 The Siri myth and ritual: A Mass possession cult of South India, *Ethnology* 14: 47-58.

Crapanzano, V. 1973 *The Hamadsha, A Study in Moroccan Ethnopsychiatry,* Berkeley: University of California Press.

D'andrade, R.G. 1974 The color of Emotion, *American Ethnologist* 1: 49-63.

——— 1987 A Folk Model Of The Mind. In *Cultural Models in Language and Thought,* D. Holland and N. Quinn (eds.), New York: Cambridge University Press, 112-48.

Deliège, R. 1992 La Possession Démoniaque chez les Intouchables Catholiques de l'Inde du Sud, *Arch. Sci. Soc.* Rel. 79 (juill. sept.): 115-34.

Douglas, M. 1970 *Natural Symbols*. London: Barrie and Jenkins.

Ernst, W. and D. Kantowsky 1983 *Mad Tales from the Raj: Case Studies from Pembroke House and Ealing Lunatic Asylum, 1818-1892.* Paper presented to the 8th European Conference on Modern South Asian Studies, Tällberg, Sweden.

Freed, R. and S. Freed 1964 Spirit Possession as Illness in a North Indian Village, *Ethnology*, 3, 2; 152-71.

———1985 *The Psychomedical Case History Of a Low-Caste Woman of North India,* Anthropological Papers of the American Museum of Natural History, vol. 60, part 2.

Freud, S. and Breuer, J. 1966 *Studies on hysteria*. New York: Avon.

Geertz, C. 1973 *The Interpretation of Culture.* New York: Basic Books.

Harper, E.B. 1957 Shamanism in South India, *Southwestern Journal of Anthropology* 13: 267-87.

——— 1969 Fear And The Status Of Women, *Southwestern Journal of Anthropology* 25: 31-85.

Kakar, S. 1978 *The Inner World: A Psychoanalysis Study of Childhood and Society in India.* New York and Delhi: Oxford University Press.

——— 1984 *Shamans, Mystics And Doctors: A Psychological Inquiry Into India and Its Healing Traditions*. London: Unwin Paperbacks.

——— 1990 Stories From Indian Psychoanalysis: context and text. In: Stigler *et al.* (eds.), q.v.

Kapferer, B. 1983 *A Celebration of Demons. Exorcism and the Aesthetics of Healing in Sri Lanka*. Bloomington: Indiana University Press.

Kleinman, A. and B. Good. 1985 *Culture and Depression.* Berkeley: University of California Press.

Leach, E.R. 1976 *Culture and Communication: The Logic by Which Symbols are Connected.* Cambridge: Cambridge University Press.

Levi-Strauss, C. 1962 *La Pensée Sauvage*. Paris: Plon.

——— 1971 *L' Homme Nu.* Paris: Plon.

——— 1973, *Anthropologie Structurale II.*

Lutz, C. 1985 Depression and the translation of Emotional Worlds. In A. Kleinman and B. Good (eds); *Culture and Depression*, q.v.

———1987 Goals, Event and Understanding in Ifaluk. Emotion Theory. In N. Quinn and D. Holland (eds.), q.v.: 291-312.

Lutz, C. and G. White. 1986 The Anthropology of Emotions, *Annual Review in Anthropology* 15: 405-36.

Lynch, M.O. 1990 *Divine Pasions The Social Construction of Emotion in India.* Delhi: Oxford University Press.

Nichter, M. 1981 Idioms of distress: alternatives in the expression of psychosocial distress: a case sudy from South India, *Culture, Medecine and Psychiatry* 5, 379-408.

Obeyesekere, G. 1970 The Idiom of Demonic Possession, A Case Study, *Social Science and Medicine* 4, 97-111.

———1981 *Medusa's Hair. An Essay On Personal Symbols and Religious Expericence.* Chicago and London: Chicago University Press.

Opler, M. 1958 Spirit Possession in a Rural Area of North India. In A. Lessa and E. Vogt (eds.), *A Reader in Comparative Religion.* Evanston: Row & Peterson: 533-66.

Pfleiderer, B. 1981 Mina Datar Dargah: A Psychiatric Institution, *Internationale Asienforum* 12, 51-75.

Quinn, N. and D. Holland (eds.), 1987 *Cultural Models in Language and Thought.* Cambridge: Cambridge University Press.

Rosaldo, M. 1980 *Knowledge and Pasion: Llongot Notions of Self and Social Life.* Cambridge: Cambridge University Press.

Rosaldo, R. 1984 Grief and the Headhunter's Rage: On the cultural Force of Emotion. In E.M. Bruner and S. Plattner (eds.), *Text, Play and Story: The Construction and Reconstruction of Self and Society.* Washington, D.C.: American Ethnological Society, 178-95.

Scheff, T.J. 1977 The Distancing of Emotion in Ritual, *Current Anthropology*, vol. 18, no. 3, Sept. 483-505.

Shweder, R. 1985 Menstrual pollution, soul loss, and the comparative study of emotions In A. Kleinman and B. Good (eds.), *Culture and Depression*, q.v.

———1979 *Catharsis In Healing, Ritual, and Drama.* Berkeley: University of California Press.

Spiro, M. 1984 Some Reflections on Cultural Determinism and Relativism with a Special Reference to Emotion and Reason. In R.A. Shweder and R.A. LeVine (eds.), *Culture Theory: Essays on Mind, Self and Emotion*, 323-46.

Stigler, J.W., R.A., Shweder and G. Herdt 1990 *Cultural Psychology. Essays on Comparative human development.* Cambridge: Cambridge University Press.

Turner, V. 1967 *The Forest of Symbols: Aspects of Ndembu Ritual.* Ithaca: Cornell University Press.

——— 1968 *The Drums Of Affliction.* Oxford: Clarendon Press.

——— 1969 *The Ritual Process. Structure And Antistructure.* Chicago: Aldine.

Trawick, M. 1990 The Ideology of Love in a Tamil Family. In. M.O. Lynch (ed.), *Divine Passions*, q.v.: 37-63.

Van Gennep, A. 1960 *The Rites of Passage*. London: Routledge & Kegan Paul.

Wikan, U. 1990 *Managing Turbulent Hearts, A Balinces Formula for Living.* Chicago: University of Chicago Press.

Zimmermann, F. 1989 *Le discours des remèdes au pays des épices. Enquête sur la médecine hindoue.* Paris: Payot.

But, They do move . . .
Religion, Illness and Therapeutics in Southern India

JACKIE ASSAYAG

It's dark: let's give free rein to our imagination.
Ah, we are in India . . . in a palace
A. Schnitzler, 'The Round' (1900)

None can ignore the fact that India abounds in places where 'Heaven meets the Earth', immediately evoking the seven major sacred sites of Hinduism: Ayodhya, Kasi, Gaya, Mathura, Ujjain, Kanchipuram and Dvaravati. We are also aware of saints, who even though lie buried in mausoleums continue to live in the eyes of their devotees, such as Mu'in al-din Chishtī in Ajmer (Currie 1989), Niẓamud'dīn in Delhi (Desiderio Pinto 1989) and Banda Namāz Gēsūdirāz in Gulbarga (Kushro Husaini 1983). We have, however, paid little attention to the myriad local 'friends' (*awliya*') of God that these incomparable Sufi Masters left in the shade: cohorts of dead *Shaikhs* who, although minor, are no less 'poles' (*qṭub*) of devout worship practised by restricted communities or associations gathered around their tombs in their 'royal palaces' (*dargāh*). In south as well as in north India, these figures are invested with a divine lieutenance (*khilāfat*) rendering uncertain the boundary between the Earth and the Sky.

Most of these figures are quite anonymous and their devotees retain only a prestigious name linked to some events revisited by hagiography; they are often lost in the mists of history but nevertheless venerated feverishly by devotees, Muslims, Hindus and sometimes Christians, on a spīritual area (*walāya*) of extremely varying dimensions. They are, in fact, spīritual preceptors (*murshid*), not so much on religious grounds as because these honourable 'elders' (*pīr*), popularly referred to as 'fathers' or 'grandfathers' (*bābā*), are formidable healers (Mayer 1967) who respond to crises, bio-medical as well as psycho-social, experienced by the sick and those prone to afflictions.

Endowed with divine attributes of Mercy and Wrath, these 'Masters' (*Mālik*) arouse a devotion all the more intense because of the knowledge (*'ilm*) of the extraordinary powers (*karāmat*) attributed to them. Isolated from the centres of Islamic orthodoxy, they have not been, till now, in the collimator of those reformist militants who have ceaselessly tried to reduce their influence in the name of the Unique (Baljon 1989; Gaborieau 1989). And the saint-doctors' *baraka*—'the beneficient force of divine origin, which causes superabundance in the physical sphere, and prosperity and happiness in the psychic order' (Rentz 1960:1032)—is there, still efficient. It is all the more effective because it has remained unchanged since their death, for the well-being of all those who came in search of and find remission, cure, relief and comfort in their mausoleums, in the votive, as well as religious, sense. Even then, we do not know what term to use because this article, which is at the confluence of therapeutics and religion, is particularly aimed at this uncertainty.

If it behoves the historian to explore the mystic origins of saint (*sufis*) worship in India, it is the job of anthropologists to describe how they respond today to health and illnesses, and more generally to misfortune and well-being, individually and collectively. This obviously concerns a cultural definition of the malady as well as the remedy, as long as one has an interest in the indigenous make-up of the body and its pathogeny. In South Asia, from a very long time, all the representations and practices, deeply embedded in an ethnomedical idiom, are shared by both Hindus and Muslims as will be seen first. But this idiom is restructured by Indian Muslims, and this will be hereafter illustrated by a description of the worship of a regionally important saint. Indeed, it is here that we can observe the manner in which legions of patients turned disciples (*murīd*) try to temporarily capture in their bodies the *baraka*, which flows continuously from the Sky to the Earth, for prophylactic and curative ends. There has been, until recently, a traditional conception of saintliness in most of the Islamic world of which Garçin de Tassigny wrote, as early as 1831, that 'for Muslims it replaced the numerous Hindu deities' (1869:15). And, like in Christianity (Wilson 1983), this saintliness is conflated, in Islam, with a space for treatment: an open-sky polyclinic still independent of (Western) medicinal systems, to which the participants resort at the same time, and which is itself, after all, a bearer of an ideology (Kakar 1982:3).

THE ROAD TO THE SAINT'S TOMB

I chose the tomb of Bābā Ḥażrat Rājnaiyyir Shāh among many others because his *dargāh* is a therapeutic centre in north Karnataka. Specializing in the treatment of 'demons'—called *bhūta* or *piśaci* by Hindus and '*shaitan*' (or *jānn*) by Muslims—the names of (Allāh)—'Guardian' (*al-Ḥafiz*), 'Powerful' (*al-Qādir*) and 'Life-giver' (*al-Muḥyī*)—are attributed to him. Moreover, the circumstances under which I learnt of his existence—while investigating a temple of the Goddess Yellamma (Assayag 1992a)—reinforced the idea that saints and divinities are not considered to be exclusive to a 'popular' religion of the low castes and untouchables, but that their powers are complemented or added, then (Bayly 1989:Ch. 3), as it is now (Assayag 1994), in south India.

On the morning of 22 November 1992, my muslim friend, Babu, was waiting for me at the bus-stand in Dharwad, daydreaming. With him was Shāh Walī, one of the priests in charge (*pīrzade*) of saint Makhdūr Hussaini of Hirekumbi village where both of them live. Shah Wali was related to the Mullahs of Bābā Rājnaiyyir, and had agreed to serve as our guide and mediator.

We boarded the bus to Chikuri and after four hours arrived at Hurikeri, a village about 15 km from the terminus. From there another bus took us to Karosi, a tiny remote village in Belgaum district. Scrutinising the faces of my companions, the words of Dupront came to me: 'therapeutic power is exogenic'. At the beginning, there is in fact a detachment, a physical distancing and getting out of 'one's place', a mental rupture with the usual, to earn a 'somewhere' which gives 'the other'. Hence, this feeling of space, the torture of the journey, tiredness of the body and spirit while waiting for the appearance of the saint, is already the beginning of the treatment and promises an effective remedy (Dupront 1987:373-8).

After quickly gulping down hot tea from a saucer, we walked through poor suburbs, passing the mosque (*masjid*) on the left and the prayer wall (*'idgāh*) on the right. Here, I am told, they sometimes prepare for devotion by means of the prayer *Fātiḥa*, 'that which opens'. In front of the sanctuary are a series of stalls where pilgrims can buy small colourful pictures of the saint and all the things needed for the rituals. Crossing the threshold of the *dargāh*, we walk about 100 m along a kind of cemetery with tens of tombs arranged in an apparently disordered manner. The path forms a circular arc; the flooring is paved and surrounded by low cement walls. We come to a rectangular courtyard, about 30 m long and 20 m wide, also surrounded by a low wall. On one side, a small river meanders in an orchard, near a few scattered tombs; on the other, fairly well-to-do families stay in pilgrims' lodges to undergo the long 'incubation' of the saint who cures (Wilson 1983:5).

In the middle of this courtyard is the sanctuary proper. Recently constructed, this edifice has a fairly banal parallelepipedic form of a house.

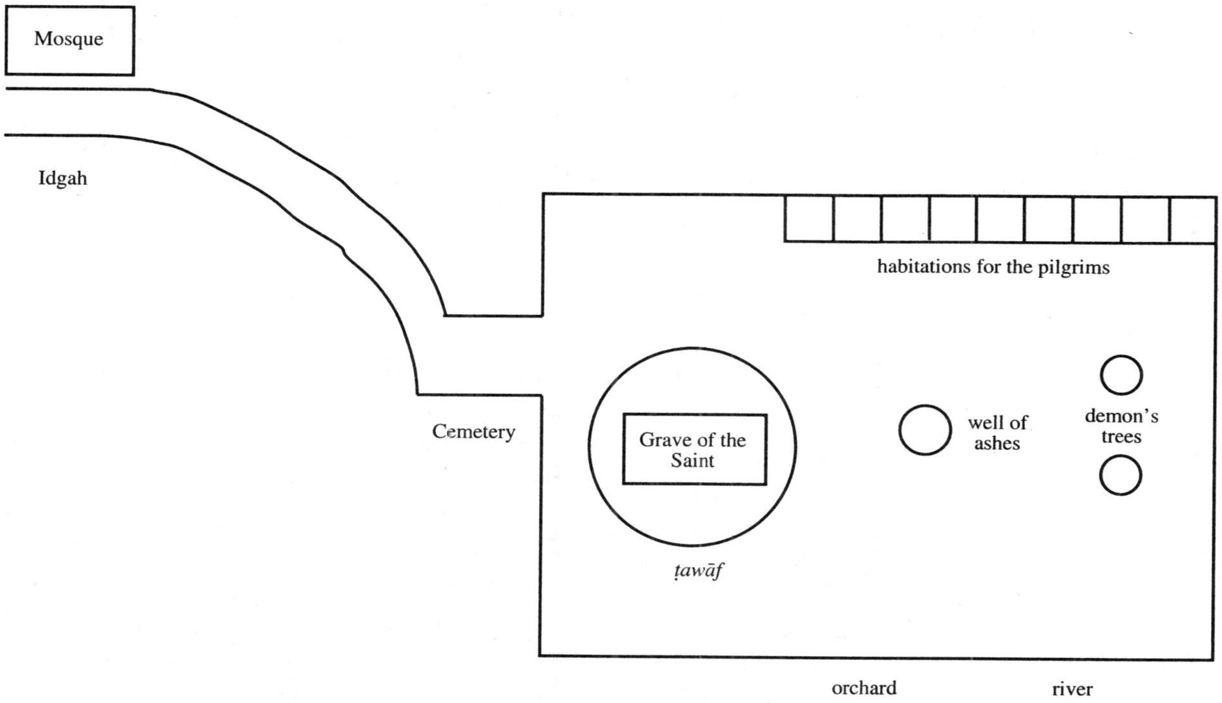

FIGURE 1: SIMPLIFIED PLAN OF THE PLACE OF WORSHIP

The sloped roof is covered by red tiles, and the green tiled walls are ornamented; windows enable us to see the sepulchre. The word 'see' is to be taken in the real sense, because the term '*darśan*' designates (among Hindus) the visual capture of a sacred being, a part of whose aura is thus absorbed. But to see the Divine, and to be seen by Him, signifies to merit it, and hence paying a superhuman price of maximal repression of one's self, demanding physical and psychic penitence which is exhausting and reinforcing at the same time. It appears that the *darśan* if fully effective only at this vacillating but ecstatic point, where the body is physically exhausted but receptive. The religious rites reach its peak in a reflective relationship where the devotee 'seen to be seen' receives the deity, 'the seer sees him'. The prototype of the religious action is deployed within the framework of this visual relationship with the Other (Assayag 1992a:379-83). But, from where we were standing, that is about 10 m from the tomb, the thin spiral of smoke rising from the ash filled concrete wells hindered our vision slightly.

For all that, before piercing this halo, we must focus on the local conception of illness and misfortune because only this explains the spectacle observed in the *dargāh*: a simple observation would only provide a superficial diagnosis of ailments. In fact, it is difficult to discriminate the kinds of illnesses (*roga*) and pains (*bēne*), and to know the nature of the problems (*upadra*) and causal agents, or even the ẹxact motives which prompt them to stay there for fairly long periods. The clear-cut nosographic categorisation is all the more uncertain because the concentration of extremely varying pathologies in this particular place leads to the belief that even when the etiology is strictly organic—an obviously impertinent dualistic hypothesis according to the fact that here it is not the illness which is treated but the whole sick person and his experience—the saint still has the power to cure all the sufferers. The pathological range is vast: from poliomyelitis to psychosis, diphtheria to neurosis, dysentery to hysteria passing through all the 'limit stages', while quite a few commonly visit the place as a sign of their devotion or to fulfill a vow (Pfleiderer 1981).

From these multiple pathologies in the field of beneficial forces, it can be inferred that these poeple unanimously confer a supernatural cause for their illnesses. In fact, even as the saint provides some comfort, the ethnophysiology, which is always linked to the climate, ecology and diet, is in itself a rich, more or less subtle, storehouse of 'physicalist' explanations; explanations partially inspired by the traditional Hindu medicinal system (*Ayurveda*) whose vitality, in spite of its historic depth, Zimmermann has demonstrated in the neighbouring state of Kerala (1989).

LOCAL ETHNOMEDICINE: AMBIGUITIES AND SPECIFICITIES

To classify or not to classify

Even outside this sancturary, the ambiguity and dynamic character of the regional perception of illnesses and afflicitions are such that it would be erroneous to confine them in a systematic and immutable classification and, consequently, infer a univocal cause as done by, for example, Ishwaran who has mechanically established a correlation between divinities and illnesses (1968:94). Not only do the people commonly label the illnesses according to numerous criteria which vary depending on the place, time, rumours, and also the power and status of individuals, but the specialists also have distinct ethnomedical, complementary or concurrent codes which advise curative strategies which are themselves distinct (Beals 1976).

The nature of the troubles is, therefore, dealt with in a different manner each time, and labelled so differently that the idiopathy superimposes labile syndromes with fairly blurred contours, even within the *dargāh*. In short, we can legitimately doubt the existence of a common cognitive code shared by all the members of the local society.

Most often, diagnosis is from 'family resemblances' based on prototypes of some illnesses experienced or observed: fever, colour, symptoms, analogies, signatures. . . . And this polythetic knowledge is so flexible that the classification is neither static, nor consistent. While the ethnomedical discourse changes the intrinsic or adventist properties of certain signs, the metaphoric uses, rich in connotations, proliferate concurrently with the patient or interlocutor, depending on the context. Nevertheless this observation is not peculiar to the traditional conceptions of the illness; it is enough to recall the polysemic usage of the (Western) idea of 'stress', 'denotatively problematic but connotatively rich' (Nichter 1989:90).

Analogically, in Karnataka, the term '*mailige*' denoting a state of impurity through contact, particularly menses, is used metaphorically or by contiguity to designate a number of contagious maladies (dermatisis, chickenpox, measles or smallpox) and also to indicate magical transfers underlying exorcism and sorcery. Moreover, the contagious etiology seems to be multicausal: 'bad air' (*gaḷi*) or 'sand' (*soṅku*), considered as direct or speeding agents of infections, behind a 'germ' (*kṛmi*) or 'tiny insect' (*kita*), may emerge as a 'malevolent spirit', specially when all the available treatments have been tried out.

However, despite this plurality of perspectives and in the absence of a monotypic definition of nosological categories, the ethnomedical medium is expressed by grammatical constructions, an implicit cognitive model, as demonstrated by Nichter (1989:113 sq.). In Kannada (and in the Dravidian languages), the disease is considered as an active agent (subject) acting on a person (object). Thus, we say 'smallpox came on me' (*nanage mailige roga banḍide*). The verb *bāru*, meaning 'to come' implies that the anger of an external agent, a 'spirit' perhaps, provoked it. Similarly, the verb *hiḍḍide*, which is synonymous but with the connotation of being 'caught', evokes a sudden seizing by force: *avanige bhūta hiḍḍide* (a demon has caught him), or that he is touched by a (bad) dream 'falling' on him. The manner of grouping the illnesses which portend a severe or unexpected seizure, for example, 'madness' (*unmāda*), leprosy (*hīre bēne*) or bad planetary influence (*bala graha*), are opposed to the state of involuntary possession, when the term *hiḍḍide* is not normally used. In the case of lunacy, a very similar term '*agu*' meaning 'to come' is more commonly used. This term is also used to designate mental changes as a result of very high fever, whether convulsive or not, during a serious illness. Afflicitions resulting from bad planetary influence (*bala graha*), is considered to be due to the influence of an evil spirit (*bala piḍe*), especially among the low castes who do not always distinguish between epilepsy (*apasmāra*) and madness (*unmada*), discounting the possibility that a *bala graha* later gets transformed into *apasmāra*!

In short, the relative precision of pathogenesis results in a terminological ambiguity which most often dominates only because of the prohibitions placed on utterances.

To tell or not to tell

On the one hand, maladies associated with divine or diabolical punishment can be conjugated neither in the first person, nor in the presence of the affected individual, because of the connotations of responsibility or sin (*pāpa*) attached to it. To publicly declare infertility or insanity is an implicit admission that one, or a member of the lineage, has sinned or violated a taboo. Women are more evasive than men, shy or ashamed (*nacike*), when it comes to expressing feelings or physical states, and refuse to describe the anatomy of their illness, contenting themselves by being vague: 'it goes from my body' (*māī inda hogutade*) or 'it came upon me' (*māī alli bīṭṭide*). It is certainly apt to refer these vague but stereotypic expressions, implying a body image where the organs have no place, to the alleged impurity of women. Even to a doctor, there is a marked reluctance to communicate anything more precise.

Moreover, one must not refer directly to maladies linked to spirits by their names; for these in themselves, contain terrible powers which would then break loose. To name skin ailments such as eczema (*gaja carma*), herpes (*sarpa suttu*) or leprosy (*hīre bēne*)—literally translated 'elephant skin', 'snake round' and 'major illness'—is to invite one or the other to enter the body or to lodge itself even more strongly. Smallpox is certainly the best known example, as this disease is attributed to *devī* or *amma*, two names of the goddess commonly associated with it. Similarly, one is loathe to invoke 'demons' (*bhūta*), quietly taking it for granted that they are responsible for the attack, to use the long drawn out metaphor of 'heating' (of bodily secretions) or 'fever'. They willingly resort to this lexical code, either to subsume a number of serious illnesses or to designate one or many efficient causes: sexual abuse, immoderate consumption of food, tea, tobacco or alcohol. Or, inversely, there is a lack of these 'hot' substances, as when they speak of 'cold fever' (*chali jvara*) or describe mental illness as 'nervous fragility' (*nāra nitrana*), just like schizophrenia which is called '*nāra doṣa*'.

Insofar as physical weakness commonly serves to designate anxiety or psychic subsidence, ethnophysiology covers ethnopsychology and vice versa, i.e. how much the emotional state is governed by variations in the thermic flux and routine cycles, besides other 'cookings' (appetite, digestion, menstruation) regulating the metabolic economy conceived as a continum of the spirit-body, as affirmed by Lynch and many others (1990:19). Thus the principle of increasing heat characterises very well some problems concerning moods, for example, anger, frustration, anxiety or sexual frenzy, while mood deficencies or leucorrhoea (*bili hoguvuḍu*) or lack of seminal excretion (*datu*) explain consumptions and depressions (Bottero 1992). *Datu* is one of the seven essential moods—*aura vitalis* for men as well as for women (Obeyesekere 1976)—whose control assures intellectual vitality (*budhi*), bodily health and correct psychic orientation (*manas*) of desire (*kāma*) from which the chaste yogi, capable of continuously maintaining his spermatic reserve, draws his powers as well as prestige by attaining (if one believes in the Indian alchemic teachings) his ultimate objective, which is immortality (O'Flaherty 1973:261 sq.).

The headaches, related to the psychological states of anxiety called *tale bisi*, literally 'hot head', also demonstrate the oscillation between the superposed principles of heat/cold:: power/weakness, because we can often recognize the sign of a burn and at the same time the signal of a forthcoming deterioration: confirmation that all mental illnesses are 'homothetic of the fever', as also observed by Zimmermann (1989:150). This statement does not invalidate the irruption of an occult social causality, that of the 'bad eye' (*drişţi*), which is believed to be the cause of a number of chronic skin ailments, digestive illnesses or diarrhoea, expressed each time by an 'overheating' which is a kind of sign thrown by the supposed enemy (Nichter 1981:392).

In a very general manner, the medical etiology is thus only a subgroup of a semantic existence which, by correlating physico-mental equilibrium to thermic homeostasy, and hence the pathology to its disorder, mixes up good health and sound behaviour, i.e. the duty (*dharma*) of the individual to conform to a social and cosmic (*dharma*) order or, more precisely, to respect the customary functions imposed upon the members of a particular caste.

The villagers do not openly admit that they suffer from a serious illness, *dodḍa roga* or *mahā roga*—and so great are the connotations of fear and stigma attached to the term '*roga*' (stronger than its synonym '*kayile*'), that it is very rarely employed. They also prefer to focus the series of symptoms on unlucky planetary conjunctions on the one hand, or, on the other, on harmful climatic conditions or bad diet as having induced them. Moreover, they never talk about the nature or causal agent (known or supposed) of the illness, near or in front of the afflicted person. They say 'he has it', and hasten to add 'but not I' (*nanage illa, avarige untu*).

Euphemism, metaphor, metonymy, catachresis and conjuration thus play a role depending on the situations, especially with reference to interlocution, because 'Indians describe emotions in terms of social situations or practices rather than in terms of individual feelings' (Lynch 1990:27). And, similarly, one does not proclaim one's illness in the village or in the hospital, in the family or in the *dargāh*. Not even to a specialist, for example an *Ayurveda* practitioner, herbalist, astrologer, exorcist or ethnologist, who only recode what they examine and hear in their own systems of classification. As for relations taking charge of the sick, it creates a propitious framework for curing illnesses or for the chronic entry in possession, specially when it is accompanied by rituals (prayers, sacrifices, magic) which help in its legitimatization by taking recourse to specialists (priests, doctors or exorcists). It is a burden for the sufferer, because of the fears and prohibitions mentioned earlier, to touch on pain without saying so, to talk of it without, however, summoning it, and on the whole, to prevent it recurring or becoming worse, even if the possessed publicly reveals some pathological symptoms in order to get the therapeutic process underway.

If the variety of clinical cases and syndromes responds to the ethno-medical coding, meaningful facts (preconstituted or from cognitive lists), explicative and inferential, only the context and practical operations sanction, in the last resort, a 'good' interpretation (Nuckolls 1991). Every therapeutic situation is, in fact, pragmatic and, by right, equivocal.

To give an example: madness (*huchu*) can be distinguished quite easily from the disordered behaviour of one possessed by a 'spirit'. Nevertheless, the former could be a temporary phase caused by sorcery or an extreme derangement of humoral equilibrium, when it is not attributed to heredity, and hence an expression of either a 'natural' deficiency or of an accidental curse. However, possession by an ancestor (*prēta*) or a family deity (*kuḷa dēvaru*) is not exactly of the same type because, by manifesting the supernatural, a positive value gets added. Those who show such a predisposition attain an elevated status, but this also depends on the 'spirit' concerned: better to be possessed by a deity (*dēvaru*) than by a 'demon', *jinn* or *bhūta*! This explains the fact that some who profess to be possessed demonstrate at will a behaviour corresponding to the ritual set-up associated with the deity. The fact remains that if the attack is accidental, possession is not supposed to affect the psycho-mental state of the one who goes through it and, consequently, not in the least considered as an idiosyncrasy of the person. Moreover, it is well known that periods of momentary impurity like menstruation or a *liminal* situation such as childbirth or mourning, are vulnerable to attacks by 'evil spirits' and, inversely, a feverish deverish devotion guarantees against this kind of intervention.

It is no less true, as has often been noted (Opler 1958; Harper 1963), that possession masks inner family conflicts, particularly between the daughter and mother in-law/daughter-in-law. It offers a good reason for labelling the latter as mad (*huchu*), and a means for the former to counterbalance the power equation inasmuch as an ancestor or a saint has chosen to express himself by his intervention. And if it is true that anthropology should refuse to liken possession to hysteria, contrary to the ethnocentric reductionism of Freed & Freed (1964), or to mental disorder as has been, in fact, disputed by Claus (1979; 1981), these manifestations rather appear to be 'solutions' of the possessed as a means of communicating his problems and grievances to others (Obeyesekere 1970:106). Faced with inordinate family pressure, the possessed thus obtains, in one shot, some substantial secondary gains depending on the institutional medium recognized: an interpretation that can be termed psychodynamic (Assayag 1992b) and which is in no way contradictory to the (very general) idea that 'demons appear to be the antithesis of deities assuring fertility and a good world order' (Deliège 1992:133), except when one reifies their respective areas of influence, which as everybody in India knows, tend to overlap.

This brief glimpse in a manner of speaking at the origin of behaviour shows to what an extent pathogenic descriptions can be conventional, i.e. variable, dynamic and negotiated. The relationship to the constituent language of varied interactions is never neutral: by crossing the asymmetric waiting horizons and differentiated learnings, it induces a kind of compromise between the self, the therapist, the illness and the other by means of a rich semantic network which is specific and at the same time open, for example, the one offered by the Rājnaiyyir's *dargāh*.

TRANCE, POSSESSION, THERAPEUTICS

Gyro-devotion

What strikes one on arrival at the *dargāh* is the stream of devotees, alone or in groups, going round the tomb. While some run, sometimes in a trance, others go around it quite slowly, and still others stop here and there, but the majority go around without stopping. In fact, it is difficult to tear one's eyes away from this incessant circulatory movement, even if it discovers little by little in this extremely agitated, obviously possessed crowd, small groups alongside who calmly go around conversing.

This ritual circumambulation from left to right, just like the pilgrims in Mecca who go around the *Ka'aba*, is also called *ṭawāf*. But while the Koran (*sura* XXII, 27) prescribes seven rounds, three running and four in normal steps, in Karosi one goes round and round till a trance is induced. Here the *ṭawāf* turns into a frenzied initiatory effort to enter into communication with the saint. Fainting becomes part of this programme of seeking a discharge of emotions, as rotation aims at depersonalization, to produce 'socially structured wild behaviour', to use Devereux's term. These are the ritual frameworks which allow 'the culturally stimulating urge to be expressed, at least in a marginal manner' (Devereux 1970: 36). And although this gyro-devotion evokes the quest of dervishes, for ecstacy (Rouget 1980:52-3), the former appear more feverish, less choreographic and altogether more pathetic than the dervish's dance. But, aimed as it is, neither at imitation of, nor identification with God (Rouget 1980:83), the *ṭawāf* remains true to the logic of transcendental religion.

Some, however, do not go round but lean against the wall of the saint's residence, crouching or lying along the floor; we find one doing a headstand and shaking his limbs, while another, with an arched back, and in an apparent stupor, periodically shaken by convulsions. Standing with forehead riveted against the window, still another converses with the saint in his posthumous abode. If one, surrounded by his family members, bemoans his fate, another seems to be sleeping, waiting for the saint to appear in a dream (*huqm*) asking for an offering or a certain penitence, as no one doubts the objective validity of the dreamlike information, conforming to the place occupied by dreams in classic Islam (Grunenbaum 1967). This does not prevent him from suddenly joining the general movement later on, turning around himself like a wild star next to those who prostrate repeatedly at regular intervals.

Hypnotized by these somewhat ostentatious anomalies, it is difficult to get rid of the impression of witnessing a strange dance by people whom no strait jacket can 'stabilize', to use the current psychiatric jargon. This impression is reinforced by the observation that the dazed pathetic penitents, with metal chains on their ankles and/or wrists and usually chained to stone pillars in an outbuilding of the *dargāh*, are taken regularly to walk with small steps around the saint and that others as numerous although not insane, join them to fulfil a vow after temporarily renting, against an emolument, these handcuffs or foot chains which are proofs of their faith to the *bābā*. All these, in a way, manifest their submission to God, i.e. Islam in the literal sense.

I should also mention the strange sonorous halo caused by the buzzing of gyrowaves, the drone and litany of plaintive moaning from which escape entreaties, hiccoughs and cries, as much as appeals directed to *bābā* Rājnaiyyir, the prayer calls punctuated by the beating of drums five times a day.

AN ACCOUNT OF THE FOUNDATION AND THE PRIESTS IN CHARGE

Once reconciled to this incessant whirl, we contacted the priests in charge of the tomb who are called not *mujavār* or *pīrzade* here, but *mullāh* and *makandār*. Descendants of the local saint, they call themselves *Sayyed*, keepers of the 'prayer mat' (*sajjāda-nashīn*), the chosen of the Chosen whom they maintain by perpetuating the spīritual chain (*silsila*) since his decease. But some claim to be 'grandsons' of the saints sister and narrate the following story:

It was during time of the emperor Akbār (1542-1605) that the saint, who came from Baghdad with his sister Bībī Masabī, preached the message of Islam in India (but others assert that he was actually related to Tipū Sulṭān (1750-1799). A very pious and learned bachelor, (*'alim*), he arrived at Karosi from Iraq, spending long periods with several well known sufi masters on his way, He met the village chief in front of a Hindu temple and told him: "I want to go to the neighbouring village, but am heavily loaded; what I carry is too heavy from one man. Could you help me by lending me a bullock so that I can continue my journey?" The village Chief refused.

At this place there was a statue of the Nandi (Śiva's) bull. When the saint saw it, he kept his heavy load on the animal and sat astride it, reciting some prayers. Suddenly, the bull came to life and began walking! The village chief was as stunned as the villagers and realised that he was dealing with a powerful saint. He then begged him to remain in Karosi. The saint accepted, descended from his mount and sat under a tree in the central yard. All the inhabitants of the village crowded around him to listen to his preachings and become his disciples, including the chief of the village who solemnly promised to serve him faithfully. Thus, when the saint passed away, the chief ordered that a mausoleum be erected over his tomb.

This place of worship belongs, in the strict sense, to this large family of muslims, and hence private property; there is absolutely no outside control or interference. The Board of Trustees comprises four members: two *mullāh* and two *makandār* who share equally the apparently non-negligible revenues that their office procures. Besides conducting the routine worship of the *pīr*, their duty is to organize the big annual festival, '*urs*—the mystical 'marriage' (with Allāh)—in which thousands of devotees participate, their numbers increasing year by year according to them. Celebrated during the eighth lunar month of Sah'ban, this festival commemorates the ascension (*mi'rāj*) of the saint from Sky to Sky, which took him to the threshold of the Divine Presence. On the ninth and tenth days preceding the commemoration, the officiating priests recite verses from the Koran continuously, and on the eleventh day paint the tomb with sandal paste (*sandal rātri*), finally covering it with a new green brocade. This ceremony is in no way exclusive to Rājnaiyyir, because it is performed in a number of *dargāh* in the subcontinent.

WORSHIP OF THE SAINT

A ritual implement, apparently insignificant, nevertheless plays an important role for the pilgrims. Kept in the 'house' sheltering the tomb, this wooden stick, about a metre long, receives and grants, if one may say so, the wishes of the devotees. Murmuring their wish to this metonymical symbol of power, the devotees wind a piece of red thread around it before offering food, usually rice or sugar. It is significant that this ritual is accompanied by the breaking of a coconut at the threshold of the tomb by the priests, just like the Hindus do, but in their case chanting the name of *bābā* and the phrase '*Bismillāh, Allāh Akbār!*' A few rupees are paid for the services. On certain occasions, which correspond to private services, rice with meat is offered, a part of which is later shared among a small group of worshippers and the priests; sometimes goats or chickens are sacrificed (*baḷi*) in front of the tomb.

It may be noted that one end of the tomb is slightly raised and hence enables the suspension of large quantities of garlands, and as the day passes bringing with it a flood of devotees, it tends to resemble the idol of a Hindu deity. Moreover, the devotees assert that the saint has a 'terrible glance' from which he gets him name, *rāj-naiyyir*, meaning 'king of light' or 'of lightning' in Urdu. Some others, playing on these words, call him '*raṇjenūr*', 'affliction'.

In return for the offerings, the priests bless the devotees, i.e. pass a fan of peacock feathers (*mūrchal*) over the head, shoulders and back, sometimes beating them quite hard, before returning to them the lemons which play an important part in the ritual. For example, before worshipping, the devotees buy a *bandam*, a small lemon covered with ash (*bhasma*) taken from the well adjoining the tomb and knotted in a white cloth, and tie it high on the fore-arm. After worship, the person accompanying the devotee who has come to ask a wish of the saint, removes the knot, reciting prayers (*namāz*) at the same time. He then takes the lemon, cuts it in halves with a small knife or razor blade, and puts them on the forehead of the suplicant. He covers each half with ash and then brushes the body, first the left side and then the right, front and back, with it and finally throws the pressed fruit in two opposite directions. In this way, the demons have been chased faraway for a long time. Talismans (*ta'widh*), tied around the wrists by the priests for a sum, have analogous protective functions, this time to ward off fate or to help recovery. However, the *bandam* or *ta'widh* are effective only if the devotees have already gone around the tomb seven times.

During the five daily prayers, circling the tomb comes to a standstill. The devotees stay where they are and turn towards the mausoleum. During the call, a majority of them press towards the door of the sanctum, bow their heads and join their hands at nose level throughout the recitation of the prayers. Powerful loudspeakers at the four corners blare out the *sura* of the Holy Koran which extoll the curative power of God represented here by one of his 'deputies'. The crowd repeats the last sentence of every prayer in unison.

The immobility of the men is in contrast to the agitation of the women who have prepared themselves for possession by an ascending hyper-ventilation mechanism, which is similar to that expressed by those possessed by Hindu deities (Assayag 1989). They now brace themselves with outstretched limbs, tirelessly describing large circular motions with their torso and head. At each gyration, their long hair (which is let loose) sweeps the floor, and they risk striking their head violently against the ground. These gesticulations testify to the torture inflicted by the *bābā's* power, and at its peak, to the 'demons' who themselves torture the possessed. Conflict shows in the convulsed bodies of these women, and which would have meant instant death had they not been unconscious: whatever happens the *bābā* protects them and only the demons suffer, they say. Expression of existential suffering is here confused with the imploring or venerating action.

Next to these sessions, public or private, but where the *ṭawāf* is imposed every time as a preface (group therapeutics) which can bring the 'demon' to the surface, we often see other types of possession affecting independent practitioners. Although in no way connected to the *dargāh*, they nevertheless benefit from the exudations of the holy *baraka* to operate more effectively. These exorcists (*ghāḷī*) engage in a dialogue with the possesssed, or more precisely with the 'demon' who speaks through their mouth, a business which quickly takes on the appearance of a domination/ submission relationship. Thus they throw fists full of ash at regular intervals on the face of the possessed till he or she suffocates, or at times they hit him or her in order to force the 'demon' to reveal his identity. The patient, who is generally lying down, contorts and his grimaces are proof of a grim battle (between the saint and 'demon') going on within him. It is not rare to see him hiccoughing or crying, while the therapist seated at his side, holds him by the hand as long as the liberation requires. Not only is the result never achieved early, but a relapse is possible and is almost always the rule. Obviously, it is not immediate because the dramatic progression of exorcism is achieved only by an entry in catatony from which the devotee emerges with great difficulty. Groggy most of the time, he does not remember anything that took place.

A brief ceremony puts the finishing touches to the session. Once recovered from the spirits, the possessed pierces three or five lemons on a long nail and ties a red thread around it, and finally attaches a rolled piece of paper containing an incantation (magical formula). It could be a wish, but information on this point differs, and it is understandable that a prudent ethnologue would not verify for himself. Whatever it may be the possessed then drives this nail into one of the trees facing the tomb reserved for this purpose. Slightly taller than a man, these dead trees are almost fully covered by nails, such that they resemble disturbed hedgehogs. The nails represent the many 'demons' solidly fixed by the power of the *bābā* and one hopes, remissions thus obtained.

MANAGEMENT AND THERAPEUTICS

Having visited many sanctuaries of this type in this region (Assayag 1995), it is very tempting to propose a structural model. The spatial opposition between the saint buried in his tomb, from which the *baraka* exudes, and the demons who ceaselessly transpose into the body of the possessed devotee, is systematic: horizontal and terrestrial opposition, if it can be so called, crossing another—vertical, celestial and paradoxical this time, because the oniric architecture of the *dargāh*, in which reposes a living ascending defunct, evokes a ladder climbing towards the low (Chodkiewicz 1986:220). Neither living nor dead, they assert that the saint has indeed climbed to the sky with eyes open, to return to the 'Paradise' (*mi'rāj*) of Allāh. Although he no longer belongs to the mortal world, he nevertheless exerts his aura over them from above. By thus opening a channel between God and the world, he diffuses his beneficial *baraka* which circulates continuously between the Sky and Earth (Ewing 1984:107). On their part, the tress planted in the soil form the link beyond the Earth, by being rooted in the subterranean world for which the demoniacal creatures have great attraction. The shining Rājnaiyyir, as his name throws light on him, is opposed to infernal regions, in accordance with a relationship of permanent hostility, a relationship which the Muslims interpret on a combat (*jihād*) model, while the Hindus transpose it to a different battlefield (*kurukṣetra*) (Assayag 1994).

At the risk of futher interpretation we can, moreover, put forward the hypothesis that it is to this topological but dynamic organization of the *dargāh* that the victims of psychic dissociation owe the possibility of dramatizing their mental 'schize' and removing their symptoms. Mainly through the medium of the *ṭawāf*, this abreaction helps overcome the barrier and starts the therapeutic process by putting aside the demands of customary reality (Rollier 1983: Chap. VI). Thanks to this passage from the latent to the manifest, it offers them the possibility of symbolising the split, to recompose an identity (which would only be momentary) torn between acceptance and rejection: 'two psychic attitudes which are different, opposed and independent from one another' (Freud 1949:82); two defence processes, one turned towards reality and the other towards drive, at least for those whose ego is sufficiently receptive to accedate to the symbolic dimension, i.e. except psychotic persons whose access to Rājnaiyyir is permanently denied.

RELIGION AND MEDICINE

A master reigning over his territory (*wilāyat*), which is itself a part of the Kingdom that Allāh, the Merciful, has granted to one of his 'substitutes' (*abdāl*) (Digby 1986:62-3), the *pīr*, protector as well as healer, sees an unending stream of sick people going around his tomb throughout the year; he literally hears, as expressed by the *ṭawāf*—this movement, pious and at the same time cathartic, showing all the symptoms in its round.

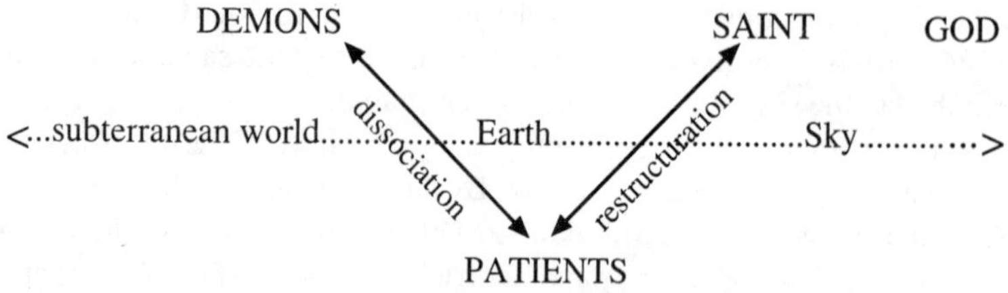

FIGURE 2: STRUCTURAL AND PSYCHOPATHOLOGICAL ORGANIZATION OF WORSHIP

Certainly, for a Westerner educated on the disjunctive model of the spirit and body, the natural and supernatural, nothing would bring together in one place pathologies which are at this point heterogeneous. But as numerous anthropological observations of 'popular' Indian religiosity testify, it is common for an interred saint figure, Muslim as well as Hindu (Blackburn 1985; Malhotra 1988), to take upon itself the hopes and desires which mix therapy with faith. This theurgy dramatizes by means of ritualistic action, i.e. gyro-devotion, not only a local ontology of the suffering but also the possibility for deranged individuals to borrow symbolically coded paths from a society closely knit, by religious ties. They are roundabout ways which enable them as much as possible to reintegrate a family order, lineage, community, etc. Social medicine, rather than pathological medicine, is directed more towards sick beings than towards a positive definition of ailment described in an anatomo-clinical atlas (Foucault 1963). That is why the facets of a nosology whose polythetic structure permits the treatment of knots of conjectural relations—

bio-medical and at the same time psychosocial—converge from all parts on the holy sepulchre, complementing the existing natural etiological and therapeuitc models, especially when these have failed to work.

All the same, while we can legitimately compare the *dargāh* to an asylum linked to an anthropological experience specific to a cure, no one has the right to reduce it to a hospital or, worse, to a lazar house, to use the term in a metaphoric sense. If the boundary between the normal and pathological is vacillating, it is primarily because the holy intercessor, by joining the Sky and the Earth, the 'divine realities' (*haqā'iq haqqiyya*) and 'mundane realities' (*haqā'iq khalqiyya*), enables the actors to build an idiom of their ailments and misfortunes on a recognized religious model, i.e. by arranging them in an order which is itself symbolic in nature. No doubt this is the best way in this peripheral context of ('popular') Islam—to seal the stamp of holiness, neither on prophecy any more than on eschatology but on the power of a saint forgotten by history. Moreover, this was not invented recently, as claimed by my informer, Shāh Walī, while leaving the place.

By this concluding remark I understood that what I had been given to observe seemed shameful to him, unworthy of the rigid moral and pietistic traditions of Islam which only accept saint worship cleansed by its therapeutic dimensions, and also unworthy of medical modernism which, to his eyes, represented the West that I was. Most certainly, my informant forgot that the traditions practised at present are not an *ex nihilo* creation, but only a reactivation of floating pictures of an autochtonous culture. This in no way prevents the same people from going to medical practitioners and taking strong medicines. All the same, Shāh Walī's reaction poses a good question: how can an analyst of a foreign culture describe the singular experience of suffering and of its treatment at the same time? Especially by avoiding psychological and psychiatric categories which are supposed to translate it; by not giving in to the temptation of reducing it to an exotic show; and lastly, by posing back-to-back, the transparent and opaque symmetrical illusions of the observer-observed with and by otherness, whose testimony, we may suppose, will interest those who study meaningful relationships between culture, society and psyche. If there is no one answer to the problem of finding a satisfactory way of narrating suffering from a distance we can, nevertheless, guarantee that the apprehension of the plurality of the worlds of imaginary and symbolic relationships, even when it questions the nature of cultural transfers, can modestly help in restarting the interrogation: who is the other?

REFERENCES

Assayag, J. 1989 Sacrifice et violence. Les genres de la possession dans le sud de l'Inde (Karnataka), *Nouvelle Revue d' Ethnopsychiatrie*, 131-57.

——— 1992a *La Colère de la déesse décapitée. Traditions, cultes et pouvoir dans le Sud de l'Inde*. Paris: CNRS Editions.

——— 1992b Compte rendu de G. Obeyesekere: *Work of Culture, Symbolic Transformation in Psychoanalysis and Anthropology, L'Homme* 121, 199-202.

——— 1994 Pouvoir contre 'puissances'. Bref essai de demonologie hindoue-musulmane, *L'Homme* 131, XXXIV (3).

——— 1995 *Au Confluent de deux rivières. Musulmans et hindous dons le Sud de l'Inde*. Paris: Editions de l'EHESS.

Baljon, I.M.S. 1989 Shah Walliullah and the Dargāh. In G.W. Troll (ed.), *Muslim Shrines in India: Their Character, History and Significance*. Delhi: Oxford University Press, 189-97.

Bayly, S. 1989 *Saints, Goddesses and Kings: Muslims and Christians in South Indian Society, 1700-1900*. Cambridge: Cambridge University Press.

Beals, A.R. 1976 Strategies of Resort to Curers in South India. In C. Leslie (ed.), *Asian Medical System: A Comparative Study*. Berkeley/Los Angeles/ London: University of California Press, 184-200.

Blackburn, S. 1985 Death and Deification: Folk Cults in Hinduism, *History of Religion* 24, 255-74.

Bottero, A. 1992 La consomption par déperdition séminale en Inde et ailleurs, *Annales de la Fondation Fyssen* 7, 17-23.

Brown, P. 1981 *The Cult of the Saints: Its Rise and Function in Latin Christianity*. Chicago: Chicago University Press.

Chodkiewicz, M. 1986 *Le Sceau des saints. Prophétie et sainteté dans la doctrine d'Ibn Arabi*. Paris: Gallimard.

Claus, P. 1979 Spirit Possession and Spirit Mediumship From the Perspective of Tulu Oral Traditions, *Culture, Medicine and Psychiatry* 3, 29-52.

——— 1984 Medical Anthropology and the Ethnography of Spirit Possession, *Contributions to Asian Studies* 18, 60-72.

Currie, P.M. 1989 *The Shrine and Cult of Mu'in Al-Din Chishti of Ajmer*. Delhi: Oxford University Press.

Deliège, R. 1992 La Possession démoniaque chez les Intouchables catholiques de l'Inde du Sud, *Archives de Sciences Sociales des Religions* 79, 115-34.

Desiderio Pinto, S.J. 1989 The Mystery of the Nizamuddin *Dargah*: The Accounts of Pilgrims. In C.W. Troll (ed.), *Muslim Shrines in India: Their Character, History and Significance*. Delhi: Oxford University Press, 112-24.

Devereux, G. 1970 Normal et anormal (1956). In G. Devereux, *Essais d' Ethnopsychiatrie générale*. Paris: Gallimard, 1-83.

Digby, S. 1986 The Sufi Shaikh as a Source of Authority in Mediaeval India. In M. Gaborieau (ed.) *Islam et société en Asie du Sud, Purusartha* 9, 57-77.

Dupront, A. 1987 *Du Sacré. Croisades et pèlerinages. Images et langages.* Paris: Gallimard.

Ewing, K. 1984 The Sufi as Saint, Curer and Exorcist in Modern Pakistan, *Contribution to Asian Studies* XVII, 106-114.

Freed S. and Freed R. 1964 Spirit Possession as Illness in a North Indian Village, *Ethnology* 3, 152-71.

Freud, S. 1949 *Abrégé de psychanalyse*. Paris: PUF (1st edn. 1938).

Foucault, M. 1963 *Naissance de la clinique. Une archéologie du regard médical.* Paris: PUF.

Gaborieau, M. 1989 A Ninetheenth Century Indian 'Wahhabi' Tract Against the Cult Of Muslim Saints: Al-Blagh al- Mubin. In C.W. Troll (ed.), *Muslim Shrines in India. Their Character, History and Significance.* Delhi: Oxford University Press, 198-239.

Garcin De Tassy, J.H. 1869 Mémoire sur les particularités de la religion, musulmane dans l'Inde. Paris: Labitte (1st edn. 1831 in *Journal Asiatique*).

Grunenbaum, G. E. von 1967 La fonction culturelle du rêve dans l'Islam classique'. In R. Caillois and G.E. von Grunenbaum (eds.): *Le Rêve et les sociétés humaines.* Paris: Gallimard, 7-23.

Harper, E.B. 1963 Spirit Possession and Social Structure. In B. Ratnam (ed.), *Anthropology on the March.* Madras: Book Centre, 165 97.

Ishwaran, K. 1968 *Shivapur: A South Indian Village.* London: Routledge and Kegan Paul.

Kakar, S. 1982 *Shamans, Mystics and Doctors: A Psychological inquiry into India and its Healing Traditions.* Delhi: Oxford University Press.

Kushro Hussaini, S.S. 1983 *Sayyid Muhammad Al-Husayni-i Gesudiraz (721/1321-825/1422): on Sufism.* Delhi. Idarah-i Adabiyat-i Delhi.

Lynch, O.M. 1990 Introduction: Emotions in Theoretical Contexts. In O.M. Lynch (ed.), *Divine Passions. The Social Construction of Emotion in India.* Berkeley/Los Angeles/Oxford: University of California Press, 3-34.

Malhotra, K.C. 1988 The Birth of a God: Ram Mauma of the Nadiwala. In E.M. Zelliot and M. Bersten (eds.), *The Experience of Hinduism. Essays on Religion in Maharashtra.* Albany: State University of New York Press, 131-41.

Mayer, A.C. 1967 Pir and Murshid: an Aspect of Religious Leadership in West Pakistan, *Middle Eastern Studies* 3, 2, 160-9).

Nichter, M. 1981 Idioms of Illness: Alternatives in the Expression of Psychosocial distress: A Case Study from South India, *Culture, Medicine and Psychiatry* 5, 379-408.

——— 1989 *Anthropology and International Health. South Asian Case Studies.* Dordrecht/Roston/London: Kluwer Academic Publishers.

Nuckolls, C.W. 1991 Culture and Causal Thinking. Diagnosis and Prediction in a South Indian Fishing Village, *Ethos* 19, 1, 3-51.

Obeyesekere, G. 1970 The Idiom of Demonic Possession: A Case Study, *Social Science and Medicine* 4, 97-111.

O'Flaherty, W.D. 1973 *Asceticism and Eroticism in the Mythology of Siva.* London: Oxford University Press.

Opler, M.E. 1958 Spirit Possession in a Rural Area of Northern India. In W.A. Lessa and E.Z. Vogt (eds.), *Reader in Comparative Religions.* New York: Row Peterson and Co., 553-6.

Pfleiderer, B. 1981 Mira Datar *Dargah*: The Psychiatry of a Muslim Shrine. In I. Ahmad (ed.), *Ritual and Religion among Muslims in India.* Delhi: Manohar, 195-233.

Rentz, G. 1960 Article: 'Barakat', in H.A.R. Gibb *et al.* (eds.), *Encyclopedia of Islam* (New Edition). Leiden: E.J. Brill and London: Cuzac et Co., 1032-3.

Rizvi, S.A.A. 1978-83 *A History of Sufism in India*, 2 vols. Delhi: Munshiram Manoharlal.

Rollier, F. 1983 *Murugmalla, Possession et rituels thérapeutiques dans un tombeau musulman d'Inde du Sud.* Etude psychiatrique. Mémoire pour le C.E.S. de psychiatrie, Université de Paris VI, Broussais/Hotel-Dieu.

Rouget, G. 1981 *La Musique et la transe. Esquisse d'une théorie générale des relations de la musique et de la possession.* Paris: Gallimard.

Subhan, T.A. 1970 *Sufism. Its Saints and Shrines. An Introduction to the Study of Sufism with Special Reference to India.* New York: Samuel Weiser Inc. (1st edn. Lahore, 1938).

Wilson, S. 1983 *Saints and their Cults. Studies in Religious Sociology, Folklore and History.* Cambridge: Cambridge University Press.

Zimmermann, F. 1989 *Le Discours des remèdes au pays des épices. Enquête sur la médecine hindoue.* Paris: Editions Payot.

Walking Round on the Straight Path in the Name of the Father: A Study of the Dispossession Trance at Murugmalla

FRANCK ROLLIER

Murugmalla is the name of a *dargāh*, that is to say the tomb of an Indian Islamic saint who belonged to the Sufi order. The *dargāh* is situated at the border of three different states of south India (Karnataka, Tamilnadu, Andhra Pradesh) and has been an important pilgrimage site since the beginning of the eighteenth century. Nowadays, the *dargāh* takes in many ailing persons which the chief *mullāh* declares 'possessed' and encourages to submit to a ritual trance called the *ṭawāf*.

Following several stays on site in 1980 I had attempted an ethnological description of Murugmalla's population, of the sites and different rituals which take place there, as well as an ethnopsychiatric observation of the possessed of Murugmalla, which is above all a retreat (Rollier 1981, 1983). I then proposed to situate the dispossession trances among the 'culturally prescribed forms of misconduct' described by Linton in the 50s (1956), a concept taken up again by Devereux who made of it a particular mode of 'ethnic disorders', as opposed to personal disorders (also known as idiosyncrasic): these 'ethnic disorders' are culturally structured and ordered and usually carry a name (1956). Devereux gives as classical examples the *berserk* behaviour of the Viking in battle or the *amok* run of the disturbed Malay. I have suggested elsewhere that this type of 'ready-made' pathology could be applied in the Western world by the end of this century to the addicitive disorders which cover a large pathological range (1985).

The *ṭawāf* thus appeared to me as a 'respectable way of going insane', as if the culture was saying: 'beware of going insane, but if you do, this is the way you should behave . . . '. This type of cultural model permits the setting up of neurotic defences following certain traumas which are frequently found in every culture. In Indian culture, in my opinion, this can apply to the nervous breakdown of the young bride, a crisis which threatens the stability of the joint family (Harper 1963; Kakar 1978; Rollier 1983).

This type of disorder 'is often used as a model by those who, for one reason or another, suffer from psychic disorders' (Devereux 1956) and in fact I observed at Murugmalla that the 'status' of the possessed is often claimed by psychotic or psycho-somatic patients.

In the present work I propose to view the problem in a different light: a psychoanalytic reading of Murugmalla's rituals and their function in the psychic economy of the possessed. We will also question the Subject's place on the path which leads from the outbreak of symptoms to the diagnosis of possession, and then from the entry into trance to the outcome of the crisis. I will concentrate on the typical case of the 'possessed' who recognizes himself by this term and agrees to enter into trance; in our observations, these cases belong to neurotic, psychotic (*Pama, Pacha*) or even psychosomatic (*Shernaz, Nisha*) pathologies. On the other hand, I will not discuss the possessed who seem indifferent or even refuse to enter into trance: they, indeed, belong either to a psychosis or to predominantly organic disorders.

My study is based on Sigmund Freud's theories and the invigorating reading of Freud by the psychoanalyst Jacques Lacan (1901-81), who proposed new concepts susceptible to clarify or continue Freud's advances. For the reader unfamiliar with this author, I refer to the index of Lacan's concepts (marked with an asterisk *) at the end of this paper. I remain, of course, responsible for the interpretation of Lacan here.

THE ENTRY INTO 'POSSESSION' IS A NAME

I shall refer to the following cases:

Bibijan: 12 years old, experienced an 'intense fear' after the death of her older sister's husband; since then, she suffers crisis of aerophagia and related pains.

Akbar: 20 years old, left his family home where he felt 'he was going insane' and had 'thoughts of committing suicide'.

Lata: 18 years old, while attending her brother's marriage, three months after her own, fainted, and consequently developed a state of nervous agitation, running away naked in the street.

Pama: 23 years old, suddenly begins raving saying that her mother-in-law wants to poison her; she refuses food and sexual relations, burns her hands and feet, and talks of crucifying herself (she is a Hindu).

Shernaz: 25 years old, suffers from chronic gastro-intestinal disorders which resist medical treatment.

Nisha: 15 years old, refuses to speak since contracting typhoid fever.

The patient is diagnosed as 'possessed' either by his/her family or entourage at the outbreak of disorders (in the first three cases mentioned), or by the *mullāh* upon arrival at the *dargāh*. The decision to go to Murugmalla may be taken immediately or weeks or months after the outbreak of the crisis: it was a taxi driver who spoke of the *dargāh* to *Pama's* husband after several months of various treatments; *Nisha* was taken there by her mother 'after having dreamed of a man who told her to go to Murugmalla'.

For the *Mullah*, any sickness or symptom—somatic or psychic—is a sign of 'possession by an evil spirit or demon' that the Saints of the *dargāh* will treat. At the level of the family group, only the appearance of psychic symptoms is recognized directly as a sign of possession. In the typical cases which we have observed, it is most often a question of a crisis of acute anguish which leads to a serious disorder in the functioning of the family.

The 'Possession' is thus first of all the experience of giving a name by the individual's entourage who is confronted with the anguish and/or delirium. The outbreak of the anguish confronts the individual with the presence of a break, a void (or an overload in the case of a delirium) which reveals that behind the social character there exists that which, with Lacan, I call a Subject*, defined as an empty place; it is from there that a lack* is felt, and therefore a desire*.

For Lacan, it is precisely 'the sudden appearance of the lack which is the source of anguish' (1962); this formulation takes up and advances the work of Freud who abandoned the hypothesis of a traumatic origin of the anguish, of which the birth would have been the model, to situate the loss as the condition which triggers the appearance of the anguish (1926).

In Murugmalla, the first symptoms of the future possessed often appear in relation with an experience of separation:

— loss of the infant love object or its representative, which may occur at the occasion of a mourning or a marriage, which is above all a separation! . . . and may sometimes take on tragic dimensions for the Indian woman who is obliged to adopt and be adopted by her family-in-law.

— the meeting of the other's desire at the occasion of the first sexual relations is also an experience of separation: it confronts the person with the difference represented by the other sex and is a moment of frequent occurrence of the anguish (etymologically the word sex comes from the Indo-European root *sek-*, then from the latin *seco*: cut in two, divide).

As soon as it is revealed, the emptiness of the Subject will be veiled, taken up by the signifier* Possession. This signifier names a foreign presence: it is a demoniac Other* who possesses the Subject, and the possession is a signifier which will henceforth represent it. This naming of the 'evil' soothes some of the anguish and also implies going to a specific site, the *dargāh*, and conforming to a ritualized behavior, the trance. From that time onward, the Subject is no longer alone before the abyss which, along with the anguish, was opened before him. The entourage's questions find an answer, and the—until now mysterious—disorder receives a name, and thus a meaning. Consequently a cause for this disorder is supposed, which will be discovered by means of the trance: it is this discovery which will allow the undoing of the 'evil'.

But what is above all expected from the trance, is that it manifests that the possession 'takes'.

THE *ṬAWĀF*: READY? ACTION: LET'S TURN AROUND!

The word *ṭawāf*, which means 'trance', refers to the action of turning and traditionally designates the ritual circuit accomplished by a pilgrim in a holy place, and above all the seven circumambulations around the Ka'ba at Mecca.

After the evening prayer, at the behest of the *mullāh*, certain 'so-called possessed' begin to turn around the tomb, the families forming a living and silent wall around them. In the midst of the cries, contortions and intoning 'Allāh Akbar' and *Ammajan-Babajan*—Mummy-Daddy—name of the Saint and his wife who rest side by side—the Spirits enter on the scene:

Shernaz tells me:

When I begin to turn, I am a little dizzy, then the *ṭawāf* takes me, my head begins to spin, I begin to run faster and then there is a conflict (*taklif*) within my body . . . an exchange of questions and answers and I say: 'No, I won't stay, I'm going to go away. . . .' After a certain time, I ask the name of the demon who has descended upon me, but he does'nt respond. *It* goes on like that for some time, and after a dispute, finally he agrees to tell his name. . . . It is then said to the demon to disturb me no more, then my head begins to spin less and everything stops.

At the end, the possessed collapses on the tomb and falls into a daze.

Upon arrival at the *dargāh* the so-called possessed identifies himself first with the signifier 'Possessed', then with the 'trance' symptom when put in the presence of those who are already turning. The identification which allows the person to enter into the *ṭawāf* results from the so-called identification 'by the symptom', described by Freud with regard to young girls at boarding school (1921); this identification allows the setting up of a community of possessed.

A DESIRE NAMED DEMON . . . IN SEARCH OF A NAME . . . AND A MASTER

At the time of the trance, the possessed experiences a dialogue, a fight between two imaginary characters with which he identifies himself; this phantasy is one of a double hold:

(*a*) By the demon supposedly responsible for the anguish or the symptoms and who now manifests his presence: that which caused the symptoms, *it* chats. . . . The possessed is his own demon, he incarnates him within his body, then lets him speak.

Possessed Muslims often call demons *Jinns*, a word which, as pointed out by S. Kakar, comes 'from the Arab *jann* which means "to cover, veil, shelter, and indicates something which is hidden like an embryo in the womb . . . " ' (1984). The Hindus—who come in great number to Murugmalla—acknowledge themselves possessed either by the God in his terrifying aspect, or by the wandering soul of a deceased person, for whom the funeral rituals were not carefully observed (the *prētas*), or whose life had been dominated by insatisfaction (the *piśacas*) or a life which has been terminated by suicide or accident (the *bhūtas*).

The *mullāh* explains to us that the demon 'descends from a deceased person upon someone who has committed a fault or who is the victim of a work of witchcraft'; the stake of the combat is the revelation of the demon's name and the faults that the individual, one of his relatives or ancestors may have commited with regard to the religious or social order, 'in this life or in a past life'; these faults will be recognized as causes of the possession. For example:

— *Pama's* family (the woman who spoke of crucifying herself), tells us that the *ṭawāf* revealed that the possession was caused by the spirit of a friend of the family, who was found dead one morning in the living room of the house, after a night of drinking.

— *Pacha*, 18 years old, came to Murugmalla to be cured of clastic crises, during the course of which 'he breaks everything in the house'. He has been doing the *ṭawāf* four times a day for two months now, and has just learned that he is possessed by the Snake ... and that before his birth a member of his family had killed a cobra in the garden, a fault which would provoke 'the brutal death of someone in the family'.

The dispossession trance is thus an invocation and an incarnation of the desire of a deceased person ... the desire of the Other*, or quite simply the desire*....

(*b*) The possessed is also taken by the 'Spirit' of the Saint, himself deceased, who comes to possess the individual in a hallucinatory form, in order to question and harass the demon: this is what L.de Heusch calls the 'joyful possession, authentically religious' (1971); it manifests the presence of God and rests on an identification with the moral values represented by the Saints, who are intermediaries between God and man. It evokes the mystical path in which access to God is immediate and refers to the figure of the *devane*, a Persian word which designates at the same time one who is insane and one with divine inspiration.

For Freud, the demon or the devil is the personification of the repressed, unconscious drive* (1908, 1923), which he calls the 'Id'. In following his second topic which distinguishes the Ego from the Id or drive agency, and both from the Superego or Ego-Ideal which is 'the carrier of tradition and parental values' (1933), we may hypothesize that during the trance the Ego takes a back seat, the perceptions of the external world being suspended, whereas the Id and the Superego are confronted, in the respective figures of the demon and the Saint. The Ego conserves, however, a role of mediator between the two instances ... authorizing the Id—the drive representative—to unload ... only if the Superego can express itself and is expected to finally win the combat.

The initial demand of the possessed is thus brought back by the trance to a game of identifications, a mechanism which bears witness to an intense transference to this place.... [Lacan: 'The transference operates in the direction of bringing demand back to identification' (1991).]

POSSESSION IS THE JOUISSANCE*

Etymologically, to possess is *potis sedere*, that is to say to be master of/to be powerful/to be able, to be seated/ which can be expressed by 'sit upon'. Possession is when one is seated on one's wealth; then one gets jouissance out of it and this is how everyone derives jouissance from his belongings, from his knowledge or from a power. . . . This aspect of jouissance is manifested here:

(*a*) First, on a physical level, in the libidinal explosion of the trance . . . beyond consciousness, beyond chronological time, and within certain limits beyond the conventions and taboos of the community; separated at the beginning of the *ṭawāf*, men and women then turn together, Muslims, Hindus or Christians, all castes and all languages intermixed. The trance mimes the sexual act with eccentric, passionate postures, with preliminary rituals, the mounting of tension, then frantic running which ends in the abandon to the wishes of the Saint. This jouissance is to be situated in a dimension beyond sexuality and sexual orgasm: it is a moment of confusion, a quest for unity, for a language common to all the possessed, a language reduced to a uniform dialogue between a demon and the *Spirit* of a Saint. Differences are abolished and above all *the* difference, which is sexuality, the difference between the sexes.

(*b*) It is also the jouissance of acquiring a new knowledge. Being 'taken', it is a question of taking, of learning something: the name of the demon possessor, perhaps the name of the one who—in the case of witchcraft—is at the origin of the possession, as well as of the faults commited.

(*c*) Jouissance is also in the process of repetition:

— during the trance the fight between the Saint and the demon in fact rests on a stereotyped thread, which fills up the majority of the possessed's speech and is found, almost identical, in every possessed person.

Thus, Akbar declaims:

> I won't come, I won't come, No Allah I won't come
> I'm coming soon, I'm coming, I'm falling at your feet
> I will never come, no never . . .
> I will come, surely, I will come into your palace, etc. . . .

the expected result being the capture of the demon by the Spirit of the Saint.

— in addition, the trance always takes place more than once, repeating every day the same combat, for weeks or even months, the demon always resisting the solicitations and punishments of the Saint.

After one of his *ṭawāf*, Akbar relates:

The demon repeats: 'how can I escape, I've been in his body for 18 years, I'm not disturbing him at all, why do you want to take me prisoner? You can punish me as much as you like, but I will never go away.'

To which Babajan responds: 'I cannot let you go on like that, I will make you my slave.'

But the demon retorts: 'I am very rich, I am the king of 121 kings, I can give him all the money he desires, I want to stay in his body.'

Babajan then says: 'no, you cannot stay in his body, you will be my slave, I will take you prisoner.'

The questions and answers continue and I hurt myself greatly.

Thus something repeats itself ad infinitum, sometimes even though the demon has already been identified—as in the case of *Shernaz*. But what is it exactly that repeats itself so? Is it the 'Id', the representative of the drive, that the theory signals as being the expression of the demon? In fact, it is rather a question of repetition of a thread woven with the signifiers of the Other—the 'demon', the 'spirit of the Saint'—signifiers which the possessed acknowledges in his words. The Other thus speaks through him and the possessed incarnates the jouissance of the Other.

As for the Id, the repressed desire, its verbal expression is continually deferred. The Superego commands: 'Submit yourself' and the Ego responds: 'No way, I'm staying'. The Ego is the centre of resistance which maintains the repression as much as possible; it is only by the repetition of threats and punishments from the Superego that one day perhaps the Id will speak.

This repetition, that I qualify as jouissance, soothes the anguish for the duration of the trance, which is however, experienced in a painful way (and sometimes even bloody for certain psychotic possessed). It is situated beyond pleasure and displeasure.

It is precisely from the clinical observation of the compulsion to repeat that Freud formulated his 'beyond the pleasure principle' in order to describe the work of the death drive, which is the unconscious search for a return to the inanimate, the inert, the All unifying (1920).

This repetition in and of the trance, this eternal return to the jousissance that culminates in the abandon of the body and the numbing of the mind at the end of each *ṭawāf*, would be thus a demonstration of the presence of the death drive, of 'that which in fact goes against life' (Lacan, 1969).

(*d*) *Finally, the jouissance of a power.* Even before the trance, the signifier possession confers a certain power:

— The individual acquires a family and social recognition that he was often lacking.
— The Subject assailed by anguish is put into words, at the same time that he is taken in hand: he is transported to Murugmalla. Thus, he benefits from a status, marginal but recognized, that gives him a real importance, especially as he is always possessed by something powerful (a divinity, the spirit of a relative or deceased friend). Although submitted to the Other's signifiers and to his entourage who transports him, surrounds and looks after him attentively, one might ask: *who, in fact, possesses whom*?

Is this submission not in fact the other side of the coin, the jouissance of a power, in particular on the family which remains mobilized for days?

The search for mastery by way of submission has a name: this is called masochism, essentially moral masochism, qualified by Freud as economic; the guilt and the need for punishment, reinforced at each *ṭawāf*, is the expression of it. For example, *Akbar* informs us, after a *ṭawāf*, of his feeling of guilt with relation to his practice of masturbation.

On the path which leads an individual from the distressing experience of a loss to the dispossession trance, he passes from separation from himself, at the time of the initial crisis, to an attempt at knowledge and mastery. This, on which the speaking *being* is in fact without a hold, this Id which is incarnated in the trance, the possessed will try to express, in order finally to name it and ideally reduce it to a *having*, which may be captured and deposed.

This desire for mastery, this masochist aspect is indeed structural and may be found in every human being; at Murugmalla, this desire is exercised by the intermediary of an accepted hold by the signifiers: the 'devil', the 'spirit of the saint' who are signifiers of the Other. If the I indeed reveals itself 'to be an Other', here it is in order to better master it, which, we note in passing, constitutes a fundamental difference with the aim of an analytical cure.

However, the stay at Murugmalla, and the trances, must end in the possessed's renouncing his jouissance and by his/her identification with the signifiers which represent the Saint only: this is the price of the dis-possession.

SOMETHING TO LOSE?

In fact the possessed end up leaving Murugmalla one day, except for certain psychotic patients. The demons and the faults having been identified, two mechanisms are determinant in initiating this departure: the loss of 'something', and the dreams.

(*a*) 'In the repetition itself, there is something that is lost' proposes Lacan (1969). What about this?

While the possessed in trance expresses his 'demon' in the stereotyped mode that we have described, and before the 'demon' allows to submit itself, certain particularities, 'flops', slip into the thread of the ready-made scenario: insults, invectives, recriminations, etc., which fall on the ears of the silent ... and smiling families, since it isn't the individual but an Other who is speaking.

Would this that escapes the speaker and the hold of the ready-made discourse of the Other, be, in fact, the Id, the repressed drive representative, which emanates from the Subject, and bears witness to the intensity of his life drive?

The *mullāh* affirms that the 'illnesses are gifts sent by God to purify us'. Is not this speech, offered as a spectacle to the attentive spectators, the 'something' that possesses the possessed and that he brings to Murugmalla 'as a gift'?

This 'loss' will be repressed after the event: obscenities, insults or claims heard have never been taken up in the account given to us of the possessed's *ṭawāf*, neither by his/her relatives or by the *mullāh*. What does the family hear of this speech, that, by the simple fact that it is pronounced under the cover of a mask, will not be analysed with regard to the individual? This is what should be stated precisely in a closer observation of these 'asides'. It must be said that this essential aspect of the trance held my attention only ... after the event! There is also, here, a 'flop' on the observer's part, something that escaped my desire to grasp and then, afterwards, makes sense ... ! One might hypothesize that this speech is not pronounced in vain, but heard in a certain way, 'signing' to the relatives of the possessed. There is thus an opening of the envelope formed by the network of the Other's signifiers, towards the letter of the desire, and towards a transmittable knowledge; it springs forth from an 'inter-diction', that is to say between two codified assertions and from the statement of the jouissance's prohibition, which is stated like what Babajan says to Akbar's demon: 'I can't let you go on like that, I will make you my slave'.

(*b*) Moreover, 'operations' are suggested to the possessed by the *mullāh* when the demons prove to be particularly resistant to the *ṭawāf*. Then he calls the signifiers of Science to the rescue: '*Ammajan-Babajan* visit the possessed in dreams' he tells us, and 'they give him injections, medications, they operate. That resembles a hospital; they remove the dirt from his body, show it to the patient, and tell him "here's what we've done to you". Then, they throw out the dirt . . .' and certain possessed show us some vague scars as proof of these symbolic operations.

The loss, which triggered the anguish crisis, which then leads to the possession, is now symbolized. This aspect appears only in a second phase of the stay at Murugmalla and is a continuation of the ritualized expression of the 'ready-made' phantasy, namely the mythic combat of the Saint with the demon that ends in the submission of the latter.

(*c*) Finally it is often a dream which concludes the stay at Murugmalla:

Shernaz declares:

Ammajan-Babajan come into my dreams, I can't see them clearly, but I see signs, symbols (*iśārā*), I can only talk about it to the *mullāh,* he explains the meanings of all that to me. I am not yet cured, I still have more *ṭawāf*s and I won't leave before having received orders in dreams from *Ammajan-Babajan*: they will show me a bus or a train, and then I can leave.

Suggested by the *mullāh* as preliminary to departure, the occurrence of the dream, then its telling, prove the desire to leave Murugmalla, but also the alienation of the Subject to the Other's signifiers, as well as the intensity of the transference to the *dargāh*. It is thus only in that way that the person recovers his/her identity and ceases to be possessed.

It is therefore a process centered on the loss which allows the dispossession. The loss, foretold by a partial renouncement of his or her identity in order to be only 'a possessed', is furthered by the submission to the ideals of the Saint. The loss is then symbolized by words, by the surprise of a speech that 'jumps the tracks'. The loss, further, is identified with any sign on the body which becomes, mythically, the trace of a cut, interpreted as the intrusion of a signifier.

Finally it is interpreted as the telling of a dream, a speech coming from the unconsciousness.

TURNING AROUND THE FATHER 'ALWAYS-ALREADY-DEAD'

The possessed spin in circles . . . this is precisely the spirit of the cult, of any cult, since the etymology of this word refers to the Indo-European root *k(w) el* = 'turn in circles, circulate around'. With the image of the round, we come back to the idea of something full, perfect, of a *whole* sufficient unto itself. But the circle is not an empty place and the possessed turns around a centre: this refers to the Prophet, 'himself a personification of the centre' writes Lings (1975), men being 'exiled' because of their separation from God.

This centre here is the place of a deceased person, a deceased Saint, of a 'dead who continues to live in the place where he is buried', as J. Assayag puts it (1992).

In the demon's ritual resistance to the solicitations of the holy Spirit, there appears the fundamental ambivalence of the possessed's relation to *Babajan*. Is not this jouissance of the mastery representative of the Freudian myth of 'Totem and Taboo', namely the murder of the father, of an *imaginary father*, adorned with the insignia of the *Saint*?

Behind this Other who makes the heads of those who approach spin, one can recognize the figure of the mythical father of the horde, a figure elaborated by Freud in 'Totem and Taboo' (1912): it is the imaginary father who takes pleasure—has 'jouissance'—without limits and who is put to death by his sons. 'It is the death, the murder of the father, that Freud proposes as being the key to the jouissance, the jouissance of the supreme object, identified with the mother, the mother as the aim of the incest' writes Lacan (1969). The desperate hand combat of the possessed with the walls and the floor of the *dargāh* can also be read as an acting out of this desire to possess the mother and thus 'become again *one*' by elimination of the father, by annulling the loss represented by the birth.

This desire for murder, if we can mark it here by the aggressivity of the 'demon's statements' and the ambivalence of the possessed who resists for a long time before submitting, can be seen explicitly in other places of dispossession: Pfleiderer tells us that at Mira Datar Dargah (Gujarat), the martyr Saint of the place is buried next to the head of a Rajput King who refused to submit to Islam and had been decapitated in such a way that 'the possessed jump violently on his head during the trance' (1981). At the Balaji Temple in Bharatpur (Rajasthan), the legend, told by Kakar, says that 'the temple was built at the exact place where a Prince was murdered, 1000 years ago, his soul clamouring for justice ever since then' (1984).

At Murugmalla, this imaginary father, adorned with the insignia of a Saint, manifests himself also under an ambivalent aspect:

— It is first of all the menacing and perhaps even sadistic agency of the Super-Ego, this Other '*jouisseur*' who cruelly punishes the recalcitrant demon and which the possessed must interiorize. *Babajan* is a dead father... immortal, who always claims more obedience and submission: it is the imaginary father, prohibitor of jouissance by the threat of castration.

  The Mullāh compares the demon to the 'filth on a piece of cloth' that must thus be 'struck against the rocks to render it wearable again': the punishment, the sanction is that which will render *sanctus*, sacred.

— His other imaginary aspect is that of *Ammajan-Babajan*, 'Mummy-Daddy' as they like to call Him, an all powerful and idealized person, carried beyond the differences of the sexes by his holiness; it is the 'Ego-Ideal' aspect, 'that by which' says Freud 'man seeks to win back the narcissistic perfection of his childhood' (1914), 'this point from which the Subject will see himself, as one says, as others see him, which will enable him to support himself' writes Lacan (1991: 268). This Other is at once a pacifier father and a benevolent mother, 'the good M(other)' as Kakar so justly writes, who expresses the nostalgia of a harmonious childhood relation; probably we can give this Ideal a healing function with regard to the young brides' separation from their family and the conflicts which are so frequent between sisters and mothers-in-law.

REBIRTH, PATERNITY AND DEBT

Alongside this imaginary father, there appears the aspect of a *symbolic father* represented, in addition to the prescription of 'operations' already mentioned, by the act of naming and the references to the 'name-of-the Father*':

— The suffering individual is pronounced as 'possessed' by the *mullāh*, that is to say that he is called by a name that he receives from the Other and subjects him to the signifier, an act which echoes the naming of a newborn.

— The reference to the Name is at the heart of the 'demons' revelations':

the possessed learns who his demon possessor is and who is the person at the origin of the possession.

— It is in the Name of God that the trance is triggered and takes place and it does not cease to be invoked by the Muslims. Let us remember, in this connection, that the invocation of the supreme Name in Sufism has a pre-eminent place with regard to all the other practices. The Name of the Saint is also repeated by all the possessed: *Babajan* is the familiar name of Faquih-ul-Lah, which means 'the scholar of Allāh', who belonged to the Sufi order and to the family of the last Muslim king of Bijapur, who was chased from his throne by the Mughal Emperor Aurangzeb in 1686. After wandering for years, Faquih-ul-Lah settled in the hills of Murugmalla where he lived 13 years in a cave on the 'hill of beasts' (*Muruga malle,* Tamil and Telugu etymology), at one time inhabited by tigers.

It is thus the story of a kingdom lost after dismissal and exile, of a life of wandering, followed by asceticism among wild beasts. I propose here a double metaphor of the origin:

— that of a birth, of the birth of every one, with all that it involves of inexorable and unspeakable loss: on this background of unavoidable Real*, the account of the life of this 'lost' man becomes the life of a Saint, that is to say a mythic support with which every 'lost' human being can identify (the myth, *muthos* in greek is that which represents 'the void, the silence . . . that which is, with regards to the truth . . . *mute*') (Martin 1991).

— and metaphor of a rebirth to a new life, heroic, pure, religious.

The 'Name-of-the-Father' symbolizes the unspeakable and permits the access to language by making the bond between father and son, because the name is what remains: through the intermediary of the myth of the Saint's life, of the naming of the demons and of the combat won against them, there is an inscription of the signifiers of the Other's desire and a recognition of being the son of someone. All the possessed become the children of *Ammajan-Babajan.*

If the possession first sets in motion an imaginary process, a passage, or rather a knotting together then takes place between the *imaginary* and the *symbolic* planes on the *Real** background.

The inscription of the Subject on the symbolic register corresponds to the overflowing of the imaginary mobilised by the trance. A code is respected for its triggering, its development and its ending: it is a question of turning, but in the 'right' direction; the trance gives a direction, a meaning to the meaningless, provided that a precise scenario is followed at the time of the confrontation between contradictory forces. The trance is an experience of language which permits the passage from an imaginary plane—in which the possessed in trance is all powerful, in the denial of castration, in the 'turning round' and the jouissance—to a symbolic plane which makes 'cuts' and actualizes the castration*.

In exchange for the 'gift from God'/illness, which is returned to its donor, the possessed receives something. The 'gift' of a name, of a myth, of the speech of the Saint, corresponds to and compensates the 'loss'.

An explicit representation of this passage is precisely the knotting of an amulet to the possessed's arm before his first trance. The amulet is a coin placed in a piece of cloth and called by the Saint's name (symbolic dimension); it is blessed by the *mullāh* on their tomb and thus becomes a carrier of curative virtues (imaginary dimension); it is tied to the suffering possessed's body (real dimension).

Then the dispossessed has access to a new dimension: that of the *debt*, debt transmitted by the deceased, whose 'faults' or *the* fault—that is to say the break, the lack of being—fall back on the Subject who becomes its bearer, indebted to God.

The unwritten law is that one cannot leave the *dargāh* without repaying a symbolic debt. Many 'duties' fall upon the possessed: he must turn, he must dream, etc., and it is also this 'flow' of words expected of him during the trance, or these gifts of money and food which are requested. This debt is addressed to the parents of the possessed, to the *mullāh*, to the *dargāh*, to the Saint, to the Father, to God and it reinforces the social bond, allowing the dispossessed to regain a place in the family community and, in a still more obvious way, it reinforces the religious bond by assembling a community of submissive supporters.

But the debt remains by nature 'unrepayable' because it concerns the *being* of every speaking Subject, something impossible to know and to master: its own cause—the 'from where do I come?'—the gaping question which is only answered by death!

At Murugmalla the game is over once the cause is heard, and then deferred to God. The *mullāh* speaks a double language, sometimes saying that the cause of the possession is an evil spirit, and at other times that 'the illnesses are gifts from God'. God is thus chosen as the cause of the symptom and the debt situated in the *have* register: the fantasy is that it can be negotiated with God's representative.

And thus persists the transference, the bond to the *dargāh* and to God, that can only be infinite.

At Murugmalla, the response to 'the lack of being' is to enter into possession with the cumbersome 'haves' in order to place them in a safe, sacred shelter. The question of being is thus transferred onto God and sacredly sealed! The possessed becomes 'an important customer' for the Other, which insures that he (or she) will remain confined as long as he continues to repay his debt 'in the interests of' the *dargāh*.

IS IT POSSIBLE TO SPEAK OF A 'THERAPEUTIC CULT'?

The word 'therapeut', in antiquity, designated 'Jewish monks who devoted themselves to a contemplative life, lived a life of mortification near Alexandria'. Is it not that the therapeut takes care, first and foremost, of himself and his own 'soul'? (in Greek *therapeuin* means 'to take care of'). At Murugmalla, is it not above all the *dargāh*, its proselyte *mullāh*, and the religion that they represent, who are the subjects of a lack, who claim recognition and aspire to be a 'centre' in a cultural environment where Muslims are in minority?

We find at Murugmalla the classic mechanisms of the edification of religions:

— The foundation of the belief and the debt to the dead Father by the intermediary of speech and submission, which here takes on particular importance if we recall that a Prophet is someone who '*speaks ahead*' (*pro-phatis*) and that the word Islam means submission.

— The interiorisation of the constraint and of the renouncement of the drive, the Superego taking charge of them (cf. Freud 1912), which opens onto the dimension of fault and guilt which soothes the anguish.

— The putting at a distance of the Real by the rite, 'an act always repeated which alone can commemorate this immemorial meeting' with the Real (Lacan 1991: 59).

— The knotting of the imaginary mechanisms to the symbolic dimension. This bond, this symbolisation of the imaginary is the religious act 'par excellence' (in Latin *religere* = attach, tie and *relegere* = reread, pick, gather); the act binds the Subject to an origin myth, attaching him to the Father of fathers, while at the same time the debt is recast, the debt of which God becomes the destination.

This cult has therefore essentially an adaptative, normative function:

(*a*) adaptation to the social and religious order for individuals in distress, by way of a neurotic 'model of misbehaviour' proposed by the culture, the search for the impossible identity of the Subject, his anguish, his revolt perhaps(?), being extinguished, masked by the religious response. Thus, the alienation of the Subject is reinforced, but one might pose, with Freud, some questions about these 'religious illusions' which 'as long as they remained strong enough, constituted for those who lived under their domination the best protection against neurosis' (1921); one may also pose some questions on the value of psychic progress represented by the 'taking charge by the Superego, the internal agency, of the external constraint' (1927).

This regeneration of the Superego, with its two aspects of submission and identification with the Ideal, evokes the setting up of the Superego in the evolution of the individual: contemporary with the abandoning of the Oedipus Complex, it is based on the identification with a 'parental agency' which replaces the authority of the parents.

I propose that Murugmalla (and other places of the same nature in India) functions as a 'center' which permits 'concentration' on, and actualization of, the Oedipian situation. Indeed, we do observe the typical dynamics of this situation, which for the child implies, at the psychic level, the dimensions of identification, seduction, agressivity and jouissance. For the parent, the Oedipian situation entails the setting up of the prohibition of incest as of limitless jouissance, permitting the establishment of the Law. Secondly, the imposed renunciation and the gift of the myth would open an issue by the transformation of a childish attitude into a religious one. The cult hides the question of the lack from the Subject, as well as from the Other. Oedipus veils castration and it is precisely in this way that it is normalizing. The response which fills the Subject's void has here for name: God.

This hypothesis may be discussed in relation to the characteristics of the psychic maturation of the child in India. I am thinking in particular of the traits describe by S. Kakar (1978) such as the 'father's lack of authority', 'the son's unconscious anger at the fathers' or their 'feminine submission to the men of the family', or even the girl's difficulties in renouncing 'a pre-Oedipian dependance on the mother', traits which might evoke a frequent fixation of the Indian young adult on an Oedipian position; the young man who, having a difficult access to the identification with the father, remains stuck to a passive and submissive identification with his mother, and the young bride who is unable to give up her affective childhood bonds.

The ritual practised at Murugmalla may thus allow the opening up of such a blocked Oedipian situation. This question might be studied more thoroughly by analysing family relations before the possession crisis and by the observation, during the trance, of the possessed's aggressivity: is this directed at *Ammajan* or at *Babajan*, depending on the sex of the patient?

(*b*) The adaptation of the community to its suffering individuals, in particular to women, probably allowing them, sometimes, 'true speech' on this 'Other scene' and obtaining for them a better status in their family.

Murugmalla functions as a place which authorizes the jouissance at the price of possession, only to master it better, and at the same time it opens the possibility of regaining a place at the price of a renouncement. Let us also remark that the patients are more readily brought to Murugmalla than to a hospital or to a clinic, where the 'good' doctor and the 'good' medication do not allow, in the cases studied, for meaning as does the *ṭawāf* in order to fill up the anguish and respond to the question of its cause.

What is the effect of this phenomenon on the economy of the family relations and the psychic functioning of a person? Is the social adaptation, the regulation of family tensions, durable? Does the patient really enter into a renouncement, or is it simply postponed? To what extent does the dispossession trance allow the reestablishment of the religious faith? We are left with so many questions; other observations should deal with further detail, particularly concentrating on 'life after Murugmalla'. For the present, we leave these questions open.

NOTES ON THE PRINCIPAL CONCEPTS OF LACAN MENTIONED

Lack . . . desire

De-sidero: to cease to see . . . the stars (*sideris* in Latin), state the absence of; consequently: to search, to desire.

'Why is desire what Freud calls sexual desire? The reason remains veiled, just as obscure as it is to the one who suffers the sexual desire, the "beyond" that he searches for behind an experience subjected to all the enticements' (Lacan 1988).

'Desire is neither the need of the biological body, nor the request to satisfy the need, but the lack which conditions both' (Levy 1994).

'Desire is a relation between being and lack; this lack is a lack of being (or "want to be") and not a lack of this or that . . . the being comes to exist in fact in function of this lack' (Lacan 1988).

'Desire . . . that is the only point of departure from which one can explain the fact that there are men who speak' (Lacan 1988).

The Other, also called *the capitalized Other*

'We must found the notion of the Other with a capital O, as being the locus of deployement of speech—the Other Scene, *eine andere schauplatz* which Freud speaks of in "The interpretation of dreams". We must state that, coming from an animal in prey of language, man's desire is the desire of the Other (Lacan 1977a, Ch. V.).

'It is the locus of speech, this third place which always exists in the relations with the other (the like one) . . . an Other who is perpetually vanishing' (Lacan 1960).

'The subject gives himself up to the locus of the Other' (Lacan 1962).

'The Other is the locus in which is situated the chain of the signifier that governs whatever may be made present of the subject' (Lacan 1991:203).

'The unconscious is the discourse of the Other . . . it is the discourse of the circuit in which I am integrated' (Lacan 1988).

'There is something prior to all that we can understand: the presence of the Other . . . Man's desire is the desire of the Other' (Lacan 1962).

The Signifier

The concept of Signifier comes straight from linguistics. Even though he was a contemporary of Ferdinand de Saussure, author of the famous 'General course in linguistics', S. Freud was not aware of the concept of Signifier. Freud speaks rather, in this way, of 'hyper-intense representations'.

'What is a signifier? A signifier is that which represents a subject, not for an other subject, but for another signifier. In order to illustrate this axiom, suppose that in the desert you find a stone covered with hieroglyphs. You do not doubt for a moment that, behind them, there was a subject who wrote them. But it is an error to believe that each signifier is addressed to you—this is proved by the fact that you might not understand any of it.

'On the other hand, you define them as signifiers, by the fact that you are sure that each of these signifiers is related to each of the others. And it is this that is at issue with the relation between the subject and the field of the Other' (Lacan 1991:198).

The Subject

'The subject is nothing other than that which "glides" in a chain of signifiers—whether or not he is conscious of which signifier he is the effect' (Lacan 1972).

'The "subject of the desire" or "subject of the unconscious" has neither a name or an image; it is to be distinguished from the grammatical subject. Man thinks that he is master of his speech, but in fact we are "spoken" by something which escapes us constantly, which is proven by our dreams, parapraxis, slips of tongue . . . the subject is divided. The barred subject is this necessary dependance with respect to the Other as such, locus of the signifier' (Lacan 1962).

'The characteristic of the subject of the unconsicous is that of being, beneath the signifier that develops its networks, its chains and its history, at an indeterminate place' (Lacan 1991:208).

The jouissance

The jouissance is not pleasure, it is even that which proves that beyond pleasure, the subject satisfies himself with something which to him is displeasure. A clinical example of it is given by Freud's famous patient 'the rat man' when he tells his phantasy of torture with an expression 'of horror at pleasure (*jouissance*) of which he himself was unaware' (Freud 'The rat man's case'). The word *lust* used by Freud carries, contrary to the word pleasure by which it is usally translated, the idea of a tension and its discharge.

'The jouissance has never been a pleasure in itself. It is a power, and it is what we seek from the moment we come out from between our mother's legs; what we are seeking for from that moment on, is to cling to' (Martin n.d. 4).

'The jouissance expects the impossible and exact relationship of the speaking being with its body' (Martin 1993).

Castration

It is never what I expected, what I desired . . . it is never what *I* desire.

'Castration does not imply any privation of organ. . . . Always symbolic, it consists of a radical impossibility of being, of having, of saying, of thinking my being. . . . It is an irreductible loss . . . which can be heard in the "I am not myself" ' (Levy 1994).

'The castration is symbolic, it is related to a certain phenomena of lack' (Lacan 1962).

'The primary fundamental castration of man is giving up finding in the partner his own lack' (Lacan 1962).

The Name-of-the-Father

'The only function of the father is that of being a myth, always and uniquely the Name-of-the-Father, that is to say nothing other than the dead father' (Lacan 1960).

'The symbolic father, what I call the Name-of-the-Father' (Lacan 1988).

'It is the name from where the father originates. . . . The Name-of-the-Father marks the descendants. It is to be distinguished from the patronym, a word which refers to the begetting. . . . The Name-of-the-Father is the name of a cut which fecondates . . . with the Name-of-the-Father, that is the name of the loss, we are on the path to desire and creativity' (Levy 1994).

The Real

'The real is that which subsists outside of the symbolisation' (Lacan 1977).

The real is to be understood 'as exterior to the subject' (ibid.) and it is 'the object *par excellence* of anguish . . . that which is unnamable behind that which is named' (Lacan 1988).

'The real is that which always comes back to the same place' (Lacan 1991:42).

The Drive

As pointed out by A. Sheridan, one of Lacan's translators, 'Lacan reinstates a distinction, already clear in Freud, between the wholly psychical *pulsion* (*Trieb*) and *instinct* (*Instinkt*), with its "biological" connotations. As Lacan has pointed out, Freud's English translators blur this distinction by translating both terms as "instinct" ' (translator's note to Lacan 1991).

REFERENCES

Assayag, J. 1992 La déesse et le saint. Acculturation et communalisme dans un lieu de culte du sud de l'Inde, in L'inventaire de la tradition, *Annales*, ESC 4; 789-813.

Devereux, G. 1956 Normal and abnormal. In *Essays on General Ethnopsychiatry*, Chicago.

Freud, S. 1908 *Charackter und Analerotik*. Standard Edition 2. London: Hogarth, 1953.

——— 1909 Bemerkungen über einen fall von Zwangsneurose (The rat's man case). Standard Edition 2, London: Hogarth, 1953.

——— 1912 *Totem and taboo*. Standard Edition 13:9. London: Hogarth, 1938.

——— 1914 *On Narcissism: an introduction on Metapsychology*, cited from La vie sexuelle. Paris: PUF, 1969.

——— 1920 *Beyond the principle of pleasure*, cited from Essais de psychanalyse. Paris: Payot, 1968.

——— 1921 *Group Psychology and analysis of the Ego*. Standard Edition 18. London: Hogarth, 1957.

——— 1923 *Eine Teufelsneurose im siebzehnten Jahrhundert*. Studienausgabe, VII, Frankfurt am Main: Fischer, 1973.

——— 1926 *Inhibition, symptom and anxiety*. Standard Edition 20. London: Hogarth, 1959.

——— 1927 *The future of an Illusion*. Standard Edition 14. London: Hogarth, 1948.

——— 1933 La décomposition de la personnalité psychique in *New lectures of introduction to psychoanalysis*. Standard Edition 22: 3. London: Hogarth, 1957.

Harper, E.B. 1963 Spirit possesion and social structure. In Bala Ratnam (ed.), *Anthropology on the march*, Madras, 167-77.

De Heusch, L. 1971 Possession et chamanisme in *Pourquoi l'épouser et autres essais* Gallimard, Paris, 1971.

Kakar, S. 1978 *The inner world: a psychoanalytic study of childhood and society in India*. Delhi: Oxford University Press.

——— 1984 *Shamans, mystics and doctors: a psychological inquiry into India and its healing traditions*. Delhi: Oxford University Press.

Lacan, J. 1960 Séminaire VIII, *The transference*, unpublished.

——— 1962 Séminaire X, *The anguish* 12-12-1962, unpublished.

——— 1969 Séminaire XVII, L'envers de la psychanalyse. Paris: Seuil, 1991.

——— 1972 Séminaire XX, *Encore*, unpublished.

——— 1977a The direction of the cure. In *Ecrits: a selection*. London: Tavistock.

——— 1977b *Ecrits; a selection*. London: Tavistock.

——— 1955 Seminar II: *The ego in Freud's theory and in the technique of psychoanalysis*. Cambridge: Cambridge University Press, 1988.

——— 1964 *The four foundamental concepts of psycho-analysis*. Harmondsworth: Penguin, 1991.

Levy, M. Qu'est-ce qu'un père? *Cahier P. Martin*, No 4. Hyěres, 1994.

Lings, M. 1975 *What is Sufism?* London: G. Allan & Unwin Ltd.

Linton, R. 1956 *Cutlure and mental disorders*, Springfield, USA: Charles Thomas Publishers.

Martin, P. 1991 Psychanalyse et religion *Trames,* No. 12, Nice: Editions Z.

——— *Cahier P. Martin No. 2.* Hyēres, 1993.

——— *Cahier P. Martin No. 4.* Hyēres, 1994.

Pfleiderer, B. 1981 Mira Datar Dargah: the psychiatry of a muslim shrine *Internationale Asienforum*, Vol. 12, No. 1, New Delhi.

Rollier, F. 1981 *Murugmalla* Film video 30mn. CNRS-SERDDAV-F. Rollier, Paris.

——— 1983 *Murugmalla, Possession et rituels thérapeutiques dans un tombeau Musulman d'Inde du sud. Etude ethnopsychiatrique.* Mémoire de Psychiatrie, Université Paris VI.

——— 1985 Possession & toxicomanie, *Revue de l'Assoc. Nationale des Intervenants en Toxicomanie.*

Editor's note: The year given here for Lacan's unpublished seminars is the first year of the actual seminars, i.e. 1960 denotes the seminar for the year 1960-1.

Jod Gomaz Dargah as a Healing Centre

Y.J. SHOBHA DEVI
G.S. BIDARAKOPPA

From the earliest times, man's concern with disease has led him to attribute its causes to a great variety of causes, natural and supernatural, and he has developed practices to deal with illness that include magical and mystical, as well as would-be scientific measures.

In India people have used Ayurvedic and herbal medicine, involving a complex theory of humoral balance, but they have also resorted to religious rituals to find solutions to their health problems. Religious shrines, dedicated to saints or goddesses, have made their own contribution to this situation of medical pluralism, acting as healing centres for a great many people all over India. Irrespective of their religious background, people visit both Muslim and Hindu shrines to find solace for their problems, especially when these are of a psychological nature.

A *dargāh* or shrine is the tomb of a Saint, which is visited by the people as they believe that the soul of the holy man continues to reside in the tomb and offer blessings to his devotees, who offer him their prayers with faith and devotion.

In the present study an attempt has been made to study the nature and social functions of one of these popular *dargāhs*, i.e. Jod Gomaz Dargah of Bijapur in north Karnataka (Plate 1).

THE METHOD AND PURPOSE OF THE STUDY

After dealing with the historical background of the *dargāh*, we shall try to throw some light on the nature of the cases brought to the centre for treatment, on the rituals practiced at the centre, and on the behaviour of the patients. We were interested in the degree of improvement, particularly among those cases who seek relief from possession by evil spirits.

An interview schedule was prepared to inquire about those who come to the shrine for the purpose of being healed. This schedule was based on the literature available and on preliminary visits of the researcher to various shrines before undertaking the present study. Further, the priests were interviewed, using an interview guide to collect information about the historical background of the shrine, the rituals practiced there and about their own role in the healing process. Besides, we used observation and case study methods in conducting the study.

THE HISTORICAL BACKGROUND OF THE SHRINE

Jod Gomaz, locally called the Jod Gomat Dargah, is also referred to as the shrine of 'twin sisters' by Henry Cousens (1890). The shrine is situated in Bijapur city in north Karnataka. It was built to commemorate the saint Syed Shah Abdul Razak Kadri and his disciple, Kawas Khan, a Hindu Brahmin by birth, and who was the commander-in-chief of Sikandar Adil Shah. Kawas Khan then converted to Islam and became a disciple of the saint. Thus in the Jod Gomaz the tombs of both the saint and his disciple are side by side, which is why it is called the Jod Gomaz—the twin tombs. Besides, we find four further tombs of other disciples of the saint. They are: Jinnah Basha (Plate 2), Kinnagi Basha (Plate 3), Chadi Basha and Bedi Basha (both, Fig. 4).

It is reported by Shah Saifullah Gadri (1896) that the saint had migrated to India from Baghdad as young man, around 400 years ago. Abdul Razak Kadri lived to the age of about 60 years and died in A.D.1641. He settled in Bijapur and started propagating Sufism among the local people, becoming popular among the local Hindu community since he helped the poor and the sick through his supernatural powers.

Daily worship and prayers are being offered at both tombs. The sick and the distressed visit the tombs. People belonging to different religions, but mainly Hindus and Muslims, frequent the shrine to find relief from various health and related problems. They share a common belief that the miraculous power of the saint's spirit will heal their sufferings. It was reported by the head priest (Mujawar) that people often visit the shrine after having already tried all possible kinds of medical treatment in different places. They see the *dargāh* as a last resort to get relief from their unresolved problems. Irrespective of caste, class or creed, people flock together here, full of faith and hope of finding a solution.

When the Mujawar was asked for his opinion concerning such beliefs and practices, he felt that it is the faith that matters. It is because people believe in the saint's supernatural power, that they are able to be cured. The priest concluded that it is necessary to offer prayers to the holy spirit as well as to take the treatment offered by the *dargāh*, if one is to be cured.

Srivastava (1971) considers that Sufism, sometimes called Islamic mysticism, come to India well before the establishment of the Delhi Sultanate in the thirteenth century A.D. Sufism in India was greatly influenced by Hindu thought, belief and practices. The Hindu concept of the relationship between God and the Soul as similar to that between the Beloved and the Lover, has been adopted by the Sufis in India. In Islam, generally speaking, the relation between God and Man reflects that of Master and Servant. Ascetic practices, such as fasting and torturing the body, were also borrowed from Hinduism and Buddhism. Several Hindu elements, such as 'bowing before the Shaikh (head of a Khanqah)', presenting water to visitors, circulating *zanbil* (a bowl made of a dried and hollow gourd), shaving the head of new entrants to the mystic circles, etc., were common among the Chistis—a Sufi order.

The Sufis had a two-fold object in view: their own spiritual development, and their service to Islam and to humanity. In order to influence Hindus they had to learn the local language and the religion of the common people. Thus Sufis studied the languages and modes of worship of the Hindus. They adopted the role and even the dress of Hindu sadhus, and they adopted some of the latter's practices and outward behaviour in order to overcome suspicion among lower-caste Hindus. But unlike Hindu sadhus who lived in the forest, Muslim Sufis established their abode (*khanqah*—hermitage) close to the settlements of lower-caste Hindus. They were accustomed to a life of poverty, and they were living on the charity of the common people. A few of them earned their daily bread by cultivating land. Living in this simple manner, they were able to impress the Hindu masses, greatly.

Perhaps the changes in the Sufi tradition has rendered it more acceptable to the local Hindu population—particularly the lower castes—and so we find both Muslims and Hindus visiting the Muslim *dargāhs* to find relief from the problems of their daily life.

RITUALS PRACTICED AT THE SHRINE

On the very day when the client comes to the shrine, he or she must pray there, and also state the reason for coming to the shrine. The client must then purchase a sacred thread from the priest, and make five knots on the thread, which is then tied round the wooden pillar installed inside the *dargāh*, in front of saint Abdul Razak Kadri's tomb. These knots may symbolize the popular belief that the patient will be relieved of his problem within forty days; if not, it is said that the holy spirit will be strangled by the knots tied by the client. Every client, therefore, must remain on the *dargāh's* premises for forty days, unless his problem is solved earlier.

The devotee also has to offer five lemon fruits to the holy spirit. These are blessed by the priest and then returned to the client, who may either eat them or apply the juice externally to his skin; lemons are, of course, a 'cooling' substance.

The client and his family or friends may stay in the open premises of the *dargāh* for the rest of the forty days. In other cases, they may return home after attending the ritual, having received the sacred water and the lemons from the priest. The water may be carried home in a bottle, and taken daily in small quantity, until the person's next visit to the shrine. The sacred water is taken from the ancient underground well situated in the vicinity of the *dargāh* (though it has now dried up).

The shrine has a vast lawn which covers nearly ten acres of ground. Tubewell water is available for the visitors' use. The people who stay there cook their food under the trees in temporary ovens which they themselves make.

On Thursdays or New Moon Days, old clients, who have earlier been cured at the shrine, visit the *dargāh* to fulfill the vows they had then made to the holy spirit. They now cook vast quantities of *biryani*, etc., which they feed to all the other visitors: the healed and the suffering are thus united in a common meal.

Also on Thursdays and New Moon Days, the clients are expected to bathe in sacred water drawn from the ancient underground well. The priest explained that the well has been blessed by the saint, so that the patients will be relieved of their suffering if they bathe in water from that well. When the researcher visited the shrine, the old well had dried up completely (Plate 5). Hence visitors draw water from a nearby step-well for their bath. Some were found to carry the water from the step-well to the platform of the 'sacred well', where they took their bath (Plate 7). Others were bathing near the step-well (Plate 6). Evidently, the saint's blessing is not confined only to the water of the old well. In general, the people visiting the shrine for healing purposes were found to be observing the rituals very religiously.

The donations of the devotees are used by the attendants of the shrine for their own maintenance. It is a private temple; there is no committee of trustees, but the Archaeological Survey of India looks after the maintenance and repair of the buildings.

THE CASES OF POSSESSION

According to Wintrob (1973) and Wijesinghe *et al.* (1976), possession is an episodic disruption of behaviour, during which it is presumed that the subject's personality has been replaced by that of a Spirit or God, whose characteristics are well known within the subject's culture. After the episode, the subject claims either partial or total amnesia regarding his behaviour during the possession.

Most of the possessed at the Jod Gomaz are women. Before entering into trance, they are seated in front of the tomb of Jinnah Basha, with their hair loose (Plate 8). Their relatives or friends smear lemon juice on the head and face of the possessed woman. Gradually, she begins to speak loudly, in an abusive manner. The people around her then start to persuade her to reveal the identity of the spirit that is possessing her (Plate 9). She may respond by mentioning several names of deceased relatives, friends or neighbours.

Once the family members of the possessed woman are convinced that she has revealed the name of the spirit, they try to extract from her the reason for possession. If the spirit expresses a desire for some material goods, the family promises to fulfill the desire, on the condition that the spirit agrees not to trouble the possessed individual in the future. As a guarantee that the spirit will really leave the person, the family ask the latter to lift a stone, of medium size, which is kept on the platform of the Jinnah Basha tomb. The stone is carried on one's head as the possessed person takes three rounds—in the *pradakṣiṇa* or auspicious direction, with the centre to the right—around the tomb (Plate 2). The spirit is then asked to touch the tomb three times, saying 'I quit I quit' (Plate 10).

Later, the relatives will help the person concerned to put down the stone carried by him or her. This, it is believed, frees the individual from the possessing spirit, which is considered to be the cause of one's sufferings.

THE OUTCOME OF THE HEALING PROCESS

The people who have been healed by the various processes mentioned above, are thereafter expected to give *hazri*—attendance—at the Jod Gomaz every Thursday, or every New Moon Day. Otherwise, it is reported, the person will again develop the same problems. During the *hazri* the person is considered to be possessed by the spirit of the Saint. Thus, the client becomes a follower of the Saint, and as a mark of respect, he or she should appear regularly for *hazri*. This also insures that the person concerned will remain free from the clutches of the 'evil spirit', which will not cause trouble in the future.

Possession by the Saint's spirit begins with a few bouts of loud belchings. She or he then enters, gradually, into an altered state of consciousness. At this stage a possessed woman will cover her face with the border of her sari, so that the people around her cannot see the holy spirit. She or he then starts swinging her body to and fro (Plate 11). It is explained by the people that, since she is possessed by the holy spirit, ordinary people cannot see her. During her state of trance the individual suggests remedies for the problems of other clients. At this stage her speech is fast and monotonous. The person remains in this altered state for some ten to fifteen minutes, before regaining her normal state. After regaining consciousness the possessed individual claims amnesia regarding the whole episode. But from then onwards, she appears agile and cheerful.

CASE 1: A MUSLIM WOMAN GETTING POSSESSED IN THE DARGAH

Family background

J. is a married Muslim woman, aged 26 years. She is illiterate, comes from a rural area, and belongs to a nuclear family. No history of possession in the family is reported.

Both her parents are alive. They live on petty business. She is the eldest of four children, and was married at the age of thirteen.

Her husband was in miltary service before his marriage. After marrying he got voluntary retirement from the service. Since then, he has been earning his livelihood by doing tinning work of brass vessels. The family income is said to be around Rs. 300 per month. They own the hut in which they live. The client herself is a housewife. Her husband is said to be a drunkard, and not to care for the needs of his wife. Besides, she lost two of her children during infancy, due to ill-health. Now she has a girl aged three. She does not want to have another child until her daughter reaches the age of eight to ten years, as she wants to take better care of her present child.

The client is said to be highly dissatisfied with her marital life. Her parents are able to help her only marginally. She says that the Jod Gomaz Dargah is the only place which can provide her with peace and solace.

Incidents preceding the possession

Six years ago J. developed headache, stomach trouble, and felt generally weak. Sometimes she would crave for sweets and *biryani* and eat excessively. These symptoms used to persist for about an hour or more every day. Afterwards, she would return to her normal state and attend to her work as usual. She consulted doctors, but there was no improvement and she continued to suffer for more than a year. Her relatives began to suspect that she was suffering because of the influence of an evil spirit. Hence she was brought to Jod Gomaz Dargah at Bijapur for relief. During her possession, she revealed that she was possessed by two spirits—one male and the other female—which were the cause of her abnormal behaviour.

On the basis of present findings we may say that the socio-spiritual environment of the shrine provides a therapeutic atmosphere for the clients, particularly when their ill-health is seen as due to possession phenomena.

CASE 2: A DAUGHTER-IN-LAW GETS POSSESSED BY GUILT RESULTING FROM THE BEHAVIOUR OF A FAMILY MEMBER

Mrs. N. is an illiterate, married woman, aged about thirty years, and hails from a rural setting. She belongs to a Hindu scheduled caste, and comes from a joint family. She has three children, two boys and a girl, aged 14, 9 and 12 years, respectively.

The researcher met her at the Jod Gomaz Dargah as she was coming to offer her regular *hazri*, which she does since she was relieved from her possession attacks at the shrine.

Family background

She comes from a nuclear family consisting of parents and seven children—three sons and four daughters. She is herself the fourth child. The financial condition of her family of origin is said to have been sound. They owned 18 acres of cultivable land and resided in their own house. The family income was estimated at about Rs. 2000 per month.

She was married at the age of fourteen to a man serving in the military. Her husband's family consisted of the father-in-law, three brothers-in-law and two sisters-in-law. Her husband voluntarily retired from military service after his marriage. He then worked in a cotton mill at Davanagere, a town in Chitradurga district of Karnataka. He had to quit that job due to the illness of his wife. At present they are living in Bijapur, where the husband is working as a peon in the Karnataka Bank.

During his leisure time he offers voluntary service at the Jod Gomaz, since his wife's condition has improved due to her visits at the shrine. The relationship between the couple, and with their children, is said to be good. Our case, in fact, is described as a well adjusted housewife.

The family has a sound economy, and their monthly income is stated to amount to some Rs. 1500 per month. Her brothers-in-law are in government service, and they have recently established their own separate households.

History of possession

The woman is said to have had attacks of possession during the past two years. Till then she had been hale and healthy. The family members tell us that the attacks of possession were precipitated by the sudden death of her younger brother-in-law, after a brief illness, some two years back.

A year earlier, her father-in-law had died. The woman herself told us that her brother-in-law, during his illness, had spoken in the voice of the deceased father-in-law, who claimed that his spirit was not being properly taken care of. The family, he said, had not observed the annual death rituals properly, by offering prayers and food. He was very angry and unhappy about this. Having thus conveyed his father's message, the sick brother-in-law passed away.

The daughter-in-law attributes his death to the wrath of the deceased father-in-law's unhappy spirit. The tragedy caused her a lot of apprehension and anxiety.

Later, arguments and quarrels developed between the woman and her in-laws concerning this issue. She began to fall ill quite frequently. She complained of tiredness, body aches and pains, and started to refuse food. These complaints may be seen to indicate a state of depression. But there was no obvious incidence of possession as long as she stayed at home.

Then, she went on a casual visit to her sister in Bijapur, and during that visit she accompanied her sister—casually—to the Jod Gomaz. Here, she had her first attack of possession, and admitted that it was the spirit of her father-in-law who manifested himself. She identified this spirit as the cause of her suffering.

Behaviour observed at the shrine

As the woman was speaking to the researcher about her experiences, she would cover her head, whenever she was not talking, with the border of her sari. Before resuming her talk she would yawn loudly two or three times, as is expected from those cases of possession who have found solace at the shrine. The yawns, considered as a sign of possession by the 'holy spirit', was not, however, followed by the monotonous talk which we have mentioned earlier in the paper.

During the interview the woman confirmed her faith in the supernatural power of the 'holy spirit' to cure disease. She added that her youngest son, who was running high temperature and did not recover when given medicine, was healed immediately when he was brought to the shrine. He was in an unconscious state when the Mujawar (priest) sprinkled holy water on him.

Appraisal

Here we have an illiterate young housewife, who is unhappy and helpless over the behaviour and attitudes of her in-laws regarding the religious rites to be performed by them after the death of their father. She also had severe apprehensions concerning the death of her younger brother-in-law, which she attributed to the wrath of the unhappy spirit of her deceased father-in-law.

This apprehension, and the resulting conflict, caused her various psychosomatic symptoms. Under these circumstances, her visit to the Gomaz, so popular for driving out evil spirits, precipitated attacks of possession in her too. It is reported she has undergone the whole healing process, and ever since she has been visiting the shrine weekly to offer *hazri*—the attendance which is expected practice from all individuals who have been relieved of possession there.

We understand that her visits to the Gomaz have given her relief from her apprehensions, and to some extent her husband, too, has become religious, as he now gives voluntary service at the Gomaz in his leisure time. This, too, has brought solace to our case. She says that she has improved 'by fifty per cent'. Sometimes she still feels body aches and pains, but this no longer causes her concern.

CONCLUSION

People from all kinds of socio-economic and religious backgrounds visit the shrine to find relief from bad health and other related problems in life. Although many of the clients reported that they have been helped to overcome their problems, it was also noticed that those who were cured did not experience complete relief, since, as explained earlier, they are expected to continue frequenting the shrine. offering prayer and *hazri* to the Saint's spirit. Otherwise, it was reported, their problems would recur or even become aggravated.

Do the visits to the shrine change the destiny of the subject? Based on our observations and experience we would say that the belief in *karma*, fate, etc., are religious factors that help the patients to reconcile themselves with their problems. Generally, they suffer from psychogenic symptoms which are caused by various psychosocial and interpersonal problems and tensions in life. It may be in human nature to forget pain after some time, and accept the situation as it is; but it may help when misfortune is seen as caused by karma or destiny in life. Moreover, the cordial atmosphere in these shrines, the emotional catharsis, and the change noticed in the behaviour of family members, all contribute to help the sick person to realize an improvement in health and well-being over a period of time.

REFERENCES

Cousens, H. 1890 Notes on the Buildings and Remains at Bijapur. *Bombay Gazetteer,* vol. XXIII: 557-67.

Shahsaifullah Qadiri 1896 *Tarjuma-e-Raudatual Auliya-e-Bijapur*, 91-4.

Srivasthva, A.L.: 1971 *Medieval Indian Culture.* Agra: Shiva Lal Agarawal, 61-78.

Wijesinghe, C.P., S.A.W. Dissanayake, and N. Mendis 1976 Possession Trance in a Semi-Urban Community in Sri Lanka, *Autstralian and New Zealand Journal of Psychiatry* 19, 135-42.

Wintrob, R.M. 1973 The Influnence of Others, Witchcraft and Root Work as Explanations of Behaviour Disturbance, *Journal of Nervous and Mental Diseases* 56, 318-26.

Plate 1: A view of the Jod Gomaz (Jod Gomat Dargah), Bijapur.

Plate 2: Picture of Jinnah Basha Tomb (A possessed woman is taking a round of the tomb with the 'stone' on her head). From: Y.J. Shobha Devi.

Plate 3: A picture of a woman offering prayer at the 'Kinnagi Basha' Tomb.

Plate 4: Chadi Basha and Bedi Basha Tomb.

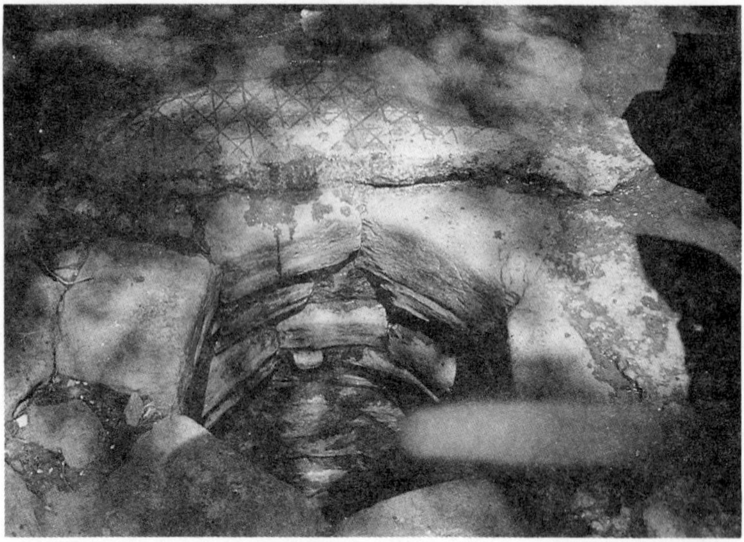

Plate 5: The ancient underground well at the site of Jod Gomaz, Bijapur.

Plate 6: The step-well from where the clients fetch water to bathe.

Plate 7: The clients bathing on the platform of the well.

Plate 8: A 'possessed' woman sitting near Jinnah Basha Tomb with her hair loose.

Plate 9: Another 'possessed' woman being coaxed by her relatives to reveal the 'possessing' spirit's identity.

Plate 10: A 'possessed' man confessing that 'I quit, I quit . . .' at Jinnah Basha Tomb.

Plate 11: A woman with the previous history of 'possession' giving *hazri* at the tomb of Holy Saint Abdul Razak Kadri of Jod Gomaz, Bijapur.
From: Y.J. Shobha Devi.

Reasserting Identity through Suffering: Healing Rituals in Bengal and Karnataka

MARINE CARRIN

Suffering is perhaps the most difficult emotion to share. As Lynch (1990) has shown, emotions in India are coded to represent the implicit part of the religious discourse. I shall try, then to show how healing rituals express basic contradictions such as purity and pollution, fortune and misfortune, health and illness.

In looking at rituals often regarded as 'therapeutic', I ask whether we can understand idioms of distress as ethno-psychiatric phenomena? Several anthropologists have stressed the relationship between symptoms of distress and the need for ritual action, and unwanted possession seems central to this problem. Anthropologists have argued that the majority of persons who get possessed are women who are denied the possibility of expressing themselves. Thus, female possession has been considered as a strategy which allows repressed individuals to express their inner desires (Harper 1963; Freed and Freed 1964). Nevertheless, Kakar (1984) analyses how men, young and old, get possessed and are often found in conflict with parental authority.

Moreover, Kakar and Obeyesekere (1981) agree that possessed individuals are characterized by hysterical personality. But this interpretation reduces the phenomenon to Western categories of psychic disorder unless the 'transcultural' concept of personality is related to the cultural concept of person. May it not be that South Asian culture provides for the expression of hysteria as offering the most natural display of inner conflicts?

We read about controlled and uncontrolled possession, induced and spontaneous possession, possession by benevolent deities and possession by harmful spirits. Of these various classifications, we need to retain, here, a distinction between what is often termed 'demonic possession', and the trance of the ritual specialist—'a spirit mediumship' (Claus 1979) acting out a certain ritual scenario, which takes place in a formalized ritual setting.

Following Bateson (1936), who emphasized the cathartic effect of Iatmul rituals, many anthropologists (Harper 1963; Turner 1968; Obeyesekere 1970, 1981) have identified psychosocial conflicts as arising from a contradiction between traditional culture and the individual. Psychiatrists such as Carstairs and Kapur (1976), trying to take social change into consideration—to wit, the evolution of matrilinearity towards patrilinearity in south Kanara—have still failed by paying insufficient attention to the social dimension, considered only as 'etiological factors', thus neglecting the possibility that the society may offer appropriate answers to affliction.

A more convincing approach is represented by M. Nichter (1981) who considers ethno-psychiatric phenomena as idioms of distress. Analysing psychosocial conflicts among Havik brahmin women, Nichter attributes the source of such disorders to the subordinate status that women occupy in the patrilineal society. Spirit possession is regarded as a disease (*kata*) to which women are particularly sensitive since they are weaker and more attractive to spirits than males. Nichter, speaking of the involvement of brahmin women in *bhakti* cults, acknowledges the therapeutic value of devotion as a 'means of gaining prestige for transforming desire and anxiety (uncontrol: emotion) into devotion (control: the sacred)'.

I shall present some cases of possession in Bengal and Karnataka to elucidate the structure of healing rituals. The question I pose is whether possession is an answer to an illness (or abnormal state), and whether the rituals are, properly speaking, therapeutic. This leads us towards the problem of culturally determined conceptions of the self, to be considered in anthropological terms, notwithstanding its obvious psychological content.

In Bengal, healing rituals are found mainly at the popular level of Hinduism. Physical illness is not here opposed to psychological suffering, rather the two are seen to intermingle in situations of crisis. People know, that in case of mental disorder (*pāgalmī*)[1], as well as illness or anxiety, the best remedy is to offer *dharnā*[2]—a religious fast—to the God Shiva. Married women fast, and offer regular vows, to protect their husbands and children from pain. In case of illness, the family takes the patient to Tarakeshwar, an important temple dedicated to Shiva Taraknath and a place of pilgrimage, north of Calcutta. Here, the pilgrim is welcomed by the priests, who purify him and tell him to lie down fasting on the floor of the temple. After one or two days, the pilgrim is expected to have a dream, which he should try to understand. If the dream is found meaningful, the patient interprets it as the message of the god; usually, the content of the dream alludes to some family conflict. The patient will try to act according to the god's message. Sometimes, he only realizes that God shows him the insufficiency of his understanding, using some very simple symbol of the ultimate truth. Thus one of my informants told me that she saw an apple in her dream; the apple was so green that she understood the value of life and the greatness of *bhakti*.

In low castes and tribal communities, such as the Santal, suffering often remains latent and is attributed to a number of causes, which may be supernatural, such as the evil eye (*najom*) or witchcraft, or, alternatively, plain natural. If the patient suffers from some recognized form of ailment, whether psychic or somatic, his family may take him to one of the shrines of the regional god Dharmo Thakur. Which are specialized in curing such somatic ailments as asthma[3], rheumatisms[4], skin diseases, or psychic disorders such as nervous fits. In such shrines dedicated to Dharmo Thakur, the cure involves bathing in a sacred pond and buying some medicinal oil, prepared by the brahmins or priests—mahto or dom. Members of any one of these three castes may serve this God.[5]

In case of minor ailments or psychological sufferings, the same patients may choose to consult an *ojha* 'diviner' who is often tribal or belongs to some low caste. The diviner classifies disease into four big categories; fevers, rheumatisms, a class which includes skin infection and stomach troubles, and finally wounds. Significantly, nervous disorders may be seen as a result of excessive 'wind' (*vayu, bao*), but may also fall outside the four categories. However, the Santal term '*bae*'—convulsion— and the Bengali '*pāgalmī*'—'madness'—often allude to situations such as evil possession, nervous disorders, or epilepsy.[6]

The patients may visit any *ojha*, who is often a devotee of the God Shiva or of the Goddess Kali.[7] In most cases, the *ojha* gives medicines and drives away the malevolent deities held responsible for the crisis. The patient explains his problems. The *ojha* then recommends him to fast and pray and even, in the case of a man, to engage himself as *bhakta* in the hook-swinging (*gājan*) of Lord Shiva.

In this ritual, the devotees are suspended by iron hooks enforced in the muscles of their back. The hooks are fixed by the Panda who is the head of the devotees. The *gājan* is not in itself a therapeutic cult, but it is the culminating point of the personal ascetic exercises (*tapas*), that the devotee offers to his god; the ritual commemorates the austerities that the god himself once performed.

In case of a female patient, the cure may also involve a series of religious trials that the Goddess Kali is imposing on her devotees.

THE SYMBOLISM OF SEXUAL IDENTITY

In Bengal, then, we find a marginal priesthood, including not only the *ojhas* of both sexes, but also priestesses and Hinduized gurus. The Santal *ojha*, despite a name borrowed from his Hindu counterpart, is clearly a tribal institution, by which the Santals bridge the gap between their own religion, centered on the cults of the *boṅga* 'Santal deities', and popular Hinduism. Most of the Santal *ojhas* trace mythical kinship through the Hindu god Shiva.[8]

This broad range of healers may be contrasted with the village priests who take care of the main agricultural rituals. Though the healers express themselves through certain Hindu concepts, such as *śakti*, 'cosmic energy', *dhorom* (*dharma*), 'socio-moral order', and *bhakti* 'devotion', their use of such concepts may differ from 'conventional' Hindu usage.

In these marginal, but nevertheless recognized, forms of priesthood, we soon come across the phenomenon of sexual ambivalence, while the language of sexual identity, here, serves to indicate certain stages of religious experience.

There remains the difference, however, between men and women. The femininity of the male *ojha*[9], is assumed, and form a part of this spiritual gift. In the case of women, increased masculinity always follows a personal crisis. In other words, before she may become a priestess, a woman is called, by the deity, to adopt certain masculine symbols, such as the matted hair (*joto*) of the Saivite religious ascetics. The *jōtō* is supposed to produce fire and to neutralize the malevolent deities; for a woman, it becomes a sign of election.

When the *joto* finally appears, in the case of Santal women, this event implies other biological and symbolic transformations: these women, generally, cease to menstruate.

Both sexes use the *joto* in order to fight malevolent deities, but women perceive the *joto* as a cumbersome acquisition. It is not an expected stage in the course of initiation or acquisition of knowledge, as in the case of the male *ojha*. Rather, for a woman, the *joto* implies a loss, the loss of feminity; while for the male *ojha*, the offering of his own blood acquires for him a double sexual identity; this blood, offered during exorcism, is called *sitkạ mạyạm*—'menstrual blood'. The feminity of the *ojhas* is occasioned by the need to deal, in the ritual sessions, with the various and sometimes changing identities of the deities of the other world. These are supposed to borrow different forms (*rup*), to lure their victims into illusion (*māyā*).

The Santal *ojha* is not the only male to get feminized. We may consider the feminity of the Hindu devotee (*bhakta*). among the Sahajio for example, who is the female lover of his god (Dimock 1989). More generally, we may wonder with Kakar (Clement and Kakar 1993) whether spiritual achievement is not often, as with the saint, expressed through the suppression of phallic revendications.

In tribal societies in India, emergence of the self occurs in the context of transgression of a taboo. The same process may be observed among members of low Hindu castes as well. We shall consider whether possession by the Goddess does not imply, in Bengali culture, the loss of masculine identity for men, while women have to abandon their feminity, their creative power.

FIRE, WATER, TAPAS, AND THE CALLING OF THE GODDESS

The 'Calling of the Goddess' is symbolically expressed through fire, as she appears in dreams, radiant with flames.

When priestesses and female *ojhas* feel that the matted hair is 'burning'[10] them, they may cut it, in rebellion against the Goddess. But the cut-off locks sometimes start moving about, spitting fire, as they are full of *śakti*. Cutting the *joto*, then, is to keep the sacred fire at a distance. When thus rejecting the Calling of the Goddess, the women also refuse possession and postpone the exercise of *tapas*. The ascetic exercises can only be postponed, as it gradually becomes psychologically evident to the disciple that he or she cannot finally, avoid answering the Goddess' Calling. Overwhelmed by heat and *tapas*, the devotee finally surrenders and performs the necessary austerities, which recall the penance of Lord Shiva himself.

For men, as we have seen *tapas* involves the performance of hook-swinging during the *gājan*. Women, on the other hand, observe different kinds of vows, implying the practice of chastity, fasting, bath in cold water, and the performance of meditation. In some cases, the possession, felt as merging with the śakti of the Goddess, is conceptualized as crossing fire and water, and implies the experience of a series of trials, which provoke dreadful visions.

We may wonder if possession, as such, is therapeutic and, if we answer in the affirmative, what is the cost of it? Before trying to answer these two questions, let us remind ourselves of Sardan's (1994) criticism of interpreting possession in therapeutic terms. Possession or trance, for him, far from being the expression of the subject manifesting its disorders, is perceived—in West Africa from where he takes his examples—as 'a partial withdrawal of the subject during the time his body is occupied by the local spirits'. Further, Sardan wonders whether the anthropologist can, legitimately, identify the roles played by the patients during possession with different characters of their personal history and even—I might add—with different instances of their psychic structure.

We shall argue that possession by the Goddess Kali means, for the devotee, going beyond the luring appearance of the world. In other words, we will question here the psychic reality of possession as it is described by the devotees themselves when coming out of the trance. Even if they seem not to remember anything, this is taken, by the audience, as indicative of a an experience. Kali as a Goddess—encompassing negative and positive aspects—offers to the devotees the possibility of transforming his/her symptom into a spiritual alliance So, when a person is possessed by Kali he becomes the goddess's devotee, and can no more shelter the inferior malevolent deities. this suggests that the patient's symptoms are identified with inferior 'demonic deities', and that possession by Kali drives away these demons, as well as the conflicts they were expressing, to give room to the authoritative charisma of a greater goddess. This schema leaves aside any identification of the possessed with the Western concept of a person, as we do not know exactly what part of the person finds solace in merging his/her identity with the Goddess. Similarly, I shall argue that the body or the image of the Goddess (sometimes merged with her statue) is conceptualized by the possessed women as the primordial body[11] from where one dies and get reborn. This reminds us of course, that as *prakṛti*, the Goddess is indeed 'the primordial body' of the world.

The devotees' comments may help the anthropologist to distinguish the behaviour relating to belief from the statements produced about it. Can we, by using such an approach, understand how the members of a culture refer to the different levels of religious knowledge? This raises another question: do all these statements about religious belief form a coherent semantic universe, and if so, with reference to what?

I shall argue that in Bengal, the context of acculturation produces a situation emphasizing the distance between the self and the other. In the following two cases, possessed women in Bengal both underwent a life-crisis and, finally, became priestesses.

THE STORY OF PARVATI

Parvati is the daughter of a diviner famous for his visionary capacities. She never married a Santal, but fell in love with a degraded Brahman, a driver working for the same contractor as herself. After a while they were married in front of Thakur (Shiva). The guru of the shrine gave each of them an amulet.

Through this marriage, they become co-disciples of the guru, a relationship which cut across caste barriers. The purity/impurity dilemma reappears as Chand, Parvati's 'husband' ties around her neck a part of his brahmanical sacred thread. By this action, her lover wanted to underline her impurity, and the sacrifice of his own purity; but the act also aims at protecting her.

According to Santal ideas, Parvati should now be considered dead[12] but her brothers, who are fond of her, refuse to perform her funeral rites. Parvati settles with her Hindu companion in the suburbs of a small Birbhum town. After a while, she realizes that she is sterile; she also finds it difficult to be accepted in Hindu society; only in the shrine of their *Shakti*st Guru are they accepted as man and wife.

Many women, like Parvati, try to overcome their sterility by turning to religion; they tend to have dreams which they interpret as the Goddess Kali driving away their feminity[13]. But Parvati emphasizes the sacrifice of her feminity to the Goddess, and by indulging in austerities (*tapas*), she is finally invested with various Hindu symbols.

She takes to wearing a *joto*, 'matted hair'. But, like some other women, Parvati then refuses to keep it: 'it feels too heavy'. Despite the threat of the Goddess who has warned her in dreams, Parvati cuts some locks and throws them angrily in a corner of the little shrine. Chand, her companion, declares that the locks are moving by themselves and some neighbours come to wonder about this miracle. A women who is suffering from skin disease, rubs her arm on the locks and is cured.

Later on, Parvati is able to carry the Shivaite trident[14] and finally has her own patients and disciples. She has gained therapeutic powers; and she is able to utter prophecies. Chand is staging her seances of possessions; sometimes, miracles take place. Parvati identifies herslf with the Goddess. At first a punitive mother figure, Kali subsequently becomes a benevolent one.

BECOMING THE CHILD OF THE GODDESS

The loss of feminity, and of the menstrual cycle, is interpreted in these stories as the gift of a new identity. The woman is reborn as the child of the Goddess. At another level, she is granted the matted hair, which transforms her into a sexually ambivalent being.

The matted hair implies the observance of chastity. The acceptance of the matted hair is often a long process, which the woman tends to compare to the gradual merging that is the union of *bhakti*. This reference to *bhakti* may imply, on another level, an opposition to the *śakti* implicit in the adoption of the matted hair.

The *joto*, of course, is supposed to express the burning power of the yogic fire. Cutting the *joto*, then, is to keep the sacred heat at a distance. To cool the heat of her *tapas*, Parvati may immerse herself in a sacred pond and take back a pot of water, which symbolizes Shiva himself.[15]

In Parvati's story, the cut matted locks represent the *śakti* of the Goddess, as well as the yogic fire. All the same, it is only after cutting the locks that her trances become more peaceful.

She cut the locks believing that she was rebelling against the Goddess; now she finds that the locks have healing powers by themselves. Thanks to the miracle of the healing locks, Parvati herself is recognized as an incarnation of the Goddess during her possession rituals.

In other words, Parvati loses part of her individual identity in order to express a more universal self. She becomes the *tapasvīn*—the one who, through austerities, is eternally in search of the Goddess.

THE STORY OF ASULA DEVI

Asula is a low-caste woman from a Bihari Lohar family, which came to Birbhum some fifty years ago. Her husband, a blacksmith, often deserts her, and she lives at the outskirts of a Hindu village with the last of her unmarried daughters.

Two years ago, after a violent quarrel with her husband, Asula began to see the Goddess Kali appearing in her dreams. Kali ordered her to build her a small temple, and to worship her regularly. As she did not have the means to build the temple, Asula just kept meditating in the cremation ground. After a while, she started to utter prophecies which were believed by the villagers. Asula then met two religious practitioners who taught her some of their divination techniques. One of them was a Santal witchfinder, and the other a Bengali *guni* (magician).

Asula referred to these two men as her gurus. She had an affair with the *guni*, who taught her how to use certain animal and human substances to prepare powerful medicines or magic charms. Of course, most of the villagers gossiped about her use of highly impure substances, such as human bones fond in the cremation ground. Certainly, these are tantric practices.

Asula does not talk much of *bhakti*, but she sometimes appeals to the

Goddess for the protection of her clients at the local shrine she has finally built in the courtyard of her house. In such cases, she addresses the Goddess by the term 'Ma'. Mothers bring their children to the shrine and make vows (*manat*) to protect them. In contrast to Parvati, who offers only vegetarian food in sacrifice, Asula sacrifices chicken in certain cases, such as the sickness of her clients.

Asula considers herself a tantric priestess, and her powers are symbolized by the triśūl she has planted in front of her little shrine. The *triśūl* has been consecrated by a sadhu famous for his powers. It seems obvious, here, that the sadhu has transmitted some part of his own *śakti* by means of the *triśūl*. Women, generally, never touch the *triśūl*, and even priestesses see the *triśūl* as an object accessible to them only when they are spiritually ready for it.

In Asula's case, then the mediation of the sadhu solves the problem of seizing the *triśūl*. While Asula's devotion generally takes as Shaktist form, she also organizes singing parties, where the devotional songs to the Goddess have, sometimes, a Bhaktist form. Asula's ideas of tantrism include her assertion that she has sexual intercourse with sadhus, on the cremation ground. On these occasions, she has received *mantras*, which she uses for meditation.

Unlike Parvati, for whom possession is the central religious experience by which she see the goddess, Asula, concentrates her meditation on the *mūrti*.

ASULA'S SOCIAL MESSAGE

The social implication of Asula's teaching has been intensified by a singular experience. Two years ago, one of her sister' sons, a boy of fourteen, was beaten to death by a rich marwari for whom he worked. The photo of the dead body of the adolescent, published in the local newspaper, has been placed at the feet of the Goddess by Asula. The Marwari was released after a while, and the family of the victim have been trying to plead their cause with local political leaders.

On the ritual level the photo of the victim is seen as a powerful symbol of *śakti*. If your heart is true, say, you can experience the vision (*darśan*) of the Goddess, crying over the body of the child. Visitors of all castes come to take oaths before Asula devi's *mūrti*. They receive the *darśan*, not only of the Goddess, but also of the young boy himself. Thus due to the injustice of his death, they body has become a minor God. Ever since the tragic event, Asula has engaged herself in austerities from time to time. She feels that she has now got the power to prevent similar injustice.

POSSESSION AND INTERPRETATION

Expression of emotion is often taken (Carstairs and Kapur 1976, Obeyesekere 1970) as a source of evidence for the study of depression, anxiety, possession and culturally related symptoms, as well as unconscious and preconscious motivations.

In the case of Asula Devi, it is clear that she manipulates possession (*rum*) as a strategy to choose a certain type of action. Asula, who has chosen a tantric way of life, is not sexually inhibited; rather, she uses possession to present her grief and feeling of injustice in order to convey to the oppressed a kind of class consciousness.

Most of the anthropological descriptions of female possession focus on hysteria. Let us recall that for Freud, the cause of hysteria is a violent shock, a physical trauma. Hysterical symptoms, as Freud wrote in a later formulation, were 'residues-precipitates' of emotional experience (Freud 1910:14). In India, the cause of hysteria is often attributed to a fear of sexuality in the context of arranged marriage. Let us add that for young brides sexuality is connected with violence, since they may fear being raped by relatives or men of their village. In many cases, as Freed and Freed (1967) report, seduction or even rape proves fatal to the young girl; she has little choice but suicide when she discovers herself to be pregnant. Often the young bride, fearing any sexual relationship, is unconsciously haunted by the suicide of a school mate or a friend. Sexuality is connected with death and guilt. But one should not forget that manifestations of psychological states depend heavily on cultural norms. As Claus remarks: 'Even if there is a strong resemblance between the behavior of a person in the state of possession and the behavior of a person in the state of hysteria, it does not necessarily mean that the preconditions are the same' (1979:33).

Even so, unwanted spirit possession, viewed as 'illness' in the literature, appears basically uniform in north India, though it is not always well documented, and most authors (e.g. Freed and Freed 1985) do not discuss the native concepts of disease. The general elements of the pattern are as follows. A person begins to act as in a strange manner and contracts an 'illness' which does not respond to ordinary remedies. The spirit is most often the ghost of a person who has died an untimely death. The patient is cured by exorcizing the ghost. Complete recovery follows.

Within this pattern, the particular details of the symptoms, events, and causation, may vary; in Bengal, we find two kinds of possession: spirit possession, and the mystic call of the Goddess. Sometimes, these two forms intermingle, especially in the case of women.

The Goddess must impose herself to drive away the demons, and it may be necessary to come to terms with them. They are not just external forces, but represent, simultaneously, the pulsions of the patient. When the demons are finally destroyed rather than just driven away, the 'healing ritual' becomes, in effect, spiritual election. The body of the devotee is submitted to a symbolic transformation through which she leaves her symptoms and hysterical fits behind, to assume the body of the *bhakta*—the true 'devotee'.

What we know for sure is that the trance allows the Goddess' disciple to express a sexual ambivalence which symbolizes a rupture in her previous identity and alludes to the complementary masculine and feminine aspects of the Goddess who, let us not forget it, is also the *śakti*—the feminine cosmic energy of Shiva. Moreover, I suggest that between the trances the devotee needs to reinterpret her altered states of consciousness (Bourguignon 1973) in terms of her ordinary life. Especially for women, there is the need to mark a qualitative rupture between possession and ordinary experience, expressed in time imagery. Thus, some accomplished devotees will say they allow the Goddess to come in the afternoon, or very Tuesday. The boundary projected in time and space recalls, of course, the Freudian circumscription of the therapeutic process in the séance. Nevertheless, I will avoid the implication that the subject who is possessed by demons differs from the subject possessed by Kali; rather I say that Kali's figure allows the subject to reconciliate his different roles and contradictory emotions, at the cost of changing his or her life. Moreover there is no evidence that a linguistic distinction is made commonly and explicitly between the two experiences of possession.

Possession by the Goddess Kali, then, offers an extreme form of liminality as it implies renunciation of mundane life. Nevertheless, once the devotee becomes a priestess, the possession constitutes, for those who observe it, a *darśan*—'the sight or vision of the deity'.[16]

We shall have to explain, then, how this transformation is possible and which psychic mechanisms are implied by it. If the opposition of possession as a symptom, and possession as *election*, is found in other cultures, such as in Africa (Sardan 1994), the way in which the Goddess imposes herself to effect this transformation seems to be quite specific to the Indian context.

In Bengal, attacks from mischievous spirit involve loss of consciousness, trance and conversion symptoms. At the beginning of the crisis, the devotee is possessed by vengeful spirits but she, simultaneously, receives the call of the Goddess. At first, the Goddess Kali appears in her threatening form (*rūp*) and provokes repeated fits in the patient's body. Some devotees remain at this stage, and never succeed in becoming the children of the Goddess. It is only the 'true' devotee, able to see the 'mother of salvation' beyond the terrible apparition of Kali who can achieve election.

THE *MŪRTI* AND THE SYMPTOM OF CONVERSION

Demon possession may be seen as a defense against disorganization of the personality. Possession by the Goddess seems rather to imply a reorganization of the personality. When a woman is possessed by the Goddess, she may be ordered by the deity to install a statue (*mūrti*) and build a shrine. But this is hardly possible unless the possession is acknowledged by others as genuine.

The *mūrti* here, is like *śakti* itself, a physical and cosmic force which is analogous to the energies of the human body. When the priestess suffers, the statue may cry, and it is the goddess who is encouraging her devotee by producing miracles. Whenever the trance is difficult, the *mūrti* seems to help the possessed woman to reorganize her mental space. When devotees talk about their visions, it is quite clear that an ideological link exists between the way the Goddess manifests herself in dreams, and her physical presence in the shrine. The *mūrti* produces at first a perceptual disorientation; one abandons everything to the Goddess' feet and then a reorientation, in which one regains vital energy, which indeed is therapeutic.

POSSESSION IN KARNATAKA

In south Kanara, each household (*illu*) and each village (*ūru*) 'replicate as a microcosm an ideal kingdom rooted in two different realms conceptualized as two different levels of reality: *māyā*—supernatural and *jōga*—natural' (Nichter 1977). Ritual possession takes place in the *bhūta* cult where the specialized mediums, belonging to three different marginal castes[17], impersonate the *bhūtas*, while their wives sing the epics. In this ritual, the audience question the *bhūtas* as oracles but there is no room for individual life crisis. The *bhūta* cults include highly elaborate ritual which reflect the hierarchical order of society and emphasize the *jajmān*-sacrificer-role, represented by a descendant of a previous king or feudal chief. Possession also takes place in Goddess temples which may be dedicated, whether to Mariamma, to Mangla Devi, or simply to Amma. In more Sanskritic kind of temples, devotees may get possessed by Durga Parameshwari, Mahishasura Mardini or another form of Durga.

In south Kanara most of the mediums of the Goddess are male. Nevertheless, I shall compare to situations involving, respectively, a male medium and a female one. In opposition to the professional mediums of the *bhūta* cult, both experienced, at first, an unwanted form of possession. But, 'In areas where there is both mediumship and unwanted spirit possession, there is obviously a cultural association between the behavior exhibited by people in both categories, i.e. they are both possessed by spirits.' (Claus 1979:29). Here too, there is no evidence that a separate linguistic category labels each of the two experiences, in spite of the rich vocabulary regarding possession.

A MEDIUM IN PUTTUR

In Puttur, there was a coolie who was employed in the building of the railway. When he was around twenty-seven, he started dreaming of the Goddess. Often, he awoke sweating in the night and crying: 'Amma'.

Then he heard that on the top of a hill, just opposite to the station, there was a house where was living a wealthy Muslim. The place was quiet but, strangely, noises were heard at night, sounding like thunder. The Muslim felt that his house was shaking and in his anxiety he consulted two astrologers: one was a Muslim and the other a Brahman famous for his predictions. This latter astrologer was quite clear: the land where the house of the Muslim had been built, almost fifty years before, belonged to the Goddess and had, at one time, been the site of a temple.

As the Muslim was thinking of ways to appease the Goddess' wrath, he fell sick, and finally both astrologers agreed that he should leave the place. Meanwhile, the Muslim and the Hindu coolie had almost the same dream; both were asked to make a place for the Goddess. The coolie, too, consulted the astrologer and became possessed by the Goddess. She wanted him to serve her, and to dedicate a temple to her. The Muslim was so convinced by the sincerity of the coolie that he agreed to sell him the house for a small sum on the condition that the latter should serve the Goddess all his life.

As soon as Samanto, the coolie, took charge of the house, devotees started coming twice a week. Samanto has staged a beautiful ritual, which is taking place in the inner shrine he has made inside the house. The Goddess Mariamma, in her terrible (*ugra*) form, is sitting inside the *garbha*, the 'inner shrine', to which a stone staircase is leading.

When the ritual begins, the devotees ring the bells with frenzy in the tiny suffocating corridor leading to the *garbha*. Then, Samanto prays, bent in front of the Goddess. Suddenly, he presents himself to the devotees garbed in the red silk saris typical of the *pātri*, 'possessed priest' wearing gold ornaments on his arms and chests, and a silver snake around his waist (Plate 12). Smiling, he shows his red palms in blessing and suddenly, starts down the staircase, jumping acrobatically on a little wooden plank (*mane*). Then he starts dancing, in a graceful and feminine manner.

Later on, the pilgrims will ask questions (*kaṇike*), like in other south Kanara shrines, giving to a mediator[18] little slips of paper where they have previously written their requests. To answer the questions, Samanto first consults the goddess and then conveys her divine message to the devotee. He will use obscene speech, insults and any possible rhetorics in order to impress on the disciple that the Goddess has indeed decided for him the right thing to do.

Obviously, there was a big gap between the tremendous trance when he was dancing in an atmosphere of incense and the fragrance of flowers, and his male, decided and abrupt voice, conveying the Goddess' orders.

In one of the sessions we attended, a young girl started to jerk unconsciously, moaning loudly, held by her mother—a thin woman who was trying in vain to control her. Samanto was asking questions but the Goddess screamed through the mouth of the girl: 'Last time . . . we went to pay homage to Durga Parameshwari in Katil and we could not take a bath in the ghat . . . there was no time . . . there was no time!' 'No time for the Devi?' Interrupted Samanto abruptly with an expression of divine anger—and he slowly turned back towards the *mūrti* as if his body had become very heavy. The scene was breathtaking; What will happen next? Samanto came back, deeply inspired and asked: 'Will you give me a golden chain? Will you give a precious ornament to your Goddess? You will do that after having returned to Katil and taken a bath to purify yourself for Durga Parameshwari!'

The girl started breathing heavily, asking in a strident voice: 'Shall I pass may exam?' Samanto replied with a tired face: 'Certainly, but listen to me, go back to Durga Parameswari and then come back to me. . . . '

During each session, there were perhaps a dozen similar situations but here, the conflict opposing the girl and her mother was quite clear. Obviously, the mother did not like to admit that they had found no time for the bath, and so she would have liked to find another cause for her daughter's failure at school. Something should have been wrong with the girl.

Here the possession revealed the authoritarian figure of the mother, crushing her daughter's personality. The Goddess, on the other hand, seemed to offer the girl an occasion to distance herself from her mother's authority at a time of her life where she was close to puberty.

One may wonder how Samanto, a low-caste man, could have staged the ritual with so much art. He was, indeed, inspired by the Goddess and became quite proud of himself. The walls of the temple were decorated with his photographs, displaying the gift of an Ambassador car by one devotee, a businessman from Bombay.

If we compare the ritual role played by Samanto as *pātri*, who is quite feminized, to the *ojha* in Bengal, we must note that he is not really indulging in *tapas*, 'austerities'; it seems enough for him to stay faithful to the Goddess and to be a vegetarian.

It seems that the Goddess in Bengal, and particularly Kali, is more exigent towards her disciples than any Goddess in Karnataka. But, observing possession in the latter region, one notices that the total hierarchy of Goddesses is always present as a frame of reference to the medium, and to the devotees as well. It is clear that Mariamma herself could not help our school-girl, but that she was showing her the way to get back to Durga Parameshwari, a more Sanskritized form of Goddess though not necessarily a more powerful one.

Returning, here, to the point of the mystic call, Samanto is definitely elected, even if circumstances have helped to a certain extent. In some other cases, it is not enough to show devotion to the Goddess in order to become possessed.

THE DEVI IN COONDAPUR

In this family, belonging to the Gowda caste,[19] two generations of women have in vain been worshipping the Goddess Kali in order to get possessed, while different kinds of disasters were falling upon the family. They are now well established in Coondapur; the father is employed as a cashier in a trading company.

Finally, the goddess came, possessing the grand-daughter, a young girl of sixteen. They have now opened a shrine, called Adi Shakti Kali Kshetra. There, the young girl is acting as a medium once a week almost for a full day. A large crowd, but mostly women, belonging to all castes, attend the shrine. The medium's mother, holding the Devi Mahatmya in one hand, is monitoring the daughter's trance.

Everybody is calling the young girl Devi, and she has become so famous that important people in town came to inaugurate the small, proper temple that is being built for the Goddess, with the financial assistance of the devotees. A *Brahma kailāsa*, 'a ritual purification of the place', has been performed in great pomp by four *tantri* brahmans[20].

The possession of the young Devi seems painful and impressive. She does not scream but rather speaks alternatively in an angry voice and a soft tune. She does not look at the *mūrti* as such, because she is, more obviously than any other medium I have seen, the Goddess herself. She does not wear a *joto*, the matted hair, as the priestesses in Bengal do. Still she does display an apparently 'virile' energy in her fits. I became even more convinced of this interpretation when her sister told me that she is also heading a *yakṣagāna*[21] theatre company, always playing male roles, such as Ravana and other *rākṣasas.*

Devi seems to pay considerable attention to the messages, representing the answers to the devotees' questions, that the Goddess writes, in red colour, on the palms of her hands, and which she has then to decipher.

Frail but concentrated during her possession, Devi was displaying a martial allure on the *yakṣagāna* stage, as is clear from the photos in her theatre album! Should we conclude that the girl has interiorized the dual aspects, feminine and masculine, of the goddess? In her case, the fits during possession were not too violent, but her devotees were sometimes falling unconscious on the floor before her, thus demonstrating the force of the Goddess.

Many of the questions (*kaṇike*) submitted to the Devi were mentioning the *nāg*, the 'chtonian deities' associated with reproductive powers. Very often, the questioner had forgotten to worship a *naga* stone somewhere on his land.

In Coondapur, the family devotion for the Goddess has been transferred from mother to daughter. It has brought forth the symptoms of hysteria and, finally, the grand daughter has been elected, on the condition that she stays a virgin and continues to serve the Goddess. Here, the sacrifice of femininity reminds us of Parvati, but, unlike her, the medium in Coondapur did not experience a life-crisis before receiving the call of the Goddess. On the contrary, in the case of the Coondapur medium, there were apprehensions of a later crisis: 'What will happen', whispered her sister, 'if somebody wanted to marry her?'

If we compare possession as a meaningful language to reassert identity in our cases from Bengal and Karnataka, we notice that in both cases possession implies sexual conversion. The medium is expected to display both female and male characteristics in order to approach the Goddess who, herself, often displays a double nature.[22] The Santal *ojhas* have a different explanation; for them mastering an ambivalent sexual identity is seen as a strategy towards the malevolent deities. Sexual conversion can be understood as a language of therapeutic powers: a male medium gets feminized in order to cure while a female medium should get virile powers.

Another aspect of sexual conversion is expressed through the symbolism of rebirth. As children of the Goddess, Parvati as well as Devi have to renounce procreation. The mystic calling introduces the elected person into a spiritual lineage, where her human descendance matters less.

If we now ask how possession is perceived by society in Karnataka, we may answer that it is highly improper to get possessed when it is not expected. It seems, here, that the ritual hierarchy is so tight that there is less room for the emergence of a 'marginal priesthood' than in Bengal; mediums try their best to assimilate themselves to mainstream Hinduism. For some high-caste people in Puttur, the shrine of Samanto was considered as a king of modern development of popular faith, but even so, one noticed many visitors belonging to high castes.

While Tulu society does not tolerate possession out of place, there is an insistence, in some cases, on having women possessed as a form of spiritual solace which can be found in coming close to certain spirits.

THE SIRI RITUAL AS A THERAPEUTIC CULT

In some villages of the Tulu country, any woman who shows a certain anxiety, or who responds to family demands in a disproportionately emotional manner, is supposed to be afflicted by some spirit.[23] The possession usually begins after the first menses, at the time when a suitable mate is being sought for the girl. The spirit attack is usually violent, and may manifest itself in a catatonic fit; but it may also produce a deterioration of the girl's energy and health. The symptoms may be somatic, but they also include the fear of marriage and female disorders associated with childbearing. A diviner has to confirm the possession, before advising the parents to bring the girl to the next Siri annual ritual.

The Siri cult has been seen as a therapeutic cult (Claus 1975). The rituals take place annually and simultaneously at six temple locations in Tulunadu and some of the cult members are regular attendants. The legend of Siri, the Siri Paddana, is sung in a formal style by the cult members in the context of the ritual. It concerns the life and misfortunes of a family of Bunts, the previous landlords of the Tulu country. Claus defines Siri spirits as 'a class of deities unto themselves consisting of four females and a male who are apotheosized beings who originally belonged to three generations of a single matrilineal family'(1979:36).

Siri, as some Goddesses, is born from a flower pad of areca nut palm. She grows up very fast and gets married. When she is getting pregnant, her husband insults her by giving her as a gift a sari already worn by his concubine. Humiliated, Siri leaves his house and gets a son Kumar. After having lost her kinsmen and wealth, Siri finally becomes the co-wife of another man.

The ritual is very elaborate and involves *tantri* brahmans as well as the local priesthood. The 'therapist', the *kumara*, is a male who acts as a possessed priest (*pātri*), but he also represents Kumara, the epic character. In all Siri rituals, there is an opposition between the mediums, who are initiated cult members associated with the different Siri spirits, and the novices who attend the Siri annual session of the first time. Possession, here, is a coded language, where the actors get possessed by the characters of the epic: the men who wear red saris around their waist are possessed by Kumara, the son of Siri.

Experienced women, regular attendants of the cult, are wearing orange saris and are possessed by Siri herself. The younger women who come for the first time are dressed in white saris and get possessed by the daughter of Siri, Sonne (Plate 13).

When one of the young women is violently possessed, Kumara and Siri ask her who is possessing her. She generally answers by the name of Siri's daughter. The Kumara and other mediums—experienced cult members—encourage the novices and welcome them in a spiritual kin group.

The scenario of the legend is presented in such an emotional way that the novice can project her own family conflicts into this broader framework. Is the effect of the ritual truly therapeutic? If it is difficult to be sure that the girl is cured, we may assert with Claus (1979:41), that her unwanted possession is transformed into mediumship. Later on this mediumship becomes a *sevā*, an honorable religious duty which ties the girl by a spiritual engagement to the Siri deities which, after all, are benevolent. But at this point, the girl has lost some of her fear of being possessed by another malevolent spirit.

The novice of the Siri cult does not have to renounce the world, or indulge in asceticism, to get cured. She just releases her inner tensions, by identifying with the tragic destiny of Siri and her children.

One may doubt whether the cult really offers an opportunity to assert one's individual identity. It does provide an image with which the subject may identify; the story of Siri becomes the mirror image of the problems of unhappy matrilineal households. 'It is a family tragedy known by everyone, yet one in which tragedy is overcome by virtue' asserts Claus (1975).

But is not virtue oppressive for women, after all? We are far, here, from Asula Devi who may choose a tantric way of life and indulge in erotic relationships on the cremation ground.

Where, then, lies the therapeutic power of the Siri cult? Is it enough for the women to attend, periodically, the same ritual, and to get possessed exclusively on this occasion? One may wonder if the ritual does not reproduce the inhibitions from which, ostensibly, it should provide a release. How do the suffering women submit to the ritual and to the sometimes authoritarian behavior of the kumar and other mediums?

In most of the village engaged in Siri rituals, women periodically undergo preparatory sessions. In some cases, the priest gets to know of the family conflict. The experienced female mediums, more secretly, receive the confidence of the novices. In this sense, Siri is a ritual where women heal other women, like the therapeutic cult of the Ndembu of Rhodesia (Turner 1968).

Sometimes the preparatory ritual is less orderly and the anthropologist cannot help noticing how it displays violent conflicts between, for example, one of the experienced female mediums and the kumara. In one case, the *kumara* was the brother of the senior female medium identified with Siri, and he, evidently, could not stand the authority of his sister in the matrilineal household. Being mother and son in the legend did not help them transcend their conflict, rather they seemed to fight each other, each one trying to get the greater influence over the devotees.

Several persons become possessed out of place and order. The priest was forcefully whipping the young novices with areca flowers, a gesture which is part of the ritual but in which he was putting more than usual emphasis. He told me, later, that he was trying to get confessions from the novices. I understood from my female assistant, who knew some of the women engaged in Siri, that this particular *pātri* was trying to 'appease' women, using a rather rough style in ritual.

But despite the priest's ritual show, which also aimed at gaining support and prestige from the more orthodox families, it seems obvious that he was boasting; the women were clever enough to conceal their secrets. They were acting out an authorized form of depression framed as the mirror image of the tragic destiny of Siri, a powerful spirit epitomizing female virtue in Tulunadu.

But, since Siri—and her grand daughters—may possess any woman at any time, women must have faith in the ritual itself if not in the priest. Yet when I again attended the preparatory ritual in the same place, the priest had become very difficult.

A large number of novices had come to the kumara's courtyard for the preparatory session. During the night, he was dragging some of the women about, screaming like an angry *bhūta*. But some girls, including his sister possessed by Siri, refused to surrender. In vain, he was shouting 'Shanti' brandishing a flowery branch of areca palm above their heads. He tried to call Narayan to his aid, but most of the women still resisted. Instead, some men, too, were getting possessed, and it become very hard to distinguish the voices of the different spirits. Siri, Kumar and Sonne seemed to have themselves come to rescue the devotes from an oppressive ritual, as if the emotions of real life could not be contained within the formal and beautiful Siri drama.

POSSESSION AS AN EXPRESSION OF THE SELF

In many cultures, illness and it symptoms are expressed in a religious idiom shared by the community as a whole. Local therapists do not disentangle the symptoms from the religious framework. In some cases, possession is conceptualized as attacks from the demons, taking place at different meaningful points in people's lives. Obeyesekere (1970:97) analyses the case of Alice Nonna, a woman in Sri Lanka who suffered from attacks of a dead ancestor after some of her pregnancies. Here, the dialogue of the demons, expressed through the dialectic of possession, convey the underlying conflict of the patient, a situation we recognize from some of our cases, both in Bengal and in Karnataka.

I think we may look at cases of possession from two related points of view. First, we may identify the problems or tensions faced by the group—in most cases resulting from the status of women—and secondly, factors specific to each life story.

Systematic repression may produce hysterical dispositions, but it seems that other factors may be as important. Thus, in an acculturation context, role models are less clear. What may be expected from Santal women in Bengal when the group becomes proletarized? Men desert their homes, and sometimes act as pimps while women may allow themselves to be seduced by their Hindu employers. Men and women show fits of rage which may lead to real violence or to witchcraft plots. Such a context may explain, partly, why some 'soft' Hindu men represent a kind of ideal for Santal women. In the same vein, such Hindu values as *bhakti* (devotion) give room for sublimation of emotions and attract individuals from a tribal background, who are conscious of having lost some of the values connected with their ancestor's customs.

In Karnataka, role evaluation is facilitated, as the culture provides alternative standards for the ideal role of adults, as expressed through the *bhūta* epics.[22] Thus, Siri represents the assertive ideal woman in a matrilineal society. Despite her tragedy, Siri takes care of her children and faces her fate. This does not mean that the Siri figure is strong enough to resolve all tensions felt by women in Tulunadu. It seems clear that some of the novices in the Siri cult have a long way to go. Obviously, too, some of them will never play the role of Siri herself, the only role of female authority in the Cult.

When Santal women are possessed by the *boṅga*, men conclude that possession is explained by their weak nature. Possession is compared with rape. Still, possession seems a way of protesting against the brutality of husbands, who may react to their wives' going away for work by taking a co-wife, and then grabbing the money earned by the first wife when she returns.

Consequently, women are tantalized to run away, and marriages become unstable. This explains, partly, why Parvati was reluctant to get married to a Santal and why the women who become devotees are not necessarily frigid. Santal women seldom seem to be. Parvati, for example, admitted that chastity was a very hard kind of *tapas*.

In this context, austerities may involve the longing to merge with the Goddess, sublimating sexual and other drives, so as to regain oneself through the mirror of spiritual election.

Tulu women, especially in a matrilineal context, are the guardians of family property; in case of conflict, they cannot run away like tribal women. In Bunt families, where cross-cousin marriage was customary, any other husband is sometimes seen as a mere substitute. Projecting one's feeling onto a demon may seem the only means to escape from the stuffy confines of married life.

While there are a limited range of conditions that produce hysterical dispositions, frigidity and sexual oppression are not the only ones. Most notably, acculturation produces situations where kinship and residence roles are losing their formal coherence. In such situations, learning a social role and coping with it becomes a complicated affair.

We have seen that possession may be expressed in number of ways and that sexual conversion is often implied. In some cases, possession by the Goddess changes the devotee's life and the experience becomes really therapeutic. Thus, in Bengal, Kali demands a lot from devotees but finally gives a lot in return. In Karnataka, Goddesses seem content with donations and proper rituals and restrict their role to the granting of boons and specific acts of appeasement. These Goddesses demand less but give less too. Even if they allow their devotees a career as a medium, such a career seems to imply a strategy and does not involve taking a chance with the devotee's reason or consciousness.

In Bengal as in Tulunadu, the possessed person who becomes a healer not only succeeds in coping with his/her initial suffering but sublimates it by taking care of others. The efficacity of the cure can be described as this transformation of an uncontrolled possession, calling for exorcism, into a spiritual alliance with a deity.

NOTES

1. The Bengali term '*pāgalmī*' means madness, insanity.
2. Dharna is, in Bengal, a fast during which the devotee is expecting a dream sent by a god, normally Shiva. Cf. also E.A. Morinis (1984).
3. In Birbhum, asthma is cured in Trilocandpur, a pilgrimage centre dedicated to Dharmo Thakur.
4. Rheumatisms (*bat*) are cured by applying a herbal oil on the patient's joints.
5. Dharmo Thakur is often said to be a 'popular' version of Shiva, but a medieval epic the *Dharmo Mangal* is dedicated to this deity. Cf. A. Bhattacharya (1952).
6. Epilepsy, *mirgī*, implies that the patient is behaving like a deer. Sometimes, the *ojha* shows him the horn of a deer to calm down his attacks.
7. Tribal and Hindu *ojhas* usally worship Shiva and Kali though these two gods are not always present together in their shrines. The *ojhas* also share a common core of knowledge including herbal medecine, *mantra* and exorcism. Cf. M. Carrin-Bouez (1986).
8. The *ojhas* consider the God Shiva as their first guru. According to the legend, there were seven gurus who founded seven lines of disciples.
9. The feminity of the *ojha* is expressed through his initiation ritual (*dikśa*) where he is supposed to be his guru's bride. In the initiation songs, possession is compared to sexual union.
10. Heat alludes to *tapas*. For a study of the relationship between asceticism and eroticism in the indian context. Cf. W.O. Flaerty (1973).
11. During the initiation ritual, the guru of the *ojha* is suposed to dismember the bodies of his disciples in the sky where they have ascended during their ritual wandering. When they get ready to go back on earth, the *guru* again assembles their bodies. But it is said that after being initiated, the *ojhas* have got a feminine part.
12. Formerly, Santal who had transgressed the taboo of endogamy were put to death or driven aways from the village.
13. When the goddess appears in their dreams, she often asks them to renounce married life.
14. To be able to catch the *triśūl* represents an important step in the devotee's life, as it implies mastering the *śakti*.

15. To bring back a pot of water and to worship it as a manifestation of the God Shiva is also an important step in the spiritual quest.
16. The priestess who has sublimated her trance is able to give the vision (*darśan*) of the goddess to her devotees.
17. There are different castes of mediums who impersonate different *bhūtas* according to their respective rank in the local hierarchy of castes. While parava and pambada, infuenced by brahmanical culture, are possessed by the *rājan daiva*, the royal *bhūtas*, the *naḷke* are possessed by Panjurli and the secundary *bhūtas*.
18. In this case the mediator is a low-caste person who helps the medium as a ritual assistant. He has been also possessed by the goddess. Samanto's wife has no ritual duty in the temple but she is responsible for giving 'pure' food to her husband and his guests.
19. The *gowda* are one of the agricultural castes of the region.
20. The *tantri* brahmans are also astrologers.
21. The *yakṣagāna* to a folk-theatre, the repertoire of which includes *Ramayana* episodes as well as local legends.
22. The *bhūtas* are spiritual beings, of which an important class are associated with territory. Guardians of the moral order, they are nonetheless involved in violent action and cannot be seen as exemplary role models for the society they protect.

REFERENCES

Assayag, J. 1989 Sacrifice et violence. Les genres de la possession dans le Sud de l'Inde (Karnataka). *Nouvelle Revue d'Ethnopsychiatrie* 13: 131-58.

Bateson, G. 1936 *Naven. A Survey of the Problems Suggested by a Composite Picture of the Culture of a New Guinea Tribe Drawn from Three Points of View.* London: Cambridge University Press.

Bhattacharya, A. 1952 *The Dharma Cult.* Bulletin of the Department of Anthropology, Govt. of India, vol. 1, no. 1.

Bourguignon, E. 1976 Possession and Trance in Cross-Cultural Studies of Mental Health. In W. Lebra (ed.) *Ethnopsychiatry and Alternative Therapies.* Honolulu: University Press of Hawaii.

——— (ed.) 1973 *Religion Altered States of Consciousness and Social Change.* Colombus: Ohio State University.

Carrin, M. 1986 *La fleur et l 'Os: symbolisme et rituel chez les Santal.* Paris: EHESS.

——— 1991 *Inner Frontiers: Santal responses to acculturations,* Bergen *CMI* 1997 *Enfants de la déesse, prêtrise et dévotion féminines au Bengale.* Paris: 'Chemins de I'ethnologie', Editions du CNRS.

Carstairs, G.M. and R.L. Kapur 1976 *The Great Universe of Kota.* London: Hogarth Press.

Claus, P. 1975 The Siri Myth and Ritual: A Mass Possession Cult of South India. *Ethnology* 14, 47-58.

——— 1979 Spirit Possession and Spirit Mediumship from The Perspective of Tulu Oral Traditions. *Culture Medicine and Psychiatry* (3): 29-52.

Clement, C. and S. Kakar 1993 *La folle et le saint.* Paris: Seuil.

Coburn, T.B. 1988 *Devi-Mahatmya: The Crystallization of the Goddess Tradition,* Delhi: Motilal Banarsidass.

Dimock, E. 1989 *The Sound of Silent Guns and Other Essays*. Delhi: Oxford University Press.

Freed, S.A. and R.S. Freed 1964 Spirit possession as illness in North Indian village. *Ethnology* 3:152-71.

——— 1985 The Psychomedical Case History of a Low Caste Woman of North India. *Anthropological Papers of the American Museum of Natural History*, vol. 60, pt. 2.

Freud, S. 1966 *Studies in Hysteria.* rpt., New York: Avon Books (lst edn. 1895).

Harper, E.B. Spirit possession and social structure. Bala Ratnam (ed.), *Anthropology on the march.* Madras, 165-77.

Houseman, M. and C. Severi 1994 *Naven ou le donner à voir Essai d'interprétation de l'action rituelle*. CNRS Editions. Editions de La Maison des Sciences de l'Homme.

Kakar, S. 1984 *Shamans, Mystics and Doctors. A Psychological Inquiry into India and its Healing Traditions*. Delhi: Oxford University Press.

Kinsley, D. 1986 Blood and Death out of Place, reflections on the Goddess Kali. In Hawley, J.S. and D.M. Wulff (eds.), *The Divine Consort.* Boston; Beacon Press, 144-52.

Levi-Strauss, C. 1973 *Anthropologie Structurale II*. Paris: Plon.

Lynch, M.O. (ed.), *Divine Passions: The Social Construction of Emotion in India.* Delhi: Oxford University Press.

Morinis, E.A. 1984 *Pilgrimage in the Hindu Tradition*. Delhi: Oxford University Press.

Nichter, M. 1977 The Joga and Maya in the Tuluva Buta. *Eastern Anthropologist* 30 (2): 139-55.

——— 1981 Idioms of Distress: Alternatives in the Expression of Psychosocial Distress: A Case Study From South India. *Culture Medicine and Psychiatry* 5, 379-408

Obeyesekere, G. 1970 The Idiom of Demonic Possession. *Social Science and Medicine* 4, 1: 97-107.

——— 1981 *Medusa's Hair*. Chicago: University of Chicago Press.

Sardan, J.P.O. De 1994 Possession, affliction et folie: les ruses de la thérapisation, *l'Homme*. Juill.-Sept. 131: 7-27.

Scheff, T.J. 1979 *Catharsis in Healing, Ritual, and Drama.* Berkeley: University of California Press.

Turner, V. 1968 *The Drums of Affliction*, Oxford: Clarendon Press.

——— 1969 *The Ritual Process. Structure and Antistructure*. Chicago: Aldine.

Plate 12: A medium in Puttur.

Plate 13: A young woman possessed by Sonne, the daughter of Siri.

The trick of the tail: Dispossessed Shamans and Witchcraft Doctors in South Indian Villages

FRÉDÉRIC BOURDIER

The aim of this work is to distinguish how, and by what logic, two dominant kinds of therapeutic practices coexist by progressively eliminating the other existing alternatives in contemporary rural Tamil society (Coimbatore district): on the one hand those of modern medicine and on the other hand those associated with a widespread set of possession cults. Our purpose is not to deal, as a lot of studies already do, with the irreductible, antagonist or complementary aspect of their respective roles according to the social context, neither to consider the possible discontinuities or continuities regarding local conceptions of health and of behaviour transformations. Our intention is to focus on the way the two medical-healing systems interact mutually in the health field, as well as in the socio-political organization of the villages, where both shamans and doctors carry on their activities.

The social context of therapeutic intervention frequently appears as a mere backdrop, on which curing processes are superimposed, without taking into consideration the complex interactions between health and social organization. Instead of emphasizing the individual shaman's personality and behaviour—is he a deviant or not?—the Indian experience, on the contrary, urges us to bring to light its collective character—does society funnel its insane people through such a compensatory institution? It will be argued that shamanism is an institution constitutive of society, and moreover, a way of conceptualizing the world, an institution whose social origins are to be found in Indo-Dravidian culture.

The symbolic foundation of shamanism explains its durability, although it is perpetuated in a changing form; somewhat degenerated, even denatured. Our purpose is to make clear the social component, too often eclipsed, and to prove that shamanic experiences have their roots in social organization and reflect socio-economical conditions as well. Finally, the relationship with biomedicine, which has not so far been compared with shamanism, may bring forth some new insight into the phenomenon. This parallel should be particularly helpful, at least to analyse their mutual socio-political position in Coimbatore rural area. By the way, in a context of medical pluralism, it appears irrelevant to envisage the different practitioners separately without evoking their interactions. Our hypothesis is that shamanism plays a major role there, not only in patterns of social relations, but also in the management of health and misfortune, in which this 'medicine man' has to cede a growing part of his prestige to the representatives of modern medicine. Hence, the socio-political stake that issues from this challenge, by means of curing and healing.

ANY SHAMANS IN TAMIL COUNTRY?

First of all, it is necessary to specify and justify our use of the term shaman, because its use may surprise quite a few anthropologists accustomed to designate and classify in an different manner the trance and possession specialists. In this article, the shaman is seen as a medicine man, a possessed priest, 'a god dancer', liable to be a diviner as well as a healer, who uses his skill to serve a family, a community, a village or even a group of hamlets. The cult he performs, which is closely but not exclusively connected with the cult of the village goddesses (i.e. the *grāmadevatās*: Mariamman and her six sisters), is based on the privileged relationships he entertains with one or more spirits. The villagers generally call him by his personal name, followed by *śāmiār* or *śāmi* when they go to see him for various disturbances occurring in their life. According to Harper (1957), the possessed priest is a man who:

> can ask his spirit to possess him whenever he wants. . . . When it happens, the shaman comes into trance and the spirit speaks through him. . . . The aim of the chamanic possession is to enable human beings to receive advices and sayings from a supernatural being whose (healing) capacities are superior to every men.

Since long, however, authors like de Heusch (1971) have dissociated possession from shamanism. The first would be associated with a god's descent and an incarnation, while the second would be confined to an ascension movement and an upward metaphysical technique. But in modern Dravidian society these two phenomena coexist in a more or less concomitant way: either joined together or in an exclusive way. Both functions operate frequently through the same person's intervention and share the fact that they enable human society to communicate with the supernatural powers transcending it. We will not enter the debate about the gap between the facts and figures as observed in south India and shamanism *stricto sensu* which, for many scholars, should be restricted to hunting and gathering societies devoid of ritual priesthood (Tumer 1972). It is indeed possible to multiply nuances and differences endlessly. But as Jean Benoist (1982) notes in his study of south Indian shamanism at Reunion Island, it is futile to attempt any classification without understanding the individual and social process. Likewise any attempt to make typologies, inevitably arbitrary, regarding various kinds of god intercessors may confine the phenomenon to reductivist considerations, precisely when it tends to express a global phenomenon. The author notes:

> The South Indian facts belong to a set of behaviours in which there is an institutionalized relationship between a specialist accepted by the society and the world of the spirits for the benefit of mankind. Instead of setting discontinuous entities versus contrasted entities, while dealing about chamanism and possession, would not it be more adequate to view this set of phenomenon as a continuum? Whatever the forms, are we not confronted with various configurations according to which some basic components are put together by adjusting themselves to history and social environment? And should we not look for their signification, beyond their explicit message, in the social system where they belong?

In that sense, the term 'shamanism', without neglecting its social and religious dimension, properly indicates the activities of various individuals (*pūśāri*, healers, exorcists, etc.) liable to come into trance or to be possessed in order to establish a link with supernatural entities, and who devote themselves to every situation which requires dealing with the spell of evil spirits. Their functions obviously go beyond health related problems but we will limit ourselves to this aspect in this paper.

AT THE CROSSROADS OF HEALING PATHS

Our observations based on field work done from November 1989 to May 1991, and later in January and February 1994, come from a group of villages[1] located some 20 km north of the industrial town of Coimbatore.

Despite the drastic socio-economic mutations and cultural changes occuring in the newly developed and dynamic region of Kongunad, rural people's health behaviour is still rooted in the healing traditions, even if these have lost their prevailing exclusiveness and share the field with modern medicine. Indeed, if various medical systems and to a certain extent classical medicine (Ayurveda, Siddha) are still rampant in the northwestern part of Tamilnadu, biomedicine is also very active. The public health delivery network has steadily extended and local and national programmes are effectively implemented and operated. There is shortage neither of paramedical workers nor of drugs. Almost all villages have either a private MBBS doctor, a dispensary tended by a qualified nurse or a moving staff who regularly visit remote places. In the main villages, located on major roads, sophisticated hospitals with all specialities available, private clinics, and well-stocked drug stores are found in abundance. Some of these medical structures are as well equipped as the best urban medical institutions, and they already receive the latest improved technologies (scanner, endoscopy and laproscopy surgery). Facing this supposedly efficient and uniform health coverage, a multiplicity of local practitioners still use their skills for the health recovery of the villagers who are eager to solicit them, not only to get relief from their pain but also to understand its signification and its origin. Their practices include a large variety of therapies from medicinal plants (*nāṭu vāydiār*), food adjustment rules and massage, to religious healing, sacred words (*maṇtra*) and so on.

Consequently, Coimbatore rural district does not reflect a typical situation, unfortunately too common in many Indian deprived areas and in most of the developed countries, in which equipment, remedies and doctors are desperately missing. This geographical accessibility to both medical systems is important for the scientist whose interests focus on health strategies which are resorted to by both healers and doctors. In the areas where there is no availability of modern facilities, traditional medicine is inevitably active, but this may be a result of the constraints. Here, in Coimbatore, *choice is really possible.*

Medical anthropology literature, frequently states that different medicines interfere with and complement each other: one is supposed to restore the biological disorder and the second is inclined to deal with the real causes of the illness, which are to be found 'somewhere else'. We do think, however, that such a distinction oversimplifies the reality. There are more subtleties, insofar as the shaman provides some technically oriented therapies as well, utilizing various food and herbal recipes, while MBBS doctors are not systematically dissociated from religion and immaterial considerations. And people's therapeutic itineraries also reflect a more complex intrication of the role they attribute to a particular medical system. We will not, however, stress this latter point which has already been analysed in a previous work (Bourdier 1994).

Contrary to the indisputable popularity of both doctor and shaman, there is a slightly decreasing interest in other curing resorts. Ayurveda and Siddha physicians desert the countryside and shift downtown.[2] And for the bulk of the families, the use of simples and minerals becomes occasional. It seems that the former two main therapeutic systems are quite capable of covering both the social, symbolic and biological dimensions of the sickness, of satisfying body and mind distress and of answering to individual and social requests. The other practitioners are only sought from time to time, and especially for some particular diseases (like leprosy, chronic ailments, etc.) and the so-called 'culture bound-syndromes' (*eduguṉam, muchupudipu*).[3]

FROM REVELATION TO CONTINUATION

One does not become a shaman especially by maternal or paternal filiation. The most common way is to receive an initiation through oral transmission. The acquisition of knowledge is realized in its early stage from 'teacher' (guru) to 'student' (*chela*), and thereafter alone with the spirits, supposed to be 'tamed' by obtaining their full confidence. The apprenticeship, strict and long—up to five years, sometimes more—necessitates increasing efforts as the learning process is going on: sexual abstinence, periods of fasting, regular food prohibitions, renunciation regarding different individually and socially 'unclean' activities (drinking, smoking, doing business, etc.). Those few who have succeeded in completing the final initiation stages, retreat for an extended period to a wild area (mostly in the Nilgiri ranges) where, as an ultimate test, they have to live as renouncers. This escape to the forest or the mountains is a key period in their magico-power acquisition process. The man has to stay alone and familiarize himself with various supernatural entities living in the cosmos. There, he will gradually learn the secrets of nature and the way to communicate with the spirits he dreams about, and who will become his privileged intercessors. Therefore, the course of this initiation, although the exorcist belongs to a backward community cannot but evoke the four stages of life in the Hindu orthodox tradition insofar as the shamanistic apprentice closely follows the 'ideal' fulfilment rules of the brahmin life. But the aim of our medicine man is not to reach deliverance (*mokśa*), because he must return to his society for the sake of the villagers.

In spite of the complexity of the initiation and the difficulty, for a majority of candidates, in reaching the final stage, village society has created a large recruitment system that starts from the earliest period of a man's life, sometimes even before his teenage years. Experienced people, mostly elderly men and women, but who are not specifically confirmed shamans, look for indications and other signs that may be interpreted as a potential aptitude among youngsters likely to assume a shaman's functions in the future. The old people proceed in fits and starts; they discreetly test the reactions of the presupposed elected children, they cursorily assess their abilities, will and desire to develop relationships with the other world. For instance, a novice will be asked to take part in a divination-possession ceremony: Is he liable to attract any spirits, and to have any intuitive relations with them? If he gets through, he will then be asked to play a slightly more important function so that the village community may test his potential skills. The whole of this selection pattern, which in fact is even more complex and diversified, demonstrates that shamanism is less an individual trend than a collective necessity. As an exorcist in Agrahara used to express it, 'it matter little that it will be my son, my brother's daughter, my wife's sister or my neighbour . . . , the real matter is that someone should take the succession'.

Shamanism is thus a main component of the social system. The general pattern in south Indian rural society, trying regularly to involve new persons into shamanism, tends to prove that reproduction of knowledge, by transmission through generations, is an essential part of the local symbolic and social organization between men and gods. Furthermore, it satisfies the imperative expectations of the village, which is to have permanently a few mediators, meant to communicate, interpret, balance and modify the invisible, but tangible, malevolent beings, facts, and intentions.

Contrary to shamans who are living among tribal communities, like those one may find in the Irula settlement near Coimbatore and who do not have any sanctuary of their own, the Hindu exorcist priest generally officiates in a minor divinity temple. Those who are not attached to any place of worship erect their own small sanctuary in the courtyard or in an appropriate room of their house. Both localisation and orientation are based on cosmic geography, myths and local legends concerning some gods (Aiyannar, Karuppan, *ammā* goddesses), demons (*muni, jadāmuni*) and other evils (*pēy, piśasu*) who are undesired but important negotiators for the human society. There is the specificity of south Indian shamanism; the medicine men are not itinerant, and unlike the orthodox brahman temple priests (*purohit*) *they do not maintain the cosmic order but deal with the disorders occurring in the village* by keeping away, and trying their best to reduce to ashes, the spirits' omens, maledictions and ill-minded intrusions in human society. Consequently in order to temper a boisterous wandering soul, the shaman calls the spirit(s), and once located and personalized he devotes a cult to him. To 'fix' the spirit means to gain a control over him and then to dominate him. The shaman's duty is, then, to prevent the desirable entities from moving freely in the villages and disturbing the inhabitants. So, he is not the one who 'goes' to reach the spirits in outer space but the one who looks for, identifies, calls them, and tries to keep them quiet in a settled place. Not completely unconnected with devotion or *bhakti* but not yet a pure devotional cult like those who are related to major Hindu gods, it is tempting to regard the observed shamanistic practices as a syncretic form derived from an old magico-religious healing pattern which has been progressively absorbed by Hindu religion.

The possessed *śāmiār* generally perform alone and in a competitive mind, but whenever some important collective ceremonies take place, they agree to cooperate, even with other priests, not versed in shamanism, but who play a separate and complementary ritual role during the festivals periods such as the Mariamman festival, the regeneration performance of the goddess, fire-walking, and so on. On these occasions, villagers will question the possessed people about the welfare of children, important life engagements and other decisions to be made. All these celebrations constitute important and decisive moments for the whole society and because of the complexity of the rituals, and the multiplicity of pujas and offerings, all the available shamans in the area join together.

SECULAR POWER VERSUS IMMATERIAL POWER

The shamans, usually coming from backward communities, mostly move in the shadow of secular community powers. Because the therapeutic activities are usually connected with sacerdotal practices, this magico-religious combination enables them to pull ahead in the informal political hierarchy.

Therefore, their priesthood functions, corollary with and indissoluble from their body and spirit healing capacity, confer on them a certain political importance, which is not easy to grasp, but which is nevertheless real and effective. The villagers use to say 'they are the *ūr* and *grāma* (territory and village) protectors' but at the same time they take part in important decisions insofar as they participate unofficially in many deliberations concerning social and agrarian life: choice of crops and cultures, of an auspicious time for starting agricultural work, divinations and predictions, arbitration in conflicts occurring among individuals, groups (*jāti*) and other social factions, preliminary advice about marriage arrangements and, more precisely, about alliances between exogamic lineages.

Consequently, the number of shamans in a panchayat village (for instance more than a dozen in Agrahara samakulam, 2300 inhabitants) is a crucial factor that contributes to their mutual emulation. They are mostly having competitive and conflictual relationships between themselves, and each one of them tends to accuse the other of being a bogus medicine man, an impostor, a quack or even a dangerous person versed in black magic. In a social universe where prestige functions and status are stressed, every shaman has to prove and to constantly reiterate his superiority against his fellows. The prestige is estimated not only from his ability to rally people's enthusiasm, but from extending his recognition within a vast geographical area: the farther the followers walk, the higher his prestige. In a village near Coimbatore (Veerapandi) a shaman we used to visit asked us to attend, on a special day, an 'important' possession performance: the patient was a respectful and well-known business contractor born in Coimbatore but presently living in Bombay. The acquisition of some precious and rare *ōlai* (compendium of *maṇtra* and *yantra* used to protect and to ward off spells, omens and misfortune) increases the reputation as well. Be that as it may, the most acknowledged consideration is accorded to the shaman who presides at major collective ceremonies. The competition among various pretenders to be chosen as the leader of a coming ceremony may lead to a good deal of intrigues and endless rivalries, as we frequently noticed at various occasions during 1990: Vannyiar's festival in Agrahara samakulam, Ammakumbabishegam in Kovilpalayam and so on. This challenge reflects the rise of a competitive spirit between possessed healers as well as the latent tensions among communities, *jāti* and other social groups which are eager to have their own representative gaining the symbolico-political control of the religious festivities. In many ways, the exacerbated relationships between possessed priests reflect the tensions and conflicts that are entertained by their respective appartenance groups. In other respects, while the official political power is negotiated between eligible panchayat memberships in charge of rural development and local pressure groups (big landowners, cast leaders, rich merchants), another set of daily occurring social and family events come under the supervision of the shaman, who is well integrated among the poorest strata of the society, usually kept apart from any decision-making process. It is thus tempting to consider the spirit mediumship as a counterpower against the institutionalised local establishment. This becomes particularly obvious during religious festivals where shamans are temporarily invested with significant power insofar as they forecast the future, control the unstable weather, prevent epidemics that threaten men, cattle and crops, and soothe the wrath of goddesses and demons creating havoc. In Kongunad most of the Hindu cults and ceremonies are celebrated from *Tai* (mid-January to mid-February) to *ādi* (mid-July to mid-August), respectively the traditional time for the end of harvest and for sowing. This period is also an occasion to strengthen linkages between different involved groups and *jāti*. At this time, public authorities are temporarily powerless, in spite of police security forces in charge of preventing people from getting out of hand during the intensely crowded and emotional ceremonies. The shaman himself decides the amount of offerings for religious festivals and the total expenditure for both individual and collective exorcisms aimed at driving away malevolent spirits causing harmful effects in the village area. During these impressive manifestations, the secular power is periodically and temporarily suspended and we may confirm, for south Indian shamanism, what Galinier (1982) judiciously pointed out in an other setting.

> The official authorities cannot attack from the front this public life shift in immaterial power allegiance without calling into question the firmly rooted pattern . . . concerning periodic and symbolic procedures for the social and cosmic order re-establishment. . . .

Having a power beyond space and time, but a power in direct relation with any cosmic destabilization threat, the shaman acts as a subterranean authority, who periodically emerges according to the auspicious days of the lunar calendar and whenever any crisis occurs (natural calamities, severe epidemics, social problems). But the status of these 'dream practitioners', an expression coined by M. Perrin (1993), is not lasting in its original form, especially with the contact of changing and modernizing factors. And if their priesthood functions are not questioned in the least, this is not the case regarding their symbolic therapeutic activities, which encroach on the practice of medical professionals.

MBBS doctors generally do not recognize the abilities of the shamans, even if some are aware of, and secretly rely on them, in case of unexplained misfortune in their own families. They do not want to conceive of the exorcist priests' ritual and involvement in social therapeutic cures in terms of efficiency (which, they would hold, has to be objectively measurable) but in terms of mere magico-religious beliefs, still rampant in a society where poverty and illiteracy make the people basically ignorant. All the more, then, they agree that shamans are doing psychological feats and tricks that may produce good results on such 'receptive and innocent' villagers. But even so, if the restoring of the body falls entirely within the doctor's competence, sanctioned by his official diploma, this does not prevent the bulk of modern practitioners to feel uncomfortable, when they have to face the *global* request of the sick man. This global request implies not only the taking of a drug, but simultaneously to understand the reason for the illness, and to find out the social and symbolic signification of the misfortune. As a medical physician employed in a Primary Health Center (PHC) stressed: 'how can we reasonably cure people who attend an exorcism after receiving a biochemical treatment?' More insidiously, the permanent presence of traditional healers, curers, *maṇtra* sayers, fortune tellers and shamans, who continuously interfere in the sphere of medicine, does not reflect, from the medical authorities' formal point of view, a rosy picture of the health situation. The endemic presence of these practitioners, despite the WHO's proposals and recommendations, runs counter to the expectations of the administrators. According to them, the health delivery system's spatial integration achievements are supposed to symbolize modernity, that is to say, the victory of scientific thought over superstitious empiricism. The vitality of shamanism further illustrates, still according to secular discursive reasoning, that obscurantism is still rampant despite state welfare development. The quality of the preventive and curative treatment freely delivered, and the reluctance of even the most deprived population to use these public services, thus call into question its adequate functioning. It is clearly to the point, that frequent strategic resort to alternative sources of healing affront the allegedly more 'adequate' and 'appropriate' planned propositions put forward by the medical establishment. This is the way in which a large number of MBBS doctors envisage the challenge of alternative practitioners.

The doctors' difficulty or incapacity to envisage the global quest of their patients, and the fact that the nature of the expectation varies according to the choice of medical system to which patients resort, paradoxically leads a majority of the representatives of both systems (cosmopolitan medicine and shamanism) to consider the others as antagonists and their own practices as irreductible, incompatible with and impossible to associate with its counterpart. If we analyse their reciprocal positions more deeply, it is tempting to argue that the parties are engaged in a power struggle, for the control and monopoly of the individual body as well as the body politic. We should remember that medicine is also a political concern, in the sense that the individuals involved use their skills to improve their social position. Furthermore, it is easy to establish the inaccuracy of this thesis of irreductibility by looking into the villager's health behaviour, which rely on both kinds of practitioners but meet them with different expectations and for complementary reasons. The practitioners' quest for power does not concern the suffering, who adapt, adjust, and demand a 'medical-healing' plural assistance.

Whenever an exorcism performance fails, the shaman's personal capacity may be called into question but not shamanism itself. On the other hand, the doctor's position is more contentious with regard to the patient's faith. Further, another distinction appears between people's reaction towards private and public services: in case of inadequate treatment in a PHC, in which the doctor is regarded as a mere drug supplier, the whole national network is incriminated and people accuse the staff of not providing proper remedies. But in the context of private medicine, the physician, who is supposed to be a man of great personal knowledge and in possession of powerful drugs, will be suspected for having wrongly diagnosed the disease. It is worth mentioning that, for the private sector, the accusation is directed toward an individual (shaman, doctor) but not toward the system, while it is the contrary for the public sector, perceived as a collective dehumanized body with irresponsible social actors. And, according to villagers, the pills manufactured by government are standardized (same colour, similar forms) and consequently have a uniform effect, whereas the pills prescribed by the private sector are different in size, colour and shape and so are made of various medicinal products whose adequacy has to be established by the doctor.

It is significant that MBBS practitioners we met in Coimbatore approve of using the traditional plants (*mūligai*) known for centuries, mentioned in classical Indian treatises and whose efficiency has been registered by experimental laboratory investigations: *Phillanthus niruri* for hepatitis, *Acorus calamus* for diarrhoea, etc. Conversely they disapprove of the therapeutic cults dealing with something else than a simple physiologic dysfunction. Doctors apparently focus specially on bodily disturbances, arguing that their technical facilities rightly prevent them from being criticized. True to their university background, which provides some keys for understanding but at the same time evades other dimensions of the disease, they do have a tendency to elude the social disorder component, which yet remains a continuation of the biological disorder. And most of the healers know it is hazardous and risky to distinguish these two complementary aspects of the same event because, in the local perception, the disease is 'a totality', and moreover just one of the possible consequences of misfortune.

A striking feature, to be observed in south Indian villages, is that MBBS doctors try, more or less clumsily, to trespass their conventional knowledge and to incorporate symbolical and psychological considerations. Then it becomes an exaggeration to confine biomedical practice to internal body alteration. A rural MBBS general practitioner is also infused with Indian culture. Generally he was born in village close by, was brought up in the local way of life and consequently knows, consciously or inconsciously, the intimate relationship between religion and health. Contrary to all expectations, an inventory of 'irrational' elements and practices in modern clinics and hospitals reveal the concern, even if not expressly formulated, to satisfy the patients' plural request. We find small sanctuaries in the building, where diseased persons along with their family go to perform their puja, Ganesha pictures in the waiting room, portraits of Dhanvantari (the god of Ayurvedic medicine) in the consulting office, Vaishnavite symbols depicted on drugstore fronts, and, as the high point of an attempt at syncretism, on hypodermic injections! Finally, these religious and symbolic references tend to demonstrate that doctors, too, share the sociological intuition that 'something more' is expected by the sick person. In the same way, the determined desire to integrate these dimensions in a therapeutic consultation corresponds to the pursuit of a power similar to the one dispensed by the shaman, considering that the doctor, too, endeavours to overcome the 'immaterial forces' and 'energies' transcending his usual role. But is there not a certain illusion, mixed with some magico-religious belief, in this desperate hope to control, through health, a skill that requires various abilities, functioning both at objective and subjective levels (physio-logical, psychological, sociocultural, mythical)?

TRADITION OR MODERNITY?

The systematic assertion that the shaman's ability has to be clearly distinguished from specialised practitioners' competence, relying on local pharmacopoeia, and especially from the modern doctors' specific knowledge, is untrue. If, theoretically speaking, each approach does have its own field of intervention, facts are more complex in the context of everyday practice, therapeutic processes are spilling over into each other, rather than mutually exclusive. Even a so-called strict biomedical representative well endowed with scientific attitude and rationality leans on a good number of cultural representations and symbols which overstep his educational background.[4] Many rural doctors are pertinently aware that these 'extra-ingredients' are more then mere components added to the administration of drugs. We have already mentioned how they use religious attitudes and symbols as a socio-cultural reference, supposed to reinforce their therapy. In this vein, coming back to a particular village, three years after our initial stay, we noted a rather remarkable change in the main private local hospital: a *pillaiyār* temple had been erected inside. The sanctuary was also dedicated to another spirit, with both benevolent and malevolent powers, supposed to roam in the surrounding area. The bedridden patients, helped by their families, came daily from their rooms to visit the holy place. Some out-patients also availed themselves of the opportunity to visit the shrine and to make an offering. Little by little the hospital turned into a pilgrimage center.

On the other hand the shaman does not move in a closed magical world. His supernatural practice makes him understand the world through its cosmic perturbations and so he looks for solutions to remedy any disorder through his spirit mediumship. His interpretation, and capacities for manipulations, regarding biological, social and psychological phenomena are not limited to a mere vertical communication within the occult world.

Nowadays, according to the testimonies recorded from among various age groups of healers, many rituals and operations are simplified, sometimes reduced to the strict minimum, while others are adjusted to the simultaneous use of biomedicine. New investitures are then arranged. For instance, a common act of worship that may be termed 'the consecrated treatment' consists in taking pills bought in a drugstore or prescribed by a doctor and then making them more efficient and less harmful (in reference to the side-effects occurring with allopathic treatment) after a passage to a holy shrine. An exorcist in Veerapandi used to explain that not only the drug itself, its substance (*caitī*) was to be speeded up, reactivated for a more efficient result. In fact, according to local perceptions, any drug, including injections, virtually contains a 'positive' and a 'negative' aspect, as in a similar way a mischievous spirit can modify the expected effect of the drug by a 'sabotage act' against the administered pill. Conversely, if religion constitutes an important factor in the healing process, it does not signify that villagers are reluctant regarding further cures. The pragmatic experience, of taking a modern medication, reiterates this constant fact.

These few examples which we have mentioned briefly (and which might easily be multiplied) illustrate how arbitrary and inadequate it is to set up a clear distinction between modern and traditional medicine in the context of pluralism. There are no closed compartments as every medical system impregnates the other, borrowing and mixing according to local distinctive features. Any attempt to draw up a rigorous classification of medical practices is therefore doomed in advance, owing to their diversity and to their mutual interference. This does not mean, however, that all the distinctions are woolly, or that any research to identify vernacular categories is illusory and cannot be traced, because the distinctions exist, basically, at a purely theoretical level. But it is more judicious to point out the prevalence of a *medicine masālā*, a cocktail made from various therapeutic alternatives and whose ingredients, put together, constitute a quite coherent unit for patients when they are seeking health recovery. Following this logic, the variations in strategic health behaviour relate less to particular kinds of resort, excluding the others, than they do to the hierarchical order of utilisation based on a multiple therapy, where every intervention is supposed to complete the others, and to deal with a specific aspect from among the religious, social, symbolic and psychologic dimensions of the illness.

So neither do biomedical doctors have the monopoly of effectiveness, nor do traditional shaman healers have the monopoly of social and symbolic meaning. Both of them share in a combination of rational and irrational factors. Furthermore, if we look at their respective position and recognition, the social power that stems from curing and healing capacities is acquired more by accumulated personal experience than by strict adhesion to a particular medical system. Individual performance is more decisive, in this respect, than their specific cultural apprenticeship background.

THE INCONSTANT GODS AND THE TEMPERED MAN

In order to complete this preliminary conceptual approach to power in medicine, it remains lastly, to look into the nature of the 'art' of mastering misfortune and illness related events. Is it possible, by looking at the aspect of signification, to gain a better understanding of the way man assigns himself a place in the universe and interferes with supernatural forces? Whether doctor or shaman, is there any analogy between the behaviour of different practitioners, especially as to their intentions to control the material and symbolic forces which are believed to govern world macrocosm and human microcosm?

First, the relationship between the shaman and the spirit has to be demystified. The possessed is, in fact, far from venerating, or even respecting, the spirit he communicates with. He sometimes qualifies them as quick-tempered, impetuous, unpredictable and thin-skinned. The malevolent beings may be identified, on the sly, as dull cretins (like *pēy-piśāsu*, for instance) who disturb people just for fun or because they have been offended, and therefore they are inclined to take revenge. Such a reaction is a simple-minded one. Exorcists confess that their duty mainly consists in coaxing and flattering the spirits just to please and control them; deceit and a treachery, to some extent. But at the same time, the potential command over spirits, minor demons and divinities becomes a handsome way for man to hold a higher position among human beings and in god's hierarchy. Like a holy man—a saṃyāsi—who is considered as a living god and therefore spiritually superior to most of the Hindu deities who are too much aware of material and sentimental considerations, the shaman maintains his superiority not only towards other people but towards the soul of the deceased, the ancestors, and the bulk of little evil beings, having extraordinary power. Moreover as de Heusch noted, proclaiming the humanity capable of transcendence implies recognizing 'god's lunacy and men's wisdom'.

Reciprocally, 'symbolic efficacity' is not the traditional healer's privilege. The therapeutic potential of any drug or injection is more than what science put into it, and a majority of villagers attribute a disproportionate 'power' to a common manufactured remedy. Some even claim that sorcerers, and a lot of malevolent beings' evil deeds, can be checked with a chemotherapy! Likewise, a woman who was said to be possessed, explained how, after repeated and expensive unsuccessful attempts by various exorcists, she finally decided to consult a radiologist. The X-ray investigations enabled the qualified doctor to detect the 'introduced object' (in fact a small tumor in the stomach) in her body, which she considered as due to a witchcraft attack. This 'object' was then removed by a surgical operation. Just after the removal, a local shaman argued that the dangerous object had been sent back to its instigator (the sorcerer). This shortened version of a more complex story is indicative of the progressive shift in meaning, from what used to be confined in the social and symbolic dimension, specially apprehended by shamans, to the medico-technological field. It is thus tempting to induce that, surprisingly, the high degree of scientific technical improvement brings the supernatural dimension into biomedecine, which in turn, and due to its apparently unlimited progress, transforms itself in a magico-religious healing system liable to reduce and to cut short the power traditionally and exclusively held by black magic, malevolent demons and some healers.

One has, further, to interpret this medical behaviour of patients stemming from a plural situation, as an attempt at a 'de-socialization' of illness, in its more oppressive forms. And we may wonder, whether the blind attraction and the unconditional popularity enjoyed by modern medicine in Coimbatore villages, even for afflictions which are not purely bio-physiological, is not a more or less conscious quest to forget; to reach oblivion, of a state where the individual is entangled in a vast complex of social relationships, more constraining than comforting, where man is submitted to the order of society, to the caste system, in a constant allegiance towards the ancestors, demons and gods overwhelming him. Perhaps, by the way, the deliberate intention to reduce the pain of the soul to its mere biological dimension is linked with an inner desire to get rid of the social pressures that relentlessly pursue the diseased (and his family) and which call into question his comportment in life and the rightness of his attitudes. How many sick men behave secretly as if they wanted to manage the misfortune by their own, that is to say, without the control and repression of the society? In south India, as in every society where modernity and tradition intermingle, the trajectory of the suffering person (as well as that of the therapist) becomes a hazardous path in the twists and turns of meaning, whose signification turns out to be multifaceted and ambivalent.

NOTES

1. We stayed continuously in one of them (Kovilpalayam) during fifteen months
2. Nowadays they mostly attract middle and high-class people, and they tend to turn to a specialized medicine in particular for chronic ailments, skin diseases, arthritis, leukemia, etc.
3. For futher explanations see: J. Benoist *et al.*, Soigner au pluriel, 1995.
4. Some anthropological studies point the fact that even medical educational training is not entirely free of the dominant socio-cultural pattern. Cf. Alice Desclaux, personal communication (AMADES).

REFERENCES

Banerji, D. 1989 Rural transformation and changes in health behaviour. *Economic and Political Weekly*, Bombay, July 1: 1474-80.

Benoist, J. 1994 *Anthropologie médicale en Société créole*, Paris, PUF.

——— 1982 Possession guérison, médiations. Un chamanisme à l'île de la Réunion, *l'Ethnographie*, Paris, 78(87-8): 227-39.

Bourdier, F. 1994 Rencontres thérapeutiques en Inde méridionale ou l'art d'utiliser le masala dans les stratégies de soins, in J. Benoist (ed.): *Soigner au pluriel*, Paris, L'Harmattan.

Carrin, M. 1980 Des maux et des mots, *l'Homme*, Juill-Sept., XX(3): 85-107.

Galinier, J. 1982. Les contraintes de l'altérité, *l'Ethnographie*, Paris, 78 (87-8): 131-47.

Harper, E.B. 1957 Shamanism in South India, *Southwestern Journal of Anthropology*, 13; 267-87.

Henry, E.O. 1976 A North Indian healer and the sources of his power, in C. Leslie, *Asian medical systems*, Berkeley: 286-305.

Heusch, Luc De 1971 *Pourquoi l'épouser? et autres essais*, Paris, Gallimard.

Joshi, P.C. and A. Mahajan 1991 *Studies in medical anthropology*, Delhi, Reliance Publishing House.

Khare, R.S. 1976 Folk medicine in a North Indian village in C. Leslie, *Asian medical systems*, Berkeley: 266-85.

Nichter, M. 1980 The layperson's perception of medicine as perspective into the utilization of multiple therapy systems in the Indian context, *Social science and medicine*, Oxford, 14B: 225-33.

Perrin, M. 1993 *Les praticiens du rêve*, Paris, PUF.

Turner, V. 1972 Religious specialists: anthropological study, *International encyclopedia of the social sciences*, New York, 13-14, Macmillan Company and the Free Press: 437-53.

'Psycho-Religious Therapy' in Kerala as a Form of Interaction between Local Traditions and (perceived) Scientific Discourse

GILLES TARABOUT

Spirit or divine possession has sometimes been reduced to a cultural expression of psychic disorders, and interpreted accordingly in reference to a therapeutic analytical framework. Exorcisms would be in this perspective a mere spontaneous psychotherapy, an application of the *pensée sauvage* to the cure of psychosomatic illnesses.[1] Such a dimension is doubtless present in a number of cases and, in India, texts like *Atharvaveda* or Ayurvedic treatises include sections about mental illnesses explained in terms of possession.[2] But this view entails quite clearly also a wide—if not wild—recoding of indigenous perspectives, reducing to a psychic level (or occasionally a 'psychosocial' one, whatever it may mean) what basically addresses a holistic relationship between various 'beings' and 'spaces'. This kind of reductionism has already been discussed by many authors[3] and it is not the purpose of this contribution to elaborate on this point. Suffice it here to state that rationalizing away thus these religious representations and practices is no more the privilege of some anthropologists or psychiatrists, but has become part, too, of a widespread ready-made outlook that 'modern' man has on 'superstitions'— in the West as well as in India.

This creates a pressure. If 'educated people' speak about possession in terms of psychic illnesses, those who do not will be looked upon as being 'folk'. The aim of this paper is to present a few consequences of this social and ideological pressure in Kerala.[4] As such this is more a study on acculturation than on therapeutic methods, and nowhere will I ask myself questions about efficacy. This is a report about locally contrasted discourses, not an evaluation of therapeutic practices.

Reducing possession and exorcism to a psychic dimension might be seen in itself as part of such an acculturative endeavour, in this case an appropriation: possession can be *understood*—encompassed—within psychology. My purpose here is to describe an obverse epistemic appropriation made by some religious therapeuts in Kerala: they use references to psychology while developing a broader religious perspective which still informs in various degrees the treatment they give. The study will focus on two specialists, one Hindu and the other Christian. The latter, a priest of the Syro-Malabar Church, Father George, depicts his activity as 'psycho-religious therapy'. This expression is not used by the other specialist, head of a Nambudiri brahman house called Poonkutil Mana, but his own method—though differing greatly from Father George's—can be put also under such a general heading. Seen in the perspective of acculturation, theirs is an effort of understanding, dialogue, and—partly only—assimilation.

This is not the only manner, though, in which (what is perceived to be) Western Psychology encounters religion in Kerala. In order to show the specificity of our two specialists, it might be worth sketching firstly other logics which can also be met. Let us limit ourselves to the discourse of specialists who consciously combine references to psychology or psychiatry—as an epitome of a 'scientific' outlook—and to religion, without taking into account the numerous exorcists or magicians who for various reasons don't make such a combination. The examples given will serve only to illustrate some contrasted opinions found in Kerala.

PSYCHIATRY AND RELIGION IN KERALA

As a first example let me recall a visit I made in 1991 to a renowned psychiatrist of Trivandrum, Dr. R. At the time, I was conducting a research on possession and a common friend told me he was the man to meet. So we went. At the onset Dr. R. brushed aside in a friendly manner, but nevertheless firmly, any questions relating to possession. The terminology itself was wrong: there was no question of a so-called 'possession syndrome' (I hadn't used the expression), but only processes of conversion of dissociation, which he was keen to explain. Ayurveda itself, in which he claimed to have been instructed for a while, didn't have any efficacy for treating mental diseases.

This was rather strong Allopathic stand, but plausibly not an uncommon one among similar specialists. In this particular case, though, the discussion happened to move towards unforeseen grounds. Dr. R. was explaining how in Kerala people believing to have an affliction caused by *dōṣam*[5] use to consult astrologers, who direct them thereafter to various specialists—religious as well as medical ones (psychiatrists included).[6] Shifting to the topic of the specific *dōṣam* caused by the action of the planet Saturn (*śanidōṣam*), Dr. R. then showed a gold ring with a red sapphire he was wearing on a finger of his left hand: this ring was precisely a protection against *śanidōṣam* and had miraculously saved his life a few years ago after a massive heart attack. The crisis had been averted due to a friend who had foretold the event—but Dr. R. thought it was unscientific at that time—and who subsequently gave the ring. The efficacy of the sapphire was but natural, explained by gemmology whose authenticity as a science was well demonstrated by the existence of Western publications on the subject and by the fact that there was an Institute of Gemmology in the U.S.A., to which Dr. R. was considering sending his son.

The way Dr. R., as a psychiatrist, was relating himself to religious representations involving illnesses was therefore somewhat contradictory. There was denegation of any epistemic and therapeutic value to anything that was not 'scientific', and this included possession. But then science was defined in a rather encompassing way. Because of his personal experience, he had been lead to accept the possibility of an evil influence by planets and of the therapeutic virtues of gemmology. The compromise was made therefore under the aegis of scientific discourse: effects of planets and gemmology were put within the purview of science, though Dr. R. must have been perfectly aware that this is far from being on the agenda of mainstream cosmopolitan medicine. The main legitimation he found was to identify scientific authority with an idealized (if not fetichized) West—an idealization shown indirectly also by an impressive private accumulation of Western curios. Behind the overt denegation of whatever was unscientific, there was then still room for some local therapeutic traditions—thanks to the mediation of the U.S.A.!

Let us go now to a very different specialist, a 'sorcerer', Kattumadam Narayanan Namputripad. Living in the central part of Kerala, not far from Trichur, he is the head of one branch of the Kattumadam House, a Nambudiri brahman house specialized since generations in magic, *mantravādam*.[7] This *mantravādi* (lit. 'expert in mantras'), though somewhat atypical for his profession, is quite representative of the complex personalities blossoming so easily in Kerala (we just have had an example). A former supporter of the Marxist Party, as self-taught dramaturgist-cum-critic who has authored a reference book in Malayalam on Ibsen, he had to take on the House's wizardry tradition after the death of his father and of his paternal uncle.

His clients include petty agriculturists living in the surroundings as well as top politicians and cinema stars coming from far away. The way of taking care of complaints is the standard one followed by high-caste *mantravādi* in Kerala. Clients would have first consulted an astrologer who establishes the diagnosis and prescribes the kind of remedial measures to be taken. The *mantravādi*, if it falls within their field of competence, will then proceed with making charms, performing pujas or oblations in fire (*hōmam*), doing rituals for appeasing *prēta* (hungry spirit of a dead person), etc. There are no blood sacrifices, but K.N.N. uses sometimes a substitute, *guruti* (lit. 'blood'), made from mixing turmeric with lime in water—a widespread practice in Kerala satisfying both dangerous divinities and *Nambudiri* purity requirements. According to K.N.N. this proves his claim that he is performing only protective 'white magic'. Ritual processes are sometimes complemented by some herbal medicines prepared in the House itself.

It happens that K.N.N. has granted some interviews in various newspapers. Let me quote a few excerpts of one of them, published in *Society* (March 1991). The journalist, Meena Narayan, comments first that: 'He is the ultimate paradox in every sense of the word: a modern rationalist practising the most primitive faith.' This is possible because, in K.N.N.'s words, 'I am a mind healer rather than a sorcerer'. He gives an example:

> The famous flutist, the late T.R. Mahalingam, had a kind of fear psychosis. He felt people were out to kill him, and consequently developed a paranoia about his audience. . . . After consulting an astrologer, I discovered that he was haunted by the spirit of his father's first wife. . . . Accordingly, we did *hōmam* to ward off her spirit, and he got cured and left for America.

In this case K.N.N. adopts and returns to his own advantage the point of view according to which exorcisms are an indigenous psychotherapy—a perspective not lost for everybody! But it is used mostly as a mere rhetorical device, a kind of 'psychological' coating on a religious practice which remains unchanged. There is no real endeavour to blend together elements belonging to both systems. At times, K.N.N. seems to be toying with the ambiguities that this position entails. For instance in another interview made by journalist T. Gopinath[8] and published under the rather well-fitting title 'From Left to Rites', he first appropriates to himself the whole psycho pathological field: 'To cure disorders of the mind, intangible means are required and here the *manthravādi* [*sic*] steps in.'

But he has later to defend his specialty against the critical remarks of the local Rationalists' League. Then he seems inclined to dissociate 'science' and religion—putting himself implicitly under the latter's label: 'Maybe we can explain ninety-nine per cent of psychic phenomena in rationalistic terms. But there is that one per cent that perplexes everybody. Psychic phenomena never yield tangible clue.'

Perhaps we could term this mode of acculturation a *superposition* process: K.N.N.'s public stand as a psychotherapist (in fact references to psychological concepts are scanty) is merely superimposed on a religious role. This suggests that, in Kerala, the negotiation of the interaction between psychology—spoken of as a science—and religious healing is marked by an asymmetry: whether there is a denial of the efficiency of religious cures (Dr. R.), or a mere superimposition of a 'scientific' terminology on exorcisms (K.N.N.), in both cases the most creditable official idiom is the scientific one, even though the two specialists mentioned differ widely in their practice. For both, too, the underlying religious traditions remain significant (though it is denied by Dr. R.). But these relationships established between psychology and religion seem to be uneasy ones, at least without any real attempt to think out the particulars of both logics.

This is not the case with the two other specialists which we shall see now. Let us visit firstly Poonkutil house.[9]

POONKUTIL HOUSE

This Nambudiri brahman House is situated in the southern part of the former Malabar district. Its hereditary occupation is the treatment of mental illnesses according to a medical tradition which, though largely grounded in Ayurveda, is claimed to be unique in Kerala and in the whole of India The House is said to have originated two hundred years ago as an offshoot of Narayana Mangalam House, being allotted in the division '*mantra* and *cikitsa*' (i.e. the practice of medicine as well as of mantras). The reference to Narayana Mangalam House is not fortuitous, for there the legendary archetypal Kerala 'madman' (*bhrāntan*), Naranath Bhrantan, is supposed to have been brought up. Bhrantan was no ordinary fool and his was a metaphysical madness: every morning before going for his begging tour, he used to roll a big stone up to the summit of a hill (there is one in Palghat district known by his name) before, with a big laugh, letting it roll down freely—a puzzling self-willing Sisyphus. Another well-known tale shows him in a cremation ground asking Goddess Kali, when she pestered him till he would accept a boon, to shift the filaria affecting his left foot to his right one.[10] Fool or sage, Naranath Bhrantan could not be but the ultimate reference for the treatment of mental illnesses.

Surrounded by paddy fields and gardens, the compound includes a main building which houses the joint family, and three other ones for inmates. Inmates number between 15 to 40 and their average stay is

15 days. A small minority of them are enchained, a practice advocated there for its psychotherapeutic value 'because it is like a treatment directly given by society: improvement might be faster'. Most of the inmates, though, are free, some of them staying with a member of their own family who cares after them. Children of Poonkutil can be seen playing with a ball among the inmates: as one member of the House pointed out, they are brought up since early childhood in close intimacy with mental patients, a fact which helps to give them intuition when they will later assume their therapeutic task. Most of the patients, though, come only for day-time consultation. There can be a hundred or more on sundays, Hindus and Muslims from the surrounding areas (no Christians live nearly). They might come several times, at regular intervals. As in the case of K.N.N., and to a lesser extent of Dr. R., many patients are sent in by local astrologers—sometimes with a prescription for a specific ritual to be done.

Though attached to their tradition, members of Poonkutil House can scarcely be reduced to old-fashioned practitioners. They have been 'reading books' about psychology. They organize annually seminars in their own place on related topics, and were quite eager to communicate with a friend who is a French psychiatrist and who visited them along with me. There is clearly a will to conduct a permanent reflection on their own practice in relation to what they know about psychiatry and psychotherapy. One of the brothers of the family, Kuttan Attan, tried to explain to us in his consulting room the essentials of his point of view—whilst conducting through a window his medical examination of patients standing outside, or giving to one of them a protective black string to be tied at the wrist.

Basically the problem is 'weak-mindedness' or *manassile durbbalam*. Some possible symptoms will be: lump in the throat, hearing aerial voices, ball of anxiety going up, shivering feverish perception without real rise in temperature. These are only broad descriptions and Kuttan Attan distinguishes, as Ayurvedic authors do, *apasmāra* (epilepsy) and *unmāda* (madness, delirium), but giving to these terms also respectively the sense of 'hysteria' and 'schizophrenia'. Of the latter, eight types are to be distinguished in relation to imbalances arising in the three humours (*dōṣam*): wind, bile, phlegm.[11] There are certain predispositions for this weakness which might be acquired even before birth. Influence of the three *guṇam* (basic qualities of the universe), personal condition of the father and the mother at the time of conception, development of pregnancy: all these factors have their effect. Generally speaking, weak-minded persons are easily affected by perturbations in their environment. The humoural imbalance which results can develop into madness. And the mental illness then becomes basically a shelter for somebody who cannot face reality. His sense organs have become disabled and he cannot experience anymore the full scope of the nine *rasa* (flavor or emotion). This should not be confused with hysteria, in which there is hyper-sensibility: in this case there is a reaction of the body which attempts to avoid mental illness—hysteria is not to be 'cured', properly speaking.

The strategy of treatment follows logically. One should endeavour to bring back the patient to reality. As mind is energy, mind should be stimulated so that the patient improves his perception of the world and awakens again to reality. Tranquilizers should never be used as they have an opposite effect: they tend to benumb the sense organs. The cooperation of the patient's family and of society is necessary since the ultimate aim is to bring back the patient to what he was before in order that he may experience again conjugal, familial and social harmony. The patient's reality is in no way an absolute, objective reality—it is his own familiar reality. Therefore, it is fruitless (and 'non-scientific') to try to educate him using Western explicative concepts—unless it is done from infancy. In Kuttan Attan's own words, 'it is better to take them back as they were'. To sum up, as a main distinction from Western psychotherapy, the cure does not aim at becoming conscious of inner conflicts and tensions so as to elucidate them, but at providing the patient serenity through his reintegration in his milieu, preserving all his previous beliefs. This can be seen as a logical outcome of an explanation of illness in terms of disharmony and disorder in the patient's relationship to his environment [and most importantly] to his social setting (Opler 1963).

As a consequence Poonkutil House does not interfere in the mental representations elaborated by the patients and their family. Quite often the illness is interpreted as the result of a possession by a *bhūta* or a *prēta*, or as an outcome of some occult attack by a sorcerer—for instance through *kaiviṣam* (hand poison), a substance (not necessarily ingested) charged with mantras and possessing occult effects such as making the victim obey and dance at the will of the magician. Poonkutil House relies in fact on its own religious prestige as an additional tool in the cure, and this for two reasons. One, as has been said, is to keep in line with the patients' expectations—which are heightened by the fact that the House is a high status brahman one and therefore credited with considerable religious power (even in the eyes of Muslims). The other is that Poonkutil doesn't itself consider its method as being merely 'medical'. Nothing can be done without the House Goddess's power and protection. Do strongly built patients accept to be fettered without attempting to resist? For Poonkutil 'this is due to the blessing of this place, the blessing of our Goddess'. The members of the house consider themselves to be only instrumental in the cure—which in fact does involve rituals.

Details of the treatments will of course vary according to the illness diagnosed. In its main lines it relies on: rest, Ayurvedic medicines to be absorbed internally, applications of Ayurvedic decoctions on the forehead, oil baths for the head. Herbal preparations are made in the House itself, according to its own specific tradition. Their efficiency is nevertheless not only a question of components or of recipe, but depends too on charging them with mantras, and on pūjas. For maintaining the power of the House there are regular pūjas performed every morning to the tutelary Goddess. But special cases can require special offerings. A vegetal 'sacrifice' (*bali*) to the *bhūtas* might be performed at the entrance of the house. Or the local astrologer will prescribe the more elaborate ceremony using the so-called 'blood' (*guruti*), already mentioned about K.N.N.'s practice.

To sum up, Poonkutil has developed an original reflection on psychology in the light of its own tradition which is largely based on Ayurveda with specific inflexions. It is difficult to assess the exact impact this encounter with (western perceived) psychology have, but it seems to be anyway rather slight in practical terms. Presenting mental illness as a 'shelter' pertains certainly to a reflection in psychological terms, as different from the predominantly eco-physiological approach inherited from Ayurveda which is also stressed here. But the argumentation opens on a theory of the 'benumbed senses' which has a distinctly classical Indian flavour: illusion is a deception of the senses, but the senses are also the means by which experimentation of the world is possible. Eventually, what Poonkutil has to say about psychology is rather negative. Take the diagnosis: Kuttan Attan explained that 'India' and 'the West' were having opposite perspectives: Western medicine goes from the concrete, *sthūla* (gross element)—let us say the liver—to the abstract, *sūkṣma* (subtle element)—let us say a virus; Indian medicine does the inverse, as for instance if we consider that hearing aerial voices can result from various causes (e.g. involving the use of drugs or not). Some parallels were drawn by Kuttan Attan between the two therapeutic processes: what Ayurveda is to psychiatry, pūjas are to psychotherapy. But according to him, since psychotherapy wants to give people a scientific conscience which they have not, there is a danger of rejection (like for any foreign body). So *pūja* is more than psychotherapy, it is beyond it. As for the use of allopathic medicines, this was right away condemned by Kuttan Attan—in fact no patient is admitted until allopathy, if previously in use, is completely stopped. It seems therefore that Poonkutil couldn't subscribe to even the first half of what a carpenter told once to McKim Marriott: 'Western Medicines are best . . . but doctors never cure anybody' (Marriott 1955:239).

In this case, then, a real attempt to relate one's own therapeutic tradition to the perceived logic of psychology ends up in interrogations, in dialogue at the most, but certainly not in compromise.

Let us turn now to Father George, this Christian priest who uses 'Psycho-Religious Therapy' to describe his activity.

FATHER GEORGE

Father George is living in the outskirts of a small town in Kottayam district—an area where Christians form an important proportion of the population. He lives and practices in a concrete one-storeyed building, his own therapeutic center. Here is for instance a list of patients coming to see him one afternoon:

— a woman, for her alcoholic husband who doesn't take anymore the medicines that Father George had prescribed him formerly;
— a Christian man brought by three other; he has suicidal mania, caused—the others say—by the spirit of a Muslim appeared in the form of a black dog;
— a 93 year old Christian man brought by his two sons and the wife of one of them: he is affected by sleeplessness, and when the sign of Cross is drawn on his forehead (at home), he protests;
— a woman, for her daughter who is doing night-shifts as a nurse in an hospital; she is regularly upset, takes sedatives, but needs anyway to go to work;
— a young man who has stopped smoking hashish.

Father George claims an impressive success to his record, having cured during the two last decades some 8000 patients, many of them declared by other doctors to be hopeless cases. His reputation is well established. A medical magazine in Malayalam, *Doktar*, has dedicated a full special issue (October 1988) to present his work, with top physicians testifying about the efficacy of his method. People in distress might come from distant places to consult him: Christians, Hindus, Muslims. Quite often they or their family consider the illness to be the result of possession—it is these cases which are considered here. Father George interprets such cases as the expression of a 'multiple personality' syndrome.[12] But his method differs quite significantly on some points from the one followed by those psychotherapists who too use the 'multiple personality' approach: both have recourse to hypnosis to make 'secondary personalities' express themselves, but while psychotherapists aim at making the patient becoming conscious of the 'personalities' as mere expressions of inner conflicts, so that therapy is an elucidation (Jagathambika 1968), Father George does nothing of the sort. His purpose, like Poonkutil, is to bring back the patient to what he was before, after removing the 'secondary personalities' through 'religious suggestion'. There is no explicitation of psychological conflicts, the cure is not an elucidation.

This method is based on an original, if not idiosyncratic, approach. Father George's own history might account partly for it. When he was in High-School a friend of him committed suicide, and from that day Father George took a deep personal interest in the human mind. He spent his years of religious formation at the Seminary in Alwaye, which has a very good library: there, he started reading books on psychology, soon training himself in self-hypnosis. He is thus an autodidact in the field and his psychological studies were undertaken simultaneously with his training for priestly life. In order to present his method let us follow the tale of one of his patients, Joseph, a 35 year old Christian man, as retold by Father George. I will keep to his own words, with only minor editing.

He wanted to stab his wife and kill her in this way, feeling she is bad, she is having affairs with others, a feeling. He is a very nice man, very good man. No bad habit. One day he got upset and he went to the toddy shop, he drank, came back, and caught hold of his wife by the hair. With a small knife, not much cutting power, he cut the neck. She cried, and the parents came and she was taken to the hospital. And this fellow was not reported to the police, he was [again] all right, there was no problem. His wife came back and [they] had a peaceful life for two weeks. He again started drinking. And he came to his house. By his very appearance she felt something is not normal. Then wanted to go home. He also went there but he could not catch her because the parents were down in the premises. Immediately the neighbours also came and he was clutched and he was taken to the psychiatrist. He was put in the asylum for few days and the doctor said there is no problem with this fellow. He drank maybe during that time. After ten days he was discharged, came back. After three days again he went to the [toddy] shop, drank and came. That time also she thought he is not normal. He immediately bounced upon her, but he was clutched and taken over here.

At this point, Father George steps in to his own tale:

What happened? I told them, just untie the legs' clutches. I took him inside and put him in hypnosis. His name is Joseph. In his hypnosis I asked him: who you are? I am Raman [italics hereafter: Raman is speaking through Joseph]. Why do you possess this one? *One year before, I committed suicide after killing my wife because my wife was not honest to me. I corrected her but she was not obedient, she did not keep well. So many times I have tried, I have given blows, I have admonished, I had done everything and anything possible, just wanted her from her bad life, but she would not. So I killed her. Soon after killing I thought I will be taken by the police, put in custody and I will be tortured. So I wanted to escape from the torture. I committed suicide.* Then, why you possess this one? *He is longing much for his wife. But all the women are like that. They are cheating people and the husbands. So one day this fellow came through where I committed suicide. When this fellow came I assumed the form of a snake and jumped in front. But he did not get frightened. Immediately I assumed the form of a bat and flew away. It was soon after the snake, and that fellow was frightened. Immediately I entered in him.*

We shall come back to this part of the story, as it is the crux of Father George's explanation for the rise of the 'second personality'. Meanwhile we may note that Raman is just bent on making Joseph repeat exactly what he himself did—mimetism is the rule:

I was given to drinks. When I possessed him he also became very desirous of drinking. So I took him to the toddy shop, make him drink, then he had the idea that his wife is dishonest. So I asked him to kill his wife. After killing his wife I wanted to direct him to commit suicide.

There are more dramatic episodes which need not retain our attention. Eventually, Father George succeeded in eliminating the spirit of Raman through hypnotic suggestion, and prayer, 'infusing courage through Jesus and the power of Christ'. Joseph didn't remember anything of the events when acting as Raman, and was reunited with his wife, Mary(!). The scar on Mary's neck was explained away by the first reason coming to mind. At no time was Joseph given a 'psychological explanation' about what had happened.

The above extract is interesting for us in that, besides allusions to aspects of domestic life which find little room in anthropological writings, it enabled Father George to explicate what he believes to be the dynamics of the 'multiple personality' syndrome. The 'second personality' is a personification of 'weird ideas' which Joseph might have had. Weird ideas are very often, but not always, linked to a guilty conscience. Then there is an association of weird ideas with some vision which leads eventually to personification:

While going alone, see something, association of ideas, the idea is there, weird ideas are there. Then comes the vision, then association of ideas, coordination of ideas, then assimilation, then last personification. Takes place altogether in some persons. In some others it slowly works and at the end it becomes personified. That depends on the quality, intensity of the guilty conscience. In some persons, when I put them in hypnosis, they say 'I see something dark'. That means personification has not taken place. The dark form is there, association of ideas, coordination is also done. but assimilation and personification has not taken place.

For instance a Muslim woman from another district had to be relieved [by the power of the Cross (cf. infra)] of a 'second personality' who was Goddess Bhadrakali, a fact that Father George attributed to the personification of weird ideas roused by a sense of guilt or fright: during her menses (ritually polluting of Hindus), the woman had been gathering dry wood in the Goddess's compound. In the case of Joseph, his fright when the bat flew produced a temporary kind of self-hypnosis which helped unconscious personification:

This process comes by itself, not through our reasoning. One person gets frightened, his personality is debilated, his five senses benumbed, whereas the intellect also is benumbed. What is seen through the eyes simply goes to the subconscious mind. That means it is an adulterated form of hypnosis, self-hypnosis. That is why without reasoning things happen. When we sleep at night, everybody, yourself and myself, anybody and everybody experience that, at night, abominable things we will do. How it happens? Because at sleep the senses are at rest, the conscious mind is at rest, and the subconscious mind is always alert, always alert. . . . During daytime suppose you wanted to commit a theft, if you are a Catholic or a Christian immediately your conscience will say, you are a Christian, don't do that, theft is a sin forbidden by the commandments, and God will punish you.[13] There comes the *censorium. Censorium.* But during sleep what happens. Senses are at rest, intellect at rest, conscious mind at rest, subconscious alert, and the gatekeeper, the *censorium*, is also at rest. . . . What happens? This idea come, knocking and knocking in the subconscious mind for a let out. There is no *censorium*, he also is at rest, there is no objection. It comes to the conscious mind, there is no objection because at rest. It comes to the senses, no objection because at rest. Then comes the realization. We feel so many things at night during sleep. . . .

At sleep it happens from the subconscious mind. Outside it happens from external forces. When we see something or hear something that causes fright, immediately we are benumbed, the whole personality is benumbed. That means hypnosis. Senses at rest, intellect at rest, conscious mind at rest, subconscious alert. So the idea enters. [The weird idea is associated with the place where a Raman is said to have actually committed suicide after killing his wife.] Raman is entering as a dog [*sic*], in a form of a dog. Raman is entering. Goes to the senses, cannot reason, they are not reasonably conscious. Enters there in the intellect, no objection there. Goes to the conscious mind, no reasoning. It goes to the subconscious mind.

And from the subconscious mind, when it comes out, the reasoning and the process were not given. So we have no memory about it. The personification is there.

What about the cure then? We should understand that health is an equilibrium between a mental side and a physical side. When there is a 'second personality' the equilibrium is lost because there is now an additional weight in the mental side.

Physicians and neurologists give medicines, sedatives or tranquilizers, but this puts an additional weight in the physical side, giving thereby an artificial and very temporary equilibrium. After giving such medicines, withdrawing them when there is an amelioration, giving again when there is a relapse, withdrawing, etc., the equilibrium is hopelessly lost (not to speak of E.C.T. which father George totally condemns: 'there is something radically lost'). There is only one proper way: to remove from the mental side that which is weighting on it—the 'second personality'. This is done through the following process: 'We put the person in hypnosis, go deep in the subconscious mind, find out the radical causes, remove it through the religious functions, give courage, infuse courage, put it right and awaken and the person is normal, there will be no relapse.'

Father George uses in addition a few Ayurvedic potions ('they are stimulative') which are sent to him from Hyderabad by the 'descendant of a saintly person'. But the method he advocates relies mainly on two tools: hypnosis, and 'religious function'. Hypnosis is achieved very simply: Father George places merely his hands on the patient's head. He then discusses the matter with the 'second personality'—who can be any being from a spirit, especially of people who committed suicide, to a Hindu god or goddess. Then comes the 'religious function'. Through enticement, menace, reasoning, the second personality is asked to leave the patient for good, and made to swear on the Holy Cross never to come back again. Additional religious suggestion under hypnosis might be given to inspire courage to the patient. The whole process takes place in a special room meant to induce a (oecumenical) 'religious atmosphere': in the middle of the wall, in front of the patient, is a cross flanked on the left side (when looking at it) by the Sanskrit symbol *Om* and on the right side by a design of a moon's crescent surmounted by a star—Father George has nevertheless his own (Christian) exegesis for that: *Om* is for the primordial word, the moon and star for creation, the Cross for redemption. This religious atmosphere is meant to instill also courage in the patient's mind.

The therapeutic process is thus also a religious one, and this for two reasons quite similar to those mentioned for Poonkutil. Firstly, as the cure is not an elucidation but aims at bringing back the patient to what he was before, Father George doesn't interfere in the mental representations of the latter and of his family. Whatever their religious affiliation, most patients brought here are believed in their social milieu to be possessed. They find in Father George somebody meeting their expectations because, in Kerala, Christian priests are credited to possess great religious power—like Nambudiri brahmans or Muslims saints. Father George knows it and relies on this expectation. According to him, Christians, Muslims and Hindus alike, all respect and know the power of the Cross. He quotes for instance a popular saying: '[running away] like a ghost seeing the Cross',[14] said for somebody who, when met, leaves immediately. There are what Father George jokingly calls 'Dracula-like stories' where powerful priests exorcise demons, ghouls and vampires (but, he might have been unaware of it, in some of these stories priests are themselves vampires!). He didn't mention it: there is the powerful figure of Kadamattattu Kattanar, a legendary priest supposed to have been a great magician and whose spirit (together with his 'demonic' maid servant, a *yakṣi*) is worshipped by some sorcerers belonging to low status castes (Uchiyamada 1995; Mullasseri 1992). So the power attributed to Christian priests is an important aspect of the therapeutic process.

The second reason is that Father George himself is of course convinced of the power of the Cross and of its efficacy in the cure. This is so because there is ultimately a lingering doubt about the root cause of the afflictions which come to his notice. When people, including some physicians, advocate the reality of diabolical possession, he is very cautious and affirms that in most cases it is only psychological. But there are also unexplained facts: people speaking in tongues, or assuming 'personalities' who give information unknown to the 'primary personality'. Father George keeps open the possibility of effective possession:

A certain fellow was taken over here, he was from Bombay side, not a Keralite. He had this suicidal mania and all the other problems, psychological problems. nausea, no appetite, always this idea of committing suicide. I put him in hypnosis. Then he told me. *I am Mohammadu Abbas, I was a prince in Saudi Arabia. Two hundred years before we came for a picnic in Uttar Pradesh. There in a pond, by chance, I fell and died. I was there. Two months before this fellow together with some others came over there in Uttar Pradesh from Bombay, just for sight-seeing, and came through the pond. I saw him, a good man, a handsome fellow, and wanted to possess him. Then I possessed him. I want to kill him and to take him to Saudi Arabia.* I eliminated the case and he was all right, perfectly all right. But I do not know how far his narrations are correct. Two hundred years before one Mohammad Abbas came here and committed suicide or not. . . .

Whether spirit possession exists or not, the power of God is said anyway to be involved in the success of the cure. Evil 'beings' are afraid of the Cross. Patients who are in a cataleptic state and who are therefore unaware when a Cross is approached, react nevertheless violently—a proof of its sheer power. But though Father George is thus strongly committed to his Christian values, the religious dimension of the therapy he advocates never means religious proselytism. His aim, like Poonkutil, is to put people back on their tracks, so that they should live a harmonious life—which means in his eyes a religious life (since the human mind is basically religious) according to each one's own religion. So he will not try to convert his patients to christianism. When talking after the hypnosis, he encourages them in fact to be devoted followers of their own faith, and has sincere respect for Islam and Hinduism: 'The Hindus they are generous people, you know, Hindus are the most generous people, they are ready to believe in any god.'

Father George had lots of fascinating stories to tell, which he did in his very humanly good-natured manner. Somewhere, it seems, he was deliberately assuming his Father-like figure. But total dedication to his work was not the only common point he had with Poonkutil. Clearly, both specialists are holding similar holistic views about mental illnesses and their therapy. There are as well vivid contrasts between the way they rationalize their method. It is time to try comparing and analyzing them.

TWO CONCEPTIONS OF MAN AND A SINGLE IDEAL FOR HEALTH

At the core mental illness is conceived here as an alteration in the perception of reality. But for our two specialists it results from very different processes. For Poonkutil it is mainly the physiology of the patient which explains weak-mindedness, which is very sensitive to the environment. This might induce a sheltering from reality, reducing the proper functioning of the sense organs. For Father George the main point is that everybody may enter into self-hypnosis through an emotional shock, which benumbs the sense organs and produces a personification of weird ideas rooted in the subconscious. Mental illness is no more a shelter but an expression of inner ideas which the *censorium*, a concept altogether absent from Poonkutil's conceptions, do precisely not censure. For both specialists the sense organs play a prominent role but hardly the same: their benumbing is a result of mental illness of Poonkutil, whereas for Father George it explains how association of ideas with external signs can be formed during self-hypnosis. In the first case delusion is more the result of endogenous processes in relation to reality; in the second the irruption of extraneous factors is decisive for the personification of internal ideas.

The distinctive way in which each specialist has worked out his set of ideas accords well with his own religious affiliation. The emphasis put on the physiology of an illness described in terms of *guṇam*, *dōṣam* and disfunctioning of the sense organs, as stated by Poonkutil, fits well with other conceptions found in classical Hindu *śastras* about the constitutive elements of man and his relationship to the world. By contrast, the clear-cut opposition between a mental side and a physical one, the role of the censorium as a specific organ of morality and guilt, the emphasis put on the splitting of personality into a good 'primary' one managed by the 'conscious mind', and an aggressive if not evil 'secondary' one rooted in the 'sub-conscious mind'—as advocated by Father George—cannot but suggest a strong Christian flavour.

It is difficult to assess to which degree clients consulting Poonkutil and Father George can be compared. The main motivation to go there should be nearly the same, because the specialists are credited with similar religious power and are reputed for their efficacy in the treatment of cases of mental illnesses and/or possession. But few Christians go to Poonkutil, for reasons of proximity, whereas they form the majority of Father George's patients (but not all of them). Whether or not this imply a real difference in pathologies reported to the specialists, it is striking to see that the emphasis is put on quite different symptoms in the two places. The prototypical patient—so to say—for Poonkutil is suffering from weak-mindedness whose signs are, we might recall, hearing aerial voices, having a lump in the throat, feeling an uprising ball, shivering, having impression of fever—all active inner manifestations linked to a lack of perception of reality. The prototypical patient for Father George is suffering from loss of appetite, sleeplessness, disinterest in work, in social relations and in everything, and suicidal mania—all passive disconnecting symptoms linked to the additional presence of a 'second personality'.

In relation with these contrasted perceptions of the illnesses, treatments follow a different logic even though both specialists insist on stimulating the reactions of the patient through Ayurvedic medicines and are very critical about the use of sedatives and tranquilizers. But for Poonkutil stimulation aims at fighting a loss—the loss of the proper functioning of the sense organs—so as to get back to reality. Active inner symptoms call here for the reactivation of the sense organs. For Father George stimulation helps the first personality to recover courage but the cure consists mostly in an elimination—that of the second personality—so as to get back to reality. Passive disconnecting symptoms call there for a removal of an inner weight. What should be stressed is that paradoxically these quite different ways of articulating theoretical and practical approaches to mental illnesses partake of the very same ideal of health: a healthy person is one who lives in conjugal, familial and social harmony. The cure aims at the patient's serenity through social reintegration, and not at trying to ameliorate his own psychological knowledge. The patient has not to be transformed into a more 'reasonable' being, but has to be brought back to his original state.

As we have seen the religious experience is important for both specialists. Not all cases can be accounted for in psychological terms. Divine power is a condition of the cure's effectiveness. In this they are quite in line with the patients. Poonkutil and Father George have thus elaborated their own rationality and therapeutical strategy in symbiosis with their cultural surroundings. Religious ideas are balanced by perceived modern and scientific ones (not necessarily Western though for Father George this is clearly the case). Nevertheless this overt rationality leaves room for unexplained events and, more fundamentally, takes sense through a predominantly religious perspective. Their approach is centered on a common ideal of harmony for man-living-in society, an ideal much valued by everybody throughout Kerala. As for what the patients themselves (and their family) might feel on the subject we may assume that, since in their eyes they come to consult an exorcist, the specialists' intellectual conceptions have no relevance whatsoever. We may as well assume also that they find in each place what they look for: respected brahmans mastering medicinal lore and mantras and performing 'pure' sacrifices, or a respected Father who can coerce spirits into leaving by the power of the Cross.

From a reading of the foregoing pages it must have become progressively apparent that this paper's main concern—the experienced relationship between Psychology, perceived as a science, and religion—was only a small part of a wider set of multiple, complex, and often ancient acculturative processes: between different religious denominations, between Allopathic and Ayurvedic medicines,[15] between medicine and religion. As we have seen also, psychology is considered to be a science not only because of its intrinsic virtues (which are sometimes critically discussed), but also because it is associated with a technologically (and politically) dominant

West. Thus, in the specific field investigated here, psychology remains the dominant and constantly thought-provoking reference largely because it comes as a cultural challenge from a powerful 'other'—whether its fate is to be fetichized, nominally appropriated, discussed, or assimilated (to name a few attitudes which do not claim to be exhaustive). The institutional aspects have not been studied, but they are obviously an important factor in this dynamic: Psychiatry has the support of the Kerala Government's health policy, which is not the case of all the other religious specialists we have seen. Quite significantly, K.N.N., Poonkutil and Father George were spontaneously defending themselves against any financial malpractice towards the patients—a regular allegation made by Kerala rationalists. The ideological tension between psychology and religion involves therefore also stakes in public recognition, in reference to a network of State institutions.

In this confrontation between contrasted paradigms, Poonkutil and Father George appear to have worked out and achieved, each in his own way, a pragmatic—and creative position.[16] More generally, the four specialists who have been evoked here can be considered as expressing in their professional field what is a widely shared experience in Kerala. The patients too are involved in this tension between 'Western' science and their own religious therapeutic traditions, and they live it mostly in a pragmatical manner since they do not hesitate to shift from one category of specialist to another. As a friend reminded me in a letter after reading a first draft of this paper, 'when people give up hope after trying various things they will be prepared to do anything'. He remembered the case of a professor of medicine offering a cock sacrifice to Goddess Mariamma for the health of his daughter who was critically ill, though it 'went very much against his ideas and principles—YET-he did all that—like a drowning man clutching to a piece of straw. I am afraid you have not brought out this aspect about patients going to the two doctors.'[17]

Sometimes also the cultural tension between science and religion is constructed to such an antagonistic point that it becomes itself the root of illness. Let me illustrate this with a last tale by Father George (this time with important cuts in an otherwise lengthy narrative):

You know, this mister Swaminathan, he is a Marxist. He was elected president of a [party's] constituency, and he started showing sleeplessness, no appetite, and he was taken to Guruvayur Hospital. Doesn't want to mingle with the people, wanted to keep away, gloomy mood, and he had the suicidal mania also. At the end, because of this kind of symptoms, they brought him over here. And the person was put in hypnosis. Then comes the Bhadrakali. Who you are? *I am Bhadrakali.* Oh, you Bhadrakali! Why do you possess him? *Because he was my child, while he was very young he used to come to my temple with the offerings. But since now some years he doesn't come. And he prevents his sisters and parents from coming to the temple. Then I wanted to take vengeance. One day when he was sleeping I appeared in full [terrifying] form. He was frightened, immediately I entered in him and I am drinking his blood, I want to teach him a lesson.* I asked what is your form? immediately he wide-opened his eyes, opened his mouth, put his tongue outside, I do not know how he can, how one can stretch the tongue so much, so much so lengthy it was, we will be wonder struck by that. All right, I asked him to withdraw. What should I do so that you may go away from him. *Only thing, let him turn to religious life, that is enough for me.*

The happy end: Bhadrakali swears on the Cross to leave, Shri Swaminathan is definitely cured. He worships now regularly the Goddess in her temple, and has written gratefully to Father George:

'Now, I can be a believer, and a Marxist.'

NOTES

1. As instances of recent papers developing a rather strict clinical—if not epidemiological approach towards possession, see Satija *et al.* (1981); Venkataramaiah *et al.* (1981); Keshavan *et al.* (1989), Chowdhury (1991).
2. General review in Thite (1982). For Ayurveda see for instance Zimmermann (1989); Weiss *et al.* (1986); for *Atharvaveda*, summary in Balodhi and Roy Chowdhary (1986).
3. See for instance in recent years Schoembucher (1993); Olivier de Sardan (1994); Assayag (1994).
4. The interviews on which this study is based were conducted during stays in 1991 and 1992. Fieldwork was funded by CNRS (Paris) and invitations to Kerala were forwarded by the International School of Dravidian Linguistics (Trivandrum) and the French Institute of Pondicherry, to which I want to express my gratitude. A first presentation of this paper was made at the 13th European Conference of Modern South Asian Studies, Toulouse, 1994. I thank L.S. Rajagopalan, F. and C. Osella, A. Bottero for their comments on a preliminary draft.
5. In this context *dōṣam* does not refer directly to one of the three humours of Ayurvedic physiology, nor to their occasional pathogenic imbalance, but rather to an occult action of divine Powers—often, but not always, the consequence of a fault.
6. This statement is corroborated by all observations. This suggests not only a widespread interaction between various medical and religious systems, but an important regulation relying specifically on the astrologers'

competence and role in Kerala society. It is part of the problem of acculturation touched upon in these pages, but cannot be elaborated here.

7. An interview was made in April 1991. Magic or 'sorcerer' are rather improper terms, used here only for commodity's sake. They should in no way presuppose an antagonism with 'religion'. For a general presentation and discussion of *mantravādam* in Kerala see Tarabout (1993).
8. *Indian Express*, Cochin edn; the newspapers was sent by a friend without a date—1994.
9. An interview was conducted in February 1991. I thank A. Leday for providing this opportunity.
10. Thomas 1989: Pillai 1991.
11. Kuttan Attan did not unfortunately elaborate on this point. The combinatory possibilities for imbalances of three *dōṣam* amount to seven only. In a local tradition of Ayurvedic psychiatry in Sri Lanka (Obeyesekere 1977) an eighth 'madness' is caused by an imbalance in bile together with blood. A hypothetic connection between the two traditions would be perhaps worth looking at.
12. According to Father George, even most of the cases diagnosed by psychiatrists as epileptics are not truly such: 80 per cent are in fact due to the existence of a second personality. On the genesis and evolution in Western thought of the 'multiple personality' diagnosis—a controversed approach—see the excellent book by Michael G. Kenny (1986). Interviews with Father George were conducted in August-September 1992.
13. In Father George's eyes, Christians would seem to have more censorium than others! Many Hindus in Kerala hold an opposite view: Christians would have loose morals because they can be absolved of their sins through confession, which enables them to act the same immediately after. . . .
14. *Kuriśu kaṇṭa piśācu pōle.*
15. The acculturation process within Ayurvedic medicine has already received the attention of many scholars—see for instance Leslie (1976), and for Kerala the short but pertinent study by Zimmermann (1978).
16. On the capacity of 'traditional specialists' to adapt creatively to external challenges, see Trawick (1987).
17. Letter from L.S. Rajagopalan (1994).

REFERENCES

Assayag, J. 1994 Religion, maladie et thérapeutique dans un lieu de culte musulman au sud de l'Inde. *Revue Internationale de Psychopathologie* 16.

Balodhi, J.P. and J. Roy Chowdhary, 1986 Psychiatric Concepts in Atharva Veda: A Review. *Indian Journal of Psychiatry* 28-1.

Chowdhury, A.N. 1991 Mass Hysteria with Animal Identification: Study from a Tribal Village of Tripura. *Journ. Indian Anthrop.* Soc., 26.

Jagathambika, R. 1968 *A Case Study of Multiple Personality or Possession-Syndrome. Its Aetilogy and Treatment.* Alwaye: Union Christian College, Department of Psycholgy (Unpublished Ph. D. Thesis).

Kenny, M.G. 1986 *The Passion of Ansel Bourne: Multiple Personality in American Culture.* Washington, Simthsonian Institution.

Keshavan, M.S., H.S. Narayanan, and B.N. Gangadhar 1989 'Bhanamati' Sorcery and Psychopathology in South India. A Clinical Study. *British Journal of Psychiatry* 154.

Leslie, C. 1976 The Ambiguities of Medical Revivalism in Modern India. In C. Leslie (ed.) *Asian Medical Systems: A Comparative Study.* Berkeley: University of California Press.

Marriott, Mckim 1955 Western Medicine in a Village of Northern India. In Benjamin D. Paul (ed.), *Health, Culture and Community. Case Studies of Public Reactions of Health Programs.* New York: Russell Sage Foundation.

Mullasseri, P.G. 1992 *Kaṭamar̲r̲attu kattanāruṭe māntrikavēlakaḷ.* Kodungallur: Devi Book Stall.

Obeyesekere, G. 1977 The Theory and Practice of Psychological Medicine in the Ayurvedic Tradition. *Culture, Medicine and Psychiatry* 1-2.

Olivier De Sardan, J.P. 1994; Possession, affliction et folie: les ruses de la thérapisation. *L'Homme*, 34-3.

Opler, M.E. 1963 The Cultural Definition of Illness in Village India. *Human Organization* 22 1.

Pillai, P.A. 1991 In memory of Naranath Bhranthan. *Indian Express* (Cochin edn.). Weekend sup., 6 April.

Satija, D.C., D. Singh, S.S. Nathawat, and V. Sharma 1981 A Psychiatric Study of Patients Attending Mehandipur Balaji Temple. *Indian Journal of Psychiatry* 23-3.

Schoembucher, E. 1993 Gods, Ghosts and Demons: Possession in South Asia. In H. Brückner, L. Lutze and A. Malik (eds), *Flags of Fame: Studies in South Asian Folk Culture.* Delhi: Manohar.

Tarabout, G. 1993 Violence et non-violence magiques. La sorcellerie au Kérala. *Purusartha* 16.

Thite, G.U. 1982 *Medicine. Its magico-religious aspects according to the Vedic and later literature.* Poona: Continental Prakashan.

Thomas, P. 1989 Naranath Bhranthan. Kerala's Arch Cynic Misnomered The Lunatic. *Malayalam Literary Survey* 11-2.

Trawick, M. 1987 The Ayurvedic Physician as Scientist. *Soc. Sci. Med.* 24-12.

Uchiyamada, Y. 1995 *Sacred Grove* (Kaavu): *ancestral land of 'landless agricultural labourers' in Kerala, India.* London: London School of Economics and Political Science (Unpubl. Ph.D.).

Venkataramaiah, V., M. Mallikarjunaiah, C.R. Chandrasekhar, C.K. Vasudeva Rao, and G.N. Narayana Reddy 1981 Possession Syndrome: An Epidemiological Study in West Karnatka. *Indian Journal of Psychiatry* 23-3.

Weiss, M.G., S.D. Sharma, R.K. Gaur, J.S. Sharma, A. Desai, and D.R. Doongaji 1986 Traditional Concepts of Mental Disorder Among Indian Psychiatric Patients: Preliminary Report of Work in Progress. *Soc. Sci. Med.* 23-4.

Zimmermann, F. 1978 Introducing Western Anatomy to the Practitioners of Classical Indian Medicine: An Ethno-Historical Analysis of the Treatises by P.S. Varier in the 1920's. In *Asie du Sud. Traditions et changements. Acts of the VIth European Confernce on Modern South Asian Studies,* Sèvres.

——— 1989 *Le discours des remèdes au pays des épices. Enquête sur la médecine hindoue*. Paris: Payot.

Places and Memories: Exorcism and Curing Among the Tharus of Western Nepal

GISÈLE KRAUSKOPFF

The Tharus of Dang Valley in western Nepal[1] view *dabāu* as a very serious health disorder. This term is generally equated to the Nepali *mirgi* that Turner translates as 'epilepsy' in his *Nepali English Dictionary* (1931:508). But the Tharu word '*dabāu*' has a wider meaning: it is derived from *dabna*, i.e. 'to be pressed down' and is also related to *dapkāunu* or 'to cause to rebuke, to be threatened'. Being pressed down—depressed could be an appropriate translation—and also being afraid, are the two main notions implied in this trouble. The '*dabāu*' state is often related to an initial threat or shock, generally marked by a loss of consciousness and followed by a psychic and physical imbalance manifested through numerous symptoms like: having the tooth blocked or 'tied up'; or the legs or arms blocked or 'tied up' losing consciousness by 'showing the white of the eyes'; slobbering like an animal; hearing the veins 'tied up'; having clots in the blood, even losing blood; having a buzzing or ringing noise in one's ears; feeling heavy like having a lid on the head; feeling dizzy; trembling, etc., . . . a set of symptoms whose list is not closed since, as it is mentioned in the healer's ritual recitation they are as numerous as the countless forms of the Goddess invoked and involved. In such kinds of disorders the Goddess incarnates herself in wild supernatural forces like the spirits of the jungle, of the river, of the uncultivated fields and so on.

I recorded several cases, from a headache quite easily cured to a very chronic case marked by regular epileptic crises during twelve years, and from a young woman whose menstruation had suddenly 'dried up' to another who was in a state of prostration after having met a witch at night. In fact, this last case was the first I heard of at the beginning of my initial fieldwork in Dang in 1982, and the young educated Tharu man who accompanied me that day used the English word 'hysteria' to define it, pointing to the psychosomatic dimension of the illness according to Westernized categories.

But *dabāu* seems to encompass a vast and open category of diseases which appears to have no direct equivalent in Western languages. It is in fact the curing process—the specific exorcism rituals done in case of *dabāu*—which define this category more precisely. This is why I will try to explore it through the discourse and representations developed in the rituals and ritual recitations.

The healing process however, cannot be merely reduced to the rituals only. As we will see, the ritual are a kind of canvas which may remain blank if the patient is not cured. What happens between the different ritual phases that makes the cure efficient is the most difficult to trace. I mean, as Sagant has shown in an illuminating paper (1987), the interpretation of the disorder by the patient himself and his close social circle which are generally unformulated, or formulated long after the first crisis had occurred. In his work concerning the shaman's cure in eastern Nepal, Sagant demonstrated how the laymen villagers' interpretation of the disease functions, that of the healer being only a part of the social process which pushes the patient to reconstruct his past with the help of his close relatives and neighbours. The anthropologist needs therefore a historical in-depth which is not always easy to come by. I personally do not have enough data to reconstruct the whole process in each of the cases I heard of. My main documents deal with the healer's interpretation, as it is exemplified in the ritual recitations and acts.

Taking up one of Sagant's formulations to define the healer's curing—the visionary shaman offers a 'symbolic horizon' to the clients (1987: 271)—this 'horizon' is certainly different from one society to another. Compared to the Nepalese hills shamanism as described by Sagant for the Limbus, what struck me in the case of the Tharu plain dwellers is the peculiar importance of the site and the environment disclosed by the healer's interpretation. As we shall see, the symptoms as well as their interpretation are directly linked to the spot and spatial context of the first attack of *dabāu,* the priest's interpretation being actually a 'route' in which each event attached to the illness' development is linked to a place. In fact this importance of the 'landscape' at the symbolic level is peculiarly developed in the Tharu conceptual world for, as I have shown elsewhere, most of the supernatural forces are classified according to environmental categories.[2]

I should first concentrate on the rituals in order to bring out the peculiar concepts and representations attached to the *dabāu* cure among the Tharus. But a contradiction arises: the 'routes' drawn during his ritual recitation by the Tharu healer along the river, the forest and other wild places, the 'landscape categories', appear as rather anonymous if not empty. Moreover, the spirits they encompass are in fact the less personalised forces of the Tharu pantheon and as such may be contrasted with the very personalised entity which may be identified by the relatives and the neighbours as the main responsible agent. The villagers' interpretation will most often point to a dead person (generally somebody who died an untimely death). Besides trying to define the *dabāu* illness, my paper will therefore indirectly deal with a question to which I do not pretend to give an answer: the enigmatic relation between the normative conceptual world of the priest and the concrete interpretation of the ordinary people which leads to a successful social as well as personal curing.

THE HEALER' DIVINATION AND THE SEVEN SISTER GODDESS

In case of a crisis as exemplified above, a Tharu priest '*gurwā*' is called for. After questioning the household's members, he asks for consecrated rice grains, *acet*, and then sits in the north west corner of the rooms for *patti baithnā*, a ritual which is done for calling the gods as well as for divination. The priest takes a terracotta oil lamp installed in a small string fitting and swings it in every direction, singing and counting the rice grains several times during the operation *acet hernā*. What has always struck me is the nearly inaudible style of this recitation (which is unusual in Tharu rituals) and the isolation of the priest; nobody except the anthropologist takes interest in this process. My close Tharu friend and best informant, who was one of the most famous priests and healers in the area I worked in, explained to me recently that *patti baithnā* was very difficult because 'many different roads appear and if you take one, suddenly another one may open'. However, in case of *dabāu*, the results point to the overall responsibility of the very powerful Seven Sisters goddesses and their army of demoniac forces.

The Seven Sisters are a very dangerous incarnation of the encompassing divine feminine force called the Goddess Devi. All the Tharu supernatural forces, even the domestic ancestors, are seen as forms, *rup*, or weapons, *ban,* of the Goddess. Devi has three main forms and it is at this level that the 'landscape' categories are more clearly drawn. As a domestic principle she is Maiya, the image of the mother, a married and relatively pacified feminine form linked to the household's ancestors. As a village principle she is Daharcandi, a much more ambiguous force, controlling all the spirits settled in the village shrine and whose domain of action includes the fields, the cultivated lands being conceived as a demarcation between the houses and the forest. In this never totally pacified space, the Goddess is coupled with a very indefinite male principal called Cabawhaguni 'the priest with four arms' who is related to the soil god, the ancestral god of the village priest. As for the Seven Sisters, they dwell mainly in the forest and 'the jungle', a wild space which infiltrates the cultivated land but remains outside the soil god's control. The Seven Sisters are actually everywhere and nowhere, as an uncontrolled (virgin and unmarried) feminine force. When I tried to question the priest on the dwelling places of the Seven Sisters, he answered with very imprecise hand gestures suggesting their omnipresence all around. Nevertheless their main retreat is 'the forest', a totally uncontrolled space, where their power is overwhelming and where the priest has to expel them.[3] The Seven Sisters rule a powerful army of wild spirits whose identity and sphere of action is detailed in the healer's recitation and supported by material representations on the altar built for the occasion.

The healing rituals done in case of *dabāu* are called *bahu karnā*.[4] They are devoted to the Seven Sisters defined as *lahara*, lines or creepers, from the youngest, *chotki* to the eldest, *barki*, depending on the seriousness of the case. This is a formal classification to provide an ideal number (seven) of classes, the youngest having in fact different names and forms Dhautahi, Pagdandi, Gurdandi. . . .

LANDSCAPE AS AN EMPTY CANVAS

Whatever the case and whoever the peculiar gods involved, the altar installed for each *dabāu* cure follow the same general pattern, being a material representation of the healer's recitation and 'symbolic horizon'. Through words and objects, it is a reduced representation of the wild space, but also of the primordial space as the evocation of the creation suggests.

A fresh gourd, always disposed at the south end of the altar, represents Aklākāl Gurubābā, the first Tharu under the primordial vegetal shape he assumed when the world—the valley of Dang—was not yet created. Then Dang was only a lake on which a lotus appeared and gave birth to the gourd.[5] On the altar's northern limit, a cup full of alcohol symbolises Patan Saura, the god of magical power and formulas, attached to the centre of the world (Patan, a sacred site in northern India) and supporting the healer's action. In between, various objects stand for the different wild forces whose classification is mainly linked to environ-mental categories: the spirits of the forest represented by an ant-hill and various wild plants, leaves and pieces of wood as well as miniature earthen ovens for the forces haunting the catechu distilleries; those of the uncultivated fields by remains of bones; and those of the river by a water pot containing small aquatic animals. Except the god of magical power, none of these representations receive sacrifices or offerings. These natural objects make for a kind of empty canvas on which the healer traces his patient's case.

Inside this natural frame, other prototypal spirits are systematically invoked in the healer's recitation but are not represented on the altar: the spirits of the outside or souls of dead persons belonging to non-Tharu groups, like the ferryman or Khun the hunter of the Magar Himalayan tribe, the potter kumar and the oil presser *teli*. They are prototypal categories of ghosts, *masān*.

It seems therefore that the wild and primordial space materialised on the healer's altar and described in his recitation is nevertheless animated by unknown souls as if the wild environment was keeping memories of even its most transitory visitors. It is noteworthy that, though anonymous, these partially human entities are not represented on the altar but receive animal sacrifices during the second and final ritual.[6] Another quite anonymous category of evil forces always invoked at the end of the healer's recitation, always nourished by animal sacrifices but, like the non-Tharu souls, never represented on the altar, are the *jog*, the evil forces of the village. They are invoked by the healer under a very formal list of prototypal agents of bad spells, the sorcerers and witches.[7] If the outside castes' spirits appear as part of the wild and primordial landscape, the *jog* signify the Tharu social and village life as one of the main agents of health disorder.

THE THARU HEALER'S INTERPRETATION: LANDSCAPE AND SOCIAL EVIL FORCES

The empty landscape framed on the altar is nevertheless particularized by the introduction of specific spirits identified by the healer as the particular agent involved in case of *dabāu*, as the following cases illustrate:

(*a*) Suddenly, one night in September 1982, an unmarried girl was extremely frightened and fell unconscious. Later on, the family's elder women explained that she had seen an old woman with a dog entering the house through the roof. The following day, the priest was called and, after talking with some members of the family, he performed his diagnostic ritual with the help of the divination procedure. A first ritual 'to raise' the evil spirits and the Seven Sisters involved was performed. The girl remained prostrate for four to five days but was easily cured. The final ritual, to expel the wild forces after nourishing them, was addressed to Gurdandi, one of the youngest forms of the Seven Sisters and was done two months later. On the wild landscape drawn on the altar, a dry gourd and a broom were installed. The gourd symbolised Siddhi Bâri and contained *bhāng*, a mixture extracted from *cannabis sativa*, ginger, *dhatura* leaves, and the yeast used to prepare beer and alcohol (a paste mainly made of wild plants). We should also remember that the girl had met an old woman before the attack, an old woman described as a witch by her family member and to whom the broom installed on the altar seems to be associated.

(*b*) In the village of Nondra, a married man was seriously ill of *khas mirgī*, 'talking like an animal, his legs trembling, sometimes jumping'. In that case the final ritual was addressed to the third of the Seven Sisters in the generational level and besides a specific form of the Goddess, Kalika, the peculiar spirit involved was Nankalya Jogyath, thought of a as wandering ascetic and sorcerer. On the altar he was symbolised by a gourd containing a pair of tongs and the same intoxicants as noted above for Siddhi Bâri. Close by, in a bamboo container, an insect called *siñghara*, a kind of grasshopper which makes 'the ear ring' was trapped.

(*c*) An old woman of Sukhdewa village was feeling dizzy and had painful headaches. The final ritual to expel the spirits was done six months after the priest' diagnosis and she was considered cured. It was addressed to Gurdandi and no peculiar supernatural figures were added to the 'landscape' spirit categories. The insistence was on the numerous village *jog* as the main agents of the illness.

(*d*) In Padampur village, an old woman lost her breath and felt pain all over her body. This time also the healer worshipped the Gurdandi form of the Seven Sisters. The peculiar spirits involved were again symbolised on the altar by a gourd full of intoxicating plants to which the healer tied a piece of bamboo fence for Thanti Masan, the bad spirit of the fence, 'the one which tied up the body'.

(*e*) In another village, the patient was a woman who had been feeling pain in her body for two years and who had been treated without success in the hospital. For the ritual a piece of fishing net, the dry gourd, as well as some pig hair were laid out. The priest added two bamboo tubes containing two sorts of grasshoppers close by. But this patient's health did not improve and the final ritual which normally signifies the spirits' expulsion was not done. In fact, in such an unsuccessful case, the priest usually corrects his diagnosis, 'finds another route', i.e. other agents and often a higher form of the Seven Sisters.

(*f*) In this case a man had been ill for 12 year—with *parsādyā*—losing consciousness during each attack—and had been unsuccessfully treated by different healers. This time, the priest addressed the final ritual to the second in hierarchy, *manli,* among the Seven Sisters. As usual, the spirit of the forest, of the uncultivated fields, of the river, of the outside, as well as the village *jog* were either installed on the altar or invoked in the recitation. In the primeval and wild empty landscape, the priest put a gourd for the spirit of the wandering ascetic, Nankalya Jogyath, and another one for Siddhi Bâri, a bamboo container with a grasshopper, another with a wasp and finally, centrally on the altar, a big water pot covered with different objects and decorations to incarnate the form of the Seven Sisters involved, which he compared to a boat to send away all the evil forces. The thievish wasp is actually an image of Sawor Bhawor, one of the most dangerous forces, who seize other people's life force. Each of the spirits as well as the *manli* form of the Seven Sisters received very expensive animal sacrifices such as sheep, goats, pigs, chicken. . . .[8]

Having observed several of these ritual, what strikes me now, after rereading my field notes, is the quite limited number of spiritual beings and objects involved in *dabāu* ritual cures. The healer fills the empty landscape canvas with prototypal evil spirits such as the omnipresent wandering ascetic—a well-known character in Dang valley, noticeably perceived as a sorcerer as the term *jog* indicates; that of the grasshopper, illustrating one of the main symptoms of *dabāu*, ringing or buzzing noise in the ears; or that of the wasp, whose life habit are at the origin of numerous symbolic elaborations in Dang—here the seizing of others' life principle.

Two stages may be distinguished in the healer's symbolic construction: first, the materialisation of the natural environment in which plants, small beasts, the river, river banks or the fields predominate; then its filling with quite a limited number of prototypal evil forces, human in nature. On one side are found the wandering souls of the migrant groups who used to establish seasonal relations with the Tharus, like the ferryman, the potter, or the northern Himalayan Magar who come down to Dang for hunting or grazing his livestock; on the other, the village evil forces, *jog*, manipulated by the Tharu witches and sorcerers. In between is the ambivalent figure of the jogi ascetic, a forest dweller, a wandering magician, a sorcerer, whose powers (*siddhi*) are overwhelming.[9]

The importance of the wild and primeval landscape is striking. Its role as an interpretative support is also stressed when the priest analyses the disease's genesis by decoding his patient's spatial movement at the time of the attack. I remember the case of a young girl whose menstrual blood had 'dried up' after an episode of prostration and depression. When he was treating her, the priest told me that the girl had been extremely afraid of a wasp and while she was running away, fell into the river where her friends found her: 'she has been attacked by a spirit of the uncultivated field, then by the bad spirit of the water, the leeches, which sucked her blood'.[10]

This wild space, where the wandering souls of the impermanent neighbours of the Tharus and of ascetics seem to have left their marks, evidently sounded like an echo of the peculiar life the Tharus used to lead until quite recently. The Tharus were the main permanent settlers, village dwellers and farmers of the Terai, infested by malaria, covered with forests and swamps, and cut by powerful rivers; an under-populated land that they used to clear for rice cultivation. They were the 'pioneers of civilization' as the nineteenth century authors defined them (Nesfield, 1885:4). They used to live in compact villages but for several reasons, agrarian as well as political, they did not maintain strong ties with the land they tilled.[11] The Terai land was itself unsettled: floods, changes in river courses during the rainy season and fire and violent storms in the dry season, regularly destroyed villages and pushed the Tharus to search for better grounds. If the new ground was 'empty' as the Tharus used to say for free land, they would settle on it. But this 'empty land' was never totally devoid of human traces since previous settlers, travellers and wandering castes had left their marks. In fact, the Terai has been cleared several times during the last two millennia and its present forests are not primeval.

Witchcraft (*jog*) on one side and the ghosts (*masān*) on the other appear as the main agents of *dabāu* disease in the 'symbolic horizon' of the healer. They are rooted in the 'wild' environment through the memories it keeps of the past, and tied to Tharu social life inside as well as outside the village. Both these aspects are linked in the genesis of the disorder.

THE SILENCE AND THE UNSAID IN THE HEALER'S INTERPRETATION

Why is the healer's interpretation built around such anonymous figures, nearly empty categories of evil forces? Is it to offer a screen to the family history, past and present clashes which should not be openly disclosed?[12] Is it up to the patient and his close social circle, as Sagant has showed in the case of the Himalayan Limbus (1987), to fill the empty landscape unfolded on the altar? Is it up to the patient to connect the unknown history of the 'wild' places he walked through to his own personal and family past and present? Does the Tharu healer, his rituals, thus give time and means to the patient and his close family and village circle to treat their social body disharmony, to reconstruct their past? If it is difficult to give a definite answer to these questions, several elements suggest that the healing ritual is only a platform and a first step in the total process of curing.

One of the most significant facts related to this complex curing process is the *dabāu* ritual procedure itself. *Bahu karnā* (with the village cloistering ritual I shall return to briefly later) is the only exorcism ritual which is done in two stages. The first step is for 'raising' the Gods, *uthān pūjā* in the days following the healer's diagnosis. It appear as the result of the healer's analysis of the case, the product of his inquiries in the house and of his divination, leading to the relatively formal interpretations we have described above. For that ritual, the priest asks for the necessary ingredients to build the altar —gourds, leaves, wood, insects—as well as for the sacrificial victims to be shown and promised to the Seven Sisters identified by the priest. Assisted by a possessed man in whom the goddesses incarnate after the recitation, the priest commands, in a quite violent and low form of address, the different spirits to leave the patient's body. There is a promise that, if the patient is cured the deities will be nourished in the second stage, a few months later. Then a ritual, quite similar to the first one, is repeated in front of the altar reinstalled with the same objects, but ending with numerous animal sacrifices, the violent destruction of the altar and the consummation of the ceremony by finishing all the meat. Nothing should be returned to the village, and the road is symbolically cut off.

Sometime the healer obtained a fast result, as in the first and most of the above cases and sometimes not. In the fifth case described, the patient used to come regularly to the priest's house, complaining of her suffering. The priest listens to her neither rushing for a new ritual, nor proposing an immediate answer to her demands. The priest's reserve and silence was striking. Nevertheless, nearly a year later he performed a new calling ritual and invoked an elder form of the Seven Sisters, which implies that the sacrifices would be more numerous and expensive. The villagers insist that this financial aspect of the ritual *bahu karnā*, the price of pay for the spirits' expulsion, is actually what differentiates the Seven Sisters involved, younger or elder. The sacrifice to the eldest form of the Seven Sisters is actually a purely theoretical one since it is supposed to be too dangerous to be done without the priest risking the balance of his own soul.

In the first case, cited earlier, a witch's curse *jog* was judged responsible for the young girl's shock and prostration, but I was unable to find out if this identification hides a more precise accusation, or how it may help in treating the girl's health problem. In the fifth case, that of the unsuccessful cure of an older woman, it was the ghost of a previous co-wife, who had died fifteen years earlier, who was designated by some of the villagers as the *masān* involved. In that case too, I do not know how the previous wife died, except evidently very young. This more precise identification seemed to have nevertheless marked an improvement of the woman's health and was followed by the final stage of the ritual. But, as we have seen, it was not a definite recovery. It is also noteworthy that both these families had many other problems, for instance economic, and in the second case, a ritual of house cloistering 'killing the masān' for restoring the prosperity of the house, was significantly done, stressing the importance of the household's health for each of its members' personal strength.

The omnipresence of the *masān* and the *jog*, as the main agents of *dabāu* (and probably of most of other illnesses) points to the social nature of the illness, to a disharmony in interpersonal relationships (*jog*) as well as of the family, and, more specifically for the Tharus, of the village body.

In the case of *masān*—the word refers to untimely or uncontrolled death in its narrow meaning—the role of the memories of unsubdued sufferings is stressed. An untimely death which is not yet correctly explained is re-evocated through somebody's illness, raising a bridge between the community's past and its present. Among the Tharus, the word '*masān*' significantly applies to nearly all the invisible forces. Inauspicious death of even unknown previous settlers fills the landscape with countless ghosts. Except for some heroic figures or great Hindu gods, the Tharu village soil god who, significantly, is an ancestor of the village priest, and the pacified ancestors (*pittar*), most of the divine forces are called *masān*. Not only the wandering souls of the dead virgins, of the women who died in childbirth (noticeably worshipped as a domestic divinity), of the suicides, of those whose life was lost by accident (especially snake bites and drowning in Dang), but also, as we have seen, the wandering unnamed and unknown souls of the migrant groups or of the ascetics. The Goddess herself in her village and wild incarnations is identified as the *masān*, when she is seen as the feminine power (*śakti*) encompassing them. The pacified ancestors are conceived as sitting in the domestic goddess Maiya's lap. The dead virgin girl, for instance, is wandering under the village Goddess Daharcandi's control, while the ascetic or the ferryman's soul make up, among others, the Forest Seven Sisters' army. At the same time, we must add that the most general Tharu term used for supernatural powers, whatever their form and status, is '*bhutwā*' which in Nepali or other north Indian languages, specifically designs a ghost.

The overwhelming presence and power of the *masan* and their link with the health of the village social body is emphasized in the village cloistering ritual called *bhut marai*, 'to kill the *bhūt*' which is done when too many people have been sick and the village prosperity has been weakened. Having built a hut in the 'forest' all the most gifted Tharu priests and healers sit in 'to kill the *masān*', by trapping them in the hut and offering them new symbolic funerals. Then, a few months later, the village is symbolically rebuilt, by erecting a new village shrine and fixing the four corners of the village.[13]

Abundantly analysed in other Nepali contexts, and elsewhere in the region, the social origin of disease may be underlined.[14] In the case of the Tharus, some remarks may be made. It does not seem that illness is predominantly linked to a present conflict, or that the healer's cure deals mainly with interpersonal relationships. Even in case of witchcraft (*jog*) it does not seem necessary to identify the witch invloved. On the contrary, the historical and environmental dimensions of disease are peculiarly marked. The healer's interpretation builds an intimate connection between the patient's body disorder and the wild and primordial environment, revealing the permanence of the memories of a long chain of human beings in the wildest places. The importance of the social memory, at least at the conceptual level, is therefore stressed so too is the leading role of the village community's harmony, as the village cloistering ritual shows.[15]

Therefore *dabāu*, even though linked to the forest goddesses and spirits, appears more as a social disease, its curing process linked to the relations inside as well as outside the village. It also seems that this psychic and physical disorder may be thought of as a kind of memory illness. The cure done in case of *dabāu* specifically requires time, through a succession of ritual steps. Maybe this is to leave time for the village community's intervention, the healer appearing therefore as a go-between, acting at the symbolic level to frame the recalling of the past and its rooting in the 'wild' environment.

NOTES

1. Different Tharu groups are living all over the Nepalese Tarai and in northern U.P. and Bihar districts of India but I refer here to the group living in Dang valley in western Nepal, known as the Dangaura Tharus.

2. For a detailed presentation of the Tharu pantheon see Krauskopff (1989: 99-122).
3. For the relation between the forest, the goddesses and the rituals, see Krauskopff 1987b.
4. I have been unable to trace the exact meaning of the word *bahu* which sometimes is equated with *bahut* 'a lot' but could be related to *bahu* or *bahurya*, daughter-in-law, pointing to this affinal relationship as a metaphor for the priest's ritual manipulation of the forest virgin Goddesses.
5. Aklākāl or *akal-kal*, lit 'the time before the time' is quite an enigmatic attribute attached to the first Tharu since *akal* is also an epithet used for 'a death before the fixed time, an untimely death' suggesting a possible link with the ghosts, the spirits of people who died of an untimely or violent death. As a gourd, Aklākāl Gurubaba is also called Pahurya Gurubaba, 'swimming Gurubaba', in reference to the primal lake of the creation.
6. For a more detailed study of animal sacrifices and their role in incarnating the supernatural forces, see Krauskopff 1993.
7. *ulti palti jog, bai biraha jog, uljha paljha jog, thengaha jog, ãnkini/dãnkini rākṣini boksini/joginiyā jog,* . . . all these terms more or less referring to types of witches.
8. For a detailed description of this specific ritual, see Krauskopff (1989: 179-85)
9. It is interesting and maybe paradoxical to remark that the Dang valley has been under the heavy and ancient presence of the Nath yogi ascetics, who were among the main landowners of the soil tilled by the Tharus. But the Naths were living in monasteries, in contrast to the image of the purely wandering, and so dangerous, ascetic developed in symbolic representations.
10. However, in that specific case, it appears that the forest spirits and the Seven Sisters were not involved and a different kind of curing ritual was done (see Krauskopff, 1987b:39).
11. The Tharus have a long history of subjection to absentee landlords. We find numerous evocations, in the nineteenth century descriptions, of their habit of moving from one site to another, particularly to escape the payment of taxes, and the harassment of landlords, as well as forced displacements under political pressure or war situations, the Terai having represented a contested frontier since at least the fourteenth century (Krauskopff 1989:36-7, note 5).
12. One feature of the Tharus' village atmosphere is the very few quarrels openly shown. Family quarrels do occur, since, for instance, they lead to splits in the big 'houses' as well as village disharmony, but conflicts unfold without noise or public display. It is the role of the village chief to settle this kind of problems.
13. For a detailed description of this ritual, see Krauskopff 1987a. 1989:218-24.
14. See for instance Blustain, 1976. For a general analysis of illness in Nepalese

high castes, see Stone (1977 and 1988). In an innovative article on Limbu shamanism, Sagant (1987) insists on the social feature of illness and on the collective aspect of the shaman's cure, a visionary man but also the one who authenticates local institutions

15. When the healer invokes the *jog* it is always as a village *jog* under the name of the village chief.

REFERENCES

Blustain, H.S. 1976 Level of Medicine in a Central Nepali Village, *Contributions to Nepalese Studies*. Vol. 3, Special Issue: 83-105.

Krauskopff, G. 1987a 'Naissance d'un village tharu. A propos des rites de claustration villageoise, *L' Ethnographie*, LXXXIII, 100-1: 131-58

——— 1987b Des paysans dans la jungle: le piégeage dans le rapport des Tharu au monde de la forêt *Etudes Rurales*, 107-8: 27-42.

——— 1989 *Maîtres et Possédés. Les Rites et l'Ordre Social chez les Tharu de Dang,* Paris: Presses du CNRS.

——— 1993 Réceptions divines. Des offrandes à l'incarnation des dieux chez les Tharu. In *Purusartha* 15: *Classer les Dieux? Des panthéons en Asie du Sud.* Paris. Ed. de l'EHESS, pp. 131-52.

Nesfield, J.C. 1885 The Tharus and Bhogshas of Upper India: *Calcutta Review* 80 (159): 1-46.

Sagant, P. 1987 La cure du chamane et l'interprétation des laïcs, *L'Ethnographie*, LXXXIII, 100-1: 247-73.

Stone, L.1977 *Illness Hierarchy and Food Symbolism in Hindu Nepal*, Ph.D. Thesis, Brown University.

———1988 *Illness Beliefs and Feeding the Dead in Hindu Nepal.* Lewiston Queenston: the Edwin Mellen Press.

Turner, R.L. 1931 *A Comparative and Etymological Dictionary of the Nepali Language.* London: Routledge & Kegan.

The Healing Practices of Mediums Living and Working on the River of Perfumes (Huê, Viêt Nam), and the Symbolic Representations of the Person[1]

DIDIER BERTRAND

INTRODUCTION

The aim of this article is to explain the symbolic representations of the person as they appear throughout the healing cults, in relation with the Viêtnamese philosophical and religious substrata. It may seem surprising to find an article about Viêt Nam, appearing in a volume, that is dealing with South Asia. As the very name Indo-China suggests, Viêtnamese culture shares an Indian influence, even though it is more common to consider it as close to the Chinese culture. The Viêtnamese empire was created by the integration of the Hindu kingdom of Champa, which had adopted Indian script and religion. Viêt Nam and India both have Austro-Asiatic populations.

In the field of healing and spiritual practices, India is for the Viêtnamese the centre of magic sciences, as we are reminded by the eleventh century epic poem (Durand 1966:346) of the famous monk Tu Dao Hanh, who left for India, to find an old woman holding the secrets and formulae (*dharani*) of a certain magic power, which would enable him to avenge the murder, by another monk, of his mandarin father.

It is interesting to consider these practices in the framework of those regional cults of southern Asia which are dedicated to spirits and surrounded by a dense and complex network of beliefs and popular practices, which are entangled in a 'somewhat chaotic syncretism' (Simon and Simon Barouh 1973:71). These practices integrate a spiritualistic and naturalistic base which is common to all the people of this region, whatever their ethnological origin with a Cham (and consequentially Indo-Brahmanic) influence, thus operating as a total syncretism of beliefs that exists in Viêt Nam:

> the traditional religion of Viêt Nam is difficult to seize in the framework which all

appear to be too rigid for the luxuriousness of reality which impregnates collective and individual life in its most solemn as well as in its most everyday form. This religion, being made up of deep beliefs and routine rituals deeply rooted in the history of the Viêtnamese people and entirely penetrated by exterior influences and imprints that in some ways reach the extremity of rich religious meditation through many other archaic religions'. (op. cit., 73)

This authentically Viêtnamese synthesis clearly reflects the multitude of influences that characterize the insertion of these people in the South Asian monsoon zone.

1. THE BOATMEN

Since many centuries, the boatmen have been leading a semi-nomadic life along the River of Perfumes. Although they are of Viêtnamese origin, they speak a slightly different Hûe dialect with a strong accent, using archaic expressions coming from the Môn-Khmer and Thai-Kadaï languages of the province. This people living on the water is not an 'ethnic', but a separate social group and its origins remain unknown. The boatmen explain that the world was created in the following way: people were needed on land to grow rice and people were needed on the water to catch fish. There are indications to show that the boatmen are descended from an isolated Cham ethnic group (songs, worship, physical, characteristics).

All boatmen are attached to a village (*van*) to which they return for their traditional festivals such as New Year, fishing rites, etc. In urban areas they leave their 'village' only on rare occasions, such as weddings, because their local network of resources has been developed to such an extent that they do not need to migrate for long periods. For much of the year, the families fish along the river, in its estuaries and in its lagoons. Sometime they go upstream into the mountains for some weeks, where they cut wood and bamboo for heating and building. On other occasions, they spend the fishing season in the Nam Dong district, which is populated by Môn-Khmer speaking mountain people, and where the fish is abundant.

The poorest of them usually live on a medium-sized boat, know as the *ghé* and used for work, while the larger and better-off family units live on a wide sampan known as the *do*, although these families mainly use an open *ghé* for work. In general, the parents live on the largest boat which is surrounded by smaller craft belonging to their sons. Everybody lives thus, in family units, with the children passing freely from one boat to another.

The boatmen are rarely able to read and write. They maintain numerous practices and beliefs concerning illness in particular. Consequently, each *van* has at least one or two mediums, the *thây dông hô* who are the first to be consulted in case of illness.

2. THE MEDIUMS

The medium is someone who heals and protects,[2] but is himself serving and protected by a powerful genius known as his *thây hô mang* (the master who serves his destiny). He regularly 're-activates' the latter (*len dông*[3]), during sessions of communication with the spirits. It is often after the spirit have cured him of a long and painful illness that, in return, the medium devotes himself to their service. He may make amulets (*bua*) or talismans (*ngay*) which protect from ghosts (*ma*), from evil spirits (*ma quy, am binh*) and from restless souls or wandering spirits (*cô hôn*).

The mediums are followers of the Holy Mother of the Sky (*Mâu Thiên Y A Na*) whose Viêtnamese name, which comes from Malayo-Polynesian language, is a reminder that the temple of *Hôn Chen*, dedicated to her, is built on an ancient Cham place of worship. The mediums venerate the tiger, who is present at the foot of all altars and who is considered to be a powerful genius for curing childhood illnesses in particular. Certain mediums treasure the bones, the teeth and the skull of the tiger for this purpose.

Healers who are mediums and who also practise traditional Viêtnamese medicine and herbalism, depend upon a complex pantheon of divinities derived not only from Taoïsm and Confucianism but including local beliefs and worship. Some of these healers are renowned along the river and its tributaries for their ability to settle relationships between men, genii (heavenly as well as human, confused in popular belief) and evil spirits.

3. THE DIFFERENT TYPES OF ILLNESS

The mediums take into account the seriousness, nature and origin of the illness. They make a primordial distinction between illnesses occurring inside the body, which are referred to a hospital after some basic treatment, and those coming from outside the body, they say are linked to beings from the spiritual world: the latter constitute their field of competence. Though this distinction comes from traditional medicine, the mediums have reappropriated it in their own way because this distinction did not originally apply to their practices.[4]

Their now follows a summary of the different categories of illness according to folk classification, with the causes as defined both by the boatmen and by the mediums.

3.1 Illnesses which are Referred to Western or Sino-Viêtnamese Medicine (Interior Illnesses)

The causes of such illnessess are usually and commonly occurring: exposure to heat or cold, wind, malnutrition, too much sun or too much work. These minor problems are cured by simple medication or elementary practices, which are sometimes performed by the patient himself.

Several illnesses are attributed to sun and water. Illnesses caused by imbalances in the *hot/cold system*, produce colds and headaches. Illnesses caused by the wind belong to an etiologic register which is common throughout Asia. The boatmen do not know where the wind comes from, nor where it goes, nor how it circulates within the body. It might comes from the outside to trouble the bodily functions; '*Bi gio*' means 'to be taken by the wind' '*bi*' is the negative and passive form of the verb 'to be'. Bad winds are driven out, using techniques with a coin such as *cao gio* meaning 'to scrape the wind'. The wind is part of the dynamic conception of illness and it enters and leaves like an aggressive force. Skin diseases, nose bleeding and illnesses caused by tiredness also fall into this category. Boatmen claim that since 1975, there have been more illnesses resulting from pollution caused by the chemical products used during the war. These mainly occur in the form of skin infections and pains and are for the most part attributed to the allegedly toxic water.[5]

These illnesses are not serious and cause little worry, although some cases are diagnosed by a medium as serious and call for rapid treatment in hospital.[6]

3.2 Illnesses Calling for the Intervention of a Medium or Healer (Exterior Illnesses)

An illness, considered as a sanction administered by the supernatural powers depends upon explicative categories, which can be identified with genii or ancestors.

ILLNESSES CAUSED BY PERSECUTION BY THE SOUL OF A DEAD PERSON

This is the type of illness most frequently treated by the boatmen and the mediums deal with it by making the distinction between the spirits of dead family members *nhà vong* (*nhà* = house, *vong* = soul), and wandering spirits of dead people. These are the 'restless dead' without a tomb. The problems associated with these restless souls are not always well defined and do not have particular name, unless it be that of the type of soul; thus, the illness *bênh* of the souls *bênh vong,* may be specified as the illness of dead soldiers, *bênh ma binh* or *benh cac quân*, or that of devils or ghosts, *bênh ma quy*. The dead soldiers receiving no veneration cause problems which may lead to madness in children. Thirty-six types of deceased (who died a violent death) can harass the living in this way. The most frequent image is that of an arrow shot by a soldier, wounding the body and causing violent local pain. Often to be found in trees, rocks, caves or in whirlpools, these souls are not necessarily malevolent, unless they are disturbed, for example by cutting down the tree. Take the case of a dead father, who now leads an unhappy existence in hell. He may capture a member of his family in order to claim ritual offerings. He manifests himself through local physical pain. In this case the medium can easily communicate with the soul and discover what should be offered. A dead person, who wishes to be buried elsewhere, will make his desire known to family members, by causing an illness.

The *Cô than ruât*, the soul of a patrilinear childless aunt, is a familiar cause of suffering. She wanders after death illness to family members—particularly children—entering and cutting their body organs and causing dreadful pain. Such an aunt leads a difficult life after death, since she has no one to venerate her. She is angry and wishes to receive ritual offerings. This prognosis is simple, and the cure in general rapid, once she has received what she wanted—money, clothes, or a vehicle made of paper.

The *Con ranh*, too (*ranh*[7] = the soul of stillborn children who inhabit children born subsequently), are also objects of fear and demand particular veneration. Parents may be persecuted by children who died young, stillborn or before being named. Boatmen who have lost young children always have an altar dedicated to them. Important family or community rituals are performed for the souls of such children drowned or dead in an accident.

Loss of soul (*mat hôn*)

The *hôn* is the superior vital principle that may be lost or caught, while the *via* are inferior souls in relation to the body. Children often lose their soul as a result of falling into the river, or from a tree. Adults can also lose their soul after an emotional shock. Without a soul, an individual may let himself waste away; he has no more energy and seems empty and apathetic. Children and old people alike are particularly sensitive to this kind of loss. According to the sampan dwellers, the *hôn* and the *via* leave the body during sleep. This is why one must avoid taking one's afternoon nap in the wrong place: such as under trees occupied by wandering spirits, who can easily slip into the body. If a person's face is painted while he sleeps, his souls will no longer recognize him and the person will die.

ILLNESSES CAUSED BY POSSESSION BY A SPIRIT (*MA NHAP*, THE GHOST ENTERS)

Most vulnerable here are young men, or young virgin women. The souls of those dead without having known love, try to steal strength and beauty from young people for their own carnal and devilish relations. These youth are subject to possession by incubi or succubi (*tinh*) attacking them while, for example, they sleep under the tree in which these spirits reside. They then go through phases of extreme frenzy which may be accompanied by exhibitionism, delirium and by a loss of energy which may lead to death.

ILLNESSES HAVING ASTROLOGICAL CAUSES

There are astrological periods during which children run the risk of illness or accident caused by *quan sat*[0] (the killer mandarin from the other world) according to their time of birth. *Thâp nhi canh ranh* (the twelve from the door of dead children) are the twelve illnesses to which a child is vulnerable from the age of one month to twelve years. For example, the child refuses to eat because of stomach pains, he is uncurably thin, he no longer eats but vomits all the same, and remains sitting in the cross-legged position with clenched fists.

4. THE THERAPEUTIC PRINCIPLES: THE MEDIUM AND HIS PRACTICE

4.1 The Diagnostic

Let us attend some sessions with a patient.

We are staying in the boat of a medium, Thây Vy, moored in a floating village upstream on the River of Perfumes, three hours away from the provincial hospital. Dung is a woman of 48 years coming with her husband seeking care because he suffers acute stomach pain. Thây Vy starts to establish the diagnostic by taking the pulse, he stares into the eyes of the patient and asks several questions concerning the circumstances of the illness (Plate 14).

The medium is using the four traditional principal of diagnosis (Phan Kê Binh 1980 i:92): looking, listening, and taking the pulse. Different types of pulse can be recognised according to different parts of the wrist, corresponding to different organs and to problems linked to the five elements (water, wood, fire, metal and earth)

Suspecting an exterior illness, Thây Vy now consults his protector (Plate 15). He burns some incense and, after some minutes of prayer and invocation, on his suggestion[9] the medium identifies the illness and the appropriate remedy. Then he utters some words of praise to the angry spirits and the appeals to them for their aid. The lady doesn't need to go to hospital for treatment, but her family has to provide rituals and offering for the local genius of her native place, where her mother still lives, and where she didn't go for over a year. To relieve the pain immediately, Thây Vy also prescribes some herbal medicine, and gives the women a drink, made from the ashes of a paper amulet that he burns and mixes with holy water taken from his altar.

4.2 The Different Types of Intervention

Remedies for *'Interior' illnesses* are linked to Sino-Viêtnamese medicine, although the effects of therapeutic syncretism imply that they do not always exactly reflect the presuppositions implicit in that system.

As far as heat-related skin diseases (*suoi*) are concerned, the crouching child is sprayed with rice alcohol. Alcohol has disinfectant qualities that are good for spots, which, like rashes, tend to suppurate slightly.

For epilepsy, the intervention is a combination of acupuncture, rituals, and Western medicine in the form of sedatives. Acupuncture is performed either with needles or with fragments of glass, on zones which have an influence on the body according to the meridians defined by oriental medicine, and known as 'nerve fibres' by the mediums. This is supposed to have a calming effect, but is often just a primary measure to relieve the suffering. Acupuncture is used, for example, on the parts of the body which are painful, to soothe headaches and colds. The treatment is also used for influenza and exterior illnesses, in order to drive out evil spirits.

For *'exterior' illnesses*, as we have seen in the case of Dung, the diagnostic is based on the vision or possession, usually naming 'those responsible'. Following the diagnostic sequence, Thây Vy proposes to organize a series of transactions with the superior genii and to call forth the genius involved in the illness, whose original story will then be revealed.

Right from the start, and by his very presence, the medium has the power of suggestion and cure. Because he is able to enter into communication with the spiritual world, he is the only person capable of indicating to the family the identity of the tormenting spirit, the nature of its demands or the means of getting rid of it.

In the treatment of *possession*, the private space occupied by the illness is made public. Let us witness another case.

Today Thây Vy's boat is surrounded by people who have come to attend the ceremony. Several offerings are being prepared: rice, alcohol, crabs, chicken. . . . Musicians start playing *châu van.*[10] Once he is possessed, Thây Vy no longer 'knows anything about himself'; he is the vehicle of his protective spirit, who belongs to the mountaineers, and he speaks what is supposed to be a Môn Khmer language, though nobody understands it. He writes, using vague Chinese ideograms, though the mediums, like most boatmen, are illiterate.

Thây Vy is assisted by different people known as servant or *dông*,[11] in whom the genius invoked by the medium may manifest itself. Today, they are all women. One *dông* dances to the tune of the châu vân, then collapses for a few seconds, indicating a more or less sudden possession. She starts to tremble and shout, signalling the arrival of the genius. Then she speaks, in the name of the genius who caused the illness, telling Thây Vy what the spirit demands. The *dông* acts out the healing process, making it visible, as in theater, to everybody. She communicates with the patient and her family, who ask questions. They promise to come back to the village soon, and to give the genius what he asks for. There will be two further ceremonies of a similar kind, followed by a long and expensive thanksgiving ceremony once Dung is cured, on a certain day determined by means of a horoscope.

It is usually possible to *conciliate* the spirits by means of offerings and through words of praise. Offerings may be of several kinds: fruit, flowers, betel leaves and areca nuts, as also paper models of various objects: clothes, shoes, houses, bicycles and even, recently, Honda motorcycles and cars. These offerings usually follow the possession.

To heal Dung, Thây Vy intervenes through his protective genius, who asks the genius possessing the women what kind of offering he demands. He then asks the latter to leave the patient in peace in return for some presents.[12] During the ceremony the malevolent spirit also receives a paper model representing the woman which he has hurt. This puppet, supposed to replace the woman, is thrown into the river or burnt, a subterfuge which will trick the spirit into leaving the woman alone.

Similarly, the medium intervenes as an intermediary in the case of trees, inhabited by avenging spirits, which people have cut down. He negotiates, with the spirit, the reparation of the damage caused, by offering him paper trees.

To fend off attacks from diabolical spirits, mediums may attempt conciliation, but may also adopt the more aggressive strategy of *exorcism*. There are different means to get rid of spirits; one may beat the patient and the area around him with a wicker cane, spray the patient with alcohol and give him a talisman, or introduce cinnabar into an amulet. One may also give the patient a drink of incense ashes mixed with holy water, or point a bow and arrow at the patient's stomach.

While exorcism is supposed to drive out evil spirits, ceremonies for calling back the soul(s) imply *adorcism*. They consist of series of rituals, venerations and offerings. Some include the use of one of the patient's shirts in order to call back his soul. The mediums also use a paper hat, worn by the patient, which is supposed to be capable of transporting and bringing back lost souls.

More generally, mediums invoke the higher deities in order to *protect* children, as well as persons who are in a liminal state, such as pregnant women. Let us give an example.

In a wooden chest placed in front of the altar and surrounded by numerous representations of the divinities (Buddha in his female form, Amithaba) and of genii (popular Viêtnamese heroes and saints), the medium places amulets such as sheets of yellow or white paper marked with ideograms in red ink, sometimes adding a seal dipped in the ink, supposed to bring good luck. These letters to the spirits (*Ngai*[13]) ask them to feed and protect a child until the age of twelve. This practice is used for children whom it is difficult to bring up or feed, and also by pregnant women who have had a stillborn or lost a baby (*con ranh*), or for families with a deceased childless aunt, *cô ruât*.

In spite of these various techniques to control spirit power, the medium only has a limited control over them, as is clear from the rite of tossing coins. After a ceremony such as the one involving Dung, Thây Vy must *verify* with the spirit whether or not he consents to the ritual. Two holed coins (sapecs), each one having one side covered in lime, are tossed; the sides represent *am* and *duong*, the male and female principles. These coins are considered to belong to the spiritual world, since people on Earth use notes instead of coin nowadays. If two female sides come up, the spirit does not give his consent. If one male and female result, consent is given. If both coins turn out male, the *Ngai* are joking and the coins must be tossed again.

This ritual keeps the attention of everyone present, and at the end of the ceremony many people take advantage of the opportunity to ask the genius' counsel about everyday life problems. The boatmen, however, do not hesitate to toss the coin again and again until they obtain the answer they want.

The coins limit the medium's omnipotence, since they introduce the notion of chance (heads or tail) as a way of asking for the opinion of superior spirits from the other world. As a divination practice, they establish a visible communication which everybody can understand.

5. THE PANTHEON

How many figures make up the pantheon used by the Viêtnamese mediums? It is extremely difficult to count them or to make an exhaustive list. There are supernatural beings, saints, genii, and the ever present spirit of the dead, in the sea, the river, the forests, and in particular places where their powers must be venerated, such as their birthplace, their place of death, or their home: trees, stones, caves, ravine, lakes, mountain passes, etc.

In fact '*most believers venerate the spirits without feeling the need to know their exact identity*' (Tran Van Toan 1967:104). The mediums know which spirits they are dealing with and are not concerned about making an inventory of them: 'the others are countless, we can only venerate them collectively, that is why before the possession ceremonies we sing the hymn to all the spirits in the four worlds' (op. cit., 106). All that is possible is to give a basic presentation of the different types who make up the pantheon inasmuch as they inform us of the part taken by the individual in the rituals.

Maû Thien Y Ana: the Holy Mother of the Sky is a Goddess from a myth, supposedly responsible for miracles and honoured by imperial recognition. She is recognised as a holy protector because she can save and cure people who have made her offerings and drunk holy water. She is at the centre of a pantheon usually known as *tam phu* (the three domains or palaces: Sky, Water, Mountains) or *tu phu* (the four domains: Sky, Water, Mountains and Earth). She usually appears with the two other mother goddesses, *Me* (or *Mau Thuong Ngan*, the Holy Mother of the Forest) and *Mâu Thuy Phu*, the Holy Mother of the Water. The goddesses are surrounded by their twelve assistants.

The divinities belong to a superior world with a distinct hierarchy, each palace being composed not only of mandarins and armies of soldiers, but also of civilians who maintain a confucian-type relationship of submission comprising great mandarins, ten princes, younger princes, younger ladies, servants and soldiers. The nobles and their servants can be called upon during the possession rituals, to intervene in the healing process and drive out the troublesome spirit or attempt a conciliation, if one of them is the cause of the harm.

The Women of the Five Elements or the Holy Ladies of the Five Elements (*Thanh Bà Ngu Hanh*)[14] are portrayed as capturing and enslaving human beings. The five elements are at the base of traditional medicine. The Holy Ladies are the creators of the universe and their altars can be found outside the temple of the Holy Mother. These characters do not always intervene in the same way in the medium's practice. They seem to be the survivals of Proto-Indochinese divinities: the Ladies of Fire and of Water are mainly known and worshipped as such, whereas the Lady of Wood is assimilated to the Holy Mother of the Forest.

RELATIONS WITH THE SPIRITUAL WORLD

None of the Viêtnamese religious influences is monotheistic; there is no single supreme being. Neither is it a question of animism in which plants, trees and even minerals are attributed a soul; the Viêtnamese pattern is a kind of spiritualism, or a permanent reference to the souls of the dead. Therefore, the healing rituals, the representations of the illness, and numerous events have an effect that goes far beyond their factual aspect. The boatmen must constantly appease the spirits and avoid disturbing them. The spirits live everywhere, doubling this world and are therefore associated with the principal events of family life.

The placets (*so*)[15] as well as the texts which are sung during the rituals are oratory precautions which carry a subtle blend of humility and praise.

These supernatural beings have gifts of power which are superior to that of humans but they depend on similar feelings and needs. Men even retain a certain control, since emperors were able to promote or hold back local genii, according to their demeanour. The relationship between all these spirits, saints and genii is quite ambivalent, spirits who are entirely harmful are rare (apart from unvenerated dead soul), but at the same time, they are feared and respected because they can be harmful if they are disturbed. The purpose of propitiatory worship is to appease vengeful spirits and to direct them towards more beneficial actions.

It is believed that through worship certain demons can become good.

The religious life of the Viêtnamese is centred, not around one well-defined religion, but is made up of ritual practices and worship with neither defined dogma nor clergy. The pantheon is complicated, to say the least; while religious beliefs are apparently collective, everybody adapts them to his individual way of thinking. It is a question less of religions, than of beliefs which must be understood as a collection of rules and respect for what is forbidden. These rules are not applied randomly, but are always used for the same particular ends, and respect for the law is combined with a confucianist moral organization, a Buddhist philosophy and a certain amount of spiritism. '*The true religion of the boatmen is the worship of the spirits*' (Cadière 1992:6) a worship from diverse origins combining a pantheon of divinities, saints, immortals and spirits in a syncretism which is astonishing in its diversity and complexity.[16] '*Religious life is made up of rituals, religious gestures, maintainance, interior acts, spiritual states which inform daily life completely*' (op. cit., 7). From representations of health, we can, at last, have an overview of the entire Viêtnamese socio-cultural universe which is deeply penetrated by religion.

6. THE IMAGE OF THE PERSON IN THERAPEUTIC RITUALS AND REPRESENTATIONS OF ILLNESS

The Mediums, coming from an oral culture and basing themselves upon individual experience of suffering and illness, have not really developed a theory of the person. It is through different field studies and reading, that the following considerations can be put forward.[17]

6.1 The Soul: Theory and Argument

At the heart of the mediums' healing practices, there seems to be a conception of the soul, while other practicians—masters of magic words (*thây phap*) or masters of rites (*thây cung*)—privilege other reasons for an illness, implying a representation of the individual which evokes standard Taoïsm or Buddhism as found in books.

Nguyen Van Chen (1963:24) gives a complex theorization directly derived from Taoïsm in which the numerous souls making up the person are attached to Yin/Yang principles. According to this metaphysical conception, the body is inhabited by souls of diverse origin linked to the five element and to the energies of nature. The *khi* is the breath of vital energy which passes through the body, animating it, and since everything is linked up, *khi* has an effect upon the humours and character of the person. These ideas have hardly been developed by the mediums, who usually refer to *Hôn* and *Via*, or, more simply, to man's having two groups of souls: three souls (*hôn*) and seven souls (*via*). Longevity depends upon the harmonious union of these two groups. In literature and in the written tradition, the *hôn* consists of three souls: the rational soul is based in the brain and fixes itself upon the gravestone, the passionate soul is based in the chest and continues to inhabit the dead body in the coffin and the material soul is based in the stomach and goes to hell after death. The *hôn* continue after death and may influence the life of descendant. The wandering spirits who disturb the living are *hôn*. The *hôn* is the soul as '*a vital component absolutely necessary for the reconstitution of a person's mental integrity* . . . and also . . . *a sacred and immaterial principle endlessly reincarnated in a thousand ways and seeming to possess an individual through a certain continuity*' (Phan Thi Dec.1966:88).

The *via* act upon the character, and are linked to the orifices. For the boatmen, they provide the difference between man and woman, since men have seven *via* and women have nine from birth. The *via* leave the body after death. People have different qualities according to their *via* of ancestors are felt by their descendants. The *via* come from the earth as an energy which is sensitive to the human and natural environment. On New Year's Day, a household will have happiness and good luck for the year to come, if its first visitors are people having good *via*.

The *hôn* and the *via* are therefore essential components of a person and are at the centre of problems concerning possession or loss of the soul.

6.2 The Living And The Dead

It is difficult to learn from the boatmen exactly what happens after death to souls who, having acquired supernatural powers after death, continue to have the same need and pleasures as on earth:

> they remain part of the world of the living and especially to members of their family. Naturally they are animated with good feelings, they help their living relatives, they watch over their happiness; but they also pass judgment if the living do not fulfill the duty imposed upon them by filial respect, those guilty of this are warned and punished with illness, with pain, with loss and with death. (Cadière1992:17)

Therefore, it is in every interest for the living to make sure their ancestors are happy and lacking for nothing. Souls made bitter by poverty can group together and cause epidemics. They become demons and devils and essentially malevolent beings with whom it is difficult to imagine conciliation. They can be conformed only by calling upon superior spirits capable of getting rid of them. These groups of spirits are organized in the same way as an army, and their generals, who are often mandarins, remain faithful to mortals who make a few offerings to them.

6.3 Destiny and Illness

It is important to consider divination practices, since they call forth various ways of dealing with a situation and imply different representations of an illness, which are seen by the boatmen as being complementary. This may be illustrated by the joint intervention in the healing rituals of the medium and the Master of magic words (*thây phap*).

The birthday cycles determine the destiny of an individual and the generals under whose protection that individual is placed, according to the year, the month, the day and the hour of birth. In a religious context where destiny is determined mainly by the stars, man can only plead for mercy and try to avoid what has been predicted.

Considering the philosophical and religious body of the three fundamental teachings (*tam giao*: Buddhism, Taoïsm and Confucianism), one may elaborate a conception of the person. But in fact personhood is expressed in different ways during the healing rituals. The healer is usually able to suggest different expressions of the individual according to his system and references.

7. CONCLUSION

An illness is interpreted as an event which is part of a mythical or family history and people are capable of taking into account certain contingencies within the administration of a family's destiny. '*The bureaucratic metaphor implies the discovery of a fault (the fault of the supernatural assailant, the fault of the sufferer, or even that of a living or dead member of a household)*' (Lemoine 1992:179). The explanation of the troubles passses by an interpretation of reality and the role of different mythological or religious characters or figures who are involved in the process. The therapy thus appears as the revelation of a system of relationships, a technique which is linked to a religious practice. The therapeutic ritual, which by means of possession calls upon those responsible for the illness, and which make them explain themselves in public, reconciles the individual with the mythical forces of his environment or of his family heritage. The legitimacy of therapeutic decision implies that there has been a search for social consensus in which the ritual process of dramatization; costumes, trances, dances, shouts, music, and incense mark the rhythm of the different stages of purification, reconciliation and reintegration, in which the bodily investment is significant.

In certain cases of possession, the individual is enslaved for life by mythical figures in order to obtain conditonal healing. He will become a *dông*, servant, and must regularly dance for, and serve his master, on pain of physical torture, in the form of violent or even lethal pain. Pathological possession thus becomes ritual possession, along with the creation of a household altar, and it reaches a dimension that is more than communal, almost sacrificial, in that the subject has offered himself (or at least his body), for regular service to the genii in exchange for being cured.

Whatever the problem it has to solve, the ritual itself shows several curative dimensions which make it efficient (even if the question of efficacy itself would need much more investigation and comment) because it encompasses globally the human being in its social, cosmological and psychological aspects.

The fabrication of medicines, which are selected for their chemical as well as symbolic properties, constitutes a kind of medical/magical action; the healing power of the master reinforce the intrinsic capacities of the drugs. Psycho-moral actions with a cosmic reach are aimed to make up for misconduct by serving the spirits, and addressing words of praise to them, that refer to parental or ancestral images, or coded scenarios that are linked to mythological configurations. The liturgy, with its more or less public dramatization, corresponds to the religious aspect, and to the beliefs about life and death, fate and luck.

The ritual is a kind of collective therapy, implicating the group at different levels, from the diagnostic to the reintegration of the patient within the community, involving the support of the audience. At another level, former patients become servants (*dông*) and participate directly in the healing process.

The medium allows a therapeutic space to be constructed from a body which is projected as an object of belief, which he then introduces into a new topological space. By initiating an associative process which turns out therapeutic, he constructs an intellectual order, the efficacity of which is possible only if it is intelligible; that is, if it pertains to the cultural foundations of the person and his representations of the body and of misfortune. Thus, we may use the term of Levi-Strauss, when he talks of *symbolic efficacy.*

The cure aims at, 'making a given situation thinkable, in affective terms at first, and make acceptable to the pain which the body refuse to tolerate' (Levi-Strauss 1975:225).

The passage to mythic language dramatizes the troubles, but introduces an order by proposing a new formal framework.

One cannot reduce the efficacy to a single symbolic or psychologic dimension. The analysis proposed by Nathan shows that this symbolic efficacy results, moreover, from 'logical constraints which allow us to explain in what way objects, ritual action and therapeutic measures may function by their intrinsic power' (Nathan 1994:116).

The therapeutic techniques are fundamentally pragmatic; they create and utilize objects for particular purposes in a context where action is efficient because of its ability to convey meaning.

The healing is effectuated by a relation of communication, and this relation is the main endeavour of the seer/healer. Its undoubted efficacy results from this fact, not in the sense that the process annihilate the pain, but to the extent that it avoids, for the patient, alienation, madness, and the break with the Other (Mohin Navet 1993:149).

The healing process rests on a social pact, which unites the illness, the healer, and society. It inscribes the therapy on a real and imaginary social order; this is why the medium has a fundamental role to play as a mediator.

NOTES

1. This research was financed by a Lavoisier grant from the French Ministery of Foreign Affairs.
2. He can only act for the good.
3. To ride or climb (*len*) the child or servant (*dông*).
4. In traditional medicine for the internal category: *noi thuong*, the source of the illness goes from the interior to the exterior and is treated with medicine. The external category: *Ngoi cam*, is caused by the wind, the cold, the heat and the damp and is treated with massage and acupuncture.
5. The same also applies for malaria; cf. D. Bertrand, 1994.
6. Once an affected organ has been reached as in the case of asthma or tuberculosis.
7. At the beginning of the twentieth century, Cadière (1992) reports the illnes of *con ranh*, a spirit who possesses and kills a child then possesses the next child in a family and so on.

8. The *quan sat* are dependent upon the horoscope (which is a twelve year cycle), therefore these attacks are treated with the co-operation of the *thây phap* (master of the sacred words) who have access to the astrological books and who refer to another pantheon.
9. And, more rarely, by visible possession at that time.
10. Music and song played during len *dông* session.
11. *Ông dông* for men and *bà dông* or *bà côt* for women. The practice of *lên dông* exist in other form which are not necessarily therapeutic but are a kind of collective seance during which they can dance to serve the spirits.
12. For example: to obtain money to play cards, the aunt sold her nephews to another spirit.
13. *Ngai* means 'He'. This is an indirect way of naming the spirits without using their name. This on one hand, denotes respect and, on the other hand, the lack of knowledge about this spirit.
14. Or Nam bà Ngu Hanh, the five ladies of the five elements: Bà Hoa (Lady of the Fire, Bà Kim (Lady of Metal, Bà Môc (Lady of Wood), Bà Thô (Lady of Earth), Bà Thuy (Lady of Water).
15. These yellow papers are either bought already printed at the market or written by the *thây phap* (master of magic words) with Chinese ideogrammes. There are different kinds according to the type of ceremony. The text is a prayer to the highest genii of the Other World asking them humbly for help and protection.
16. Insofar as, for all unwritten religions there are many variations of interindividual names or interpretations that make it necessary to accept a plural reality even though it is still necessary to refer to original sources.
17. A more detailed study, dealing with not only therapeutic rituals, but also the different rituals and ceremonies marking the lives of the boatmen, would doubtlessly provide more elements concerning the representation of the person.

REFERENCES

Bertrand, D. 1994 *Le paludisme, son origine et son traitement chez les sampaniers de la Rivère des Parfums*. Informations medicales d'Asie Francophone. Riasem, Nice; September 1994; 14-17.

Cadiere, L. 1992 *Croyances et pratiques religieuses des Viêtnamiens*. Paris: réimpressions de l'Ecole Française d'Extrême Orient, T. I.

Dao, Thai Hanh, 1914 Histoire de la déesse Thiên Y Ana, Huê, *Bulletin des Amis du Vieux Huê* 162-81.

Dumoutier, G. 1908 Essai sur les Tonkinois superstitieux, *Revue indochinoise* 25-76.

Durand, M. 1959 *Technique et panthéon des médiums viêtnamiens* (*dông*). Paris: EFEO, vol. XLV.

——— 1966 *Viêt Nam, le monde du sorcier*. Paris: Seuil.

Lafond, P.B. 1959 Pratiques médicales des Thai noirs du Laos de l' Ouest, *Anthropos* 54; 819-40.

Lagerwey, J. 1993 *Le continent des esprits, la Chine dans le miroir du Tao´sme.* Bruxelles: Maisonneuve et Larose.

——— (ed.) 1992 Comportement rituel et corps social en Asie, Paris: BEFEO no. 79.2.

Lemoine, J. 1992 *Variations miao-yao dans l'intervention chamanique*. BEFEO no. 79, 2 (Lagerwey, ed., op. cit.).

Levi-Strauss, C. 1975 L' efficacité symbolique. In *Anthropologie structurale.* Paris: Plon I.

Mercier, J. 1993 Corps pour corps, corps à corps, Paris: L'Homme 125, 67-87.

Mohia Navet, N. 1993 *Le thérapies traditionnelles dans la société kabyle*. Paris: I'Harmattan.

Nathan, T. 1994 *L'influence qui guérit*. Paris: Odile Jacob.

Nguyen, Duong Binh 1966 Les vestiges des religions primitives chez les minorités du Nord Viêt Nam, Hà Noi, Revue, *Thông bao khoa Hoc* 42-6.

Nguyen, Phong 1990 *Chau Van possession ritual from Viêt Nam*. USA: World Music Enterprise.

Nguyen, Thê Anh 1991 Thiên Y A Na ou la récupération de la déesse Cam Pô Nagar par la monarchie confucéenne viêtnamienne. In *Cultes populaires et sociétés asiatiques*. Paris: L'Harmattan, 73-86.

Nguyen, Van Chien 1963 *La famille viêtnamienne dans son rapport avec les croyances religieuses*. 3rd cycle doctorate thesis in sociology, Strasbourg.

Nguyen, Van Huyên 1994 *Le culte immortel en Annam*. Hanôi: Imprimerie d'Extrême Orient.

Nguyen, Van Khoan 1933 *Le repêchage de l'âme*. Paris: BEFEO XXXIII; 11-34.

Phan Kê Binh 1980 *Moeurs et coutumes du Viêt Nam*, traduction par Nicole Louise-Hénard. Paris: Textes et Document EFEO.

Phan Thi Dac 1966 *La situation de la personne au Viêtnam*. Paris: CNRS.

Schipper, K. 1982 *Le corps taoïste*. Paris: Fayard.

Simon, P.J. et Simon Barouh, I 1973 Hâu Bong, un culte viêtnamien de possession transplanté en France, *Cahiers de l'Homme*. Paris: Mouton, EHESS.

Tran, Van Toan 1966 La sainte religion de l'immortelle céleste dans la région de Huê (Centre Viêt Nam), *Revue du Sud Est Asiatique*. Belgique, no. 1; 77-102, no. 2; 241-58.

——— 1967 La sainte religion de l'immortelle céleste dans la région de, Huê, Thiên Thanh giao (Centre Viêt Nam), *Revue du Sud Est Asiatique*. Belgique, no. 1, 103-30.

——— 1969 Note sur la sainte religion de l'immortelle céleste dans la région de Huê, Thien Tiên Thanh giao. *Bulletin de la société de études indochinoises*, XLVI: 245-82.

Truong, Dinh Hoè 1988 *Les immortels viêtnamiens d' aprés le Hôi Chân Biên*. Paris: EFEO, TDI no. XVI.

Plate 14: The medium takes the pulse of the patient (River of Perfumes).

Plate 15: The medium consults his protector.

La prise en charge de l'affliction: possession et cultes thérapeutiques en Asie du Sud

MARINE CARRIN

Les contributions réunies dans ce volume montrent à quel point la frontière entre maladie et infortune est ténue. En effet, les systèmes médicaux du sous-continent, loin d'exprimer une dualité toute cartésienne du corps et de l'esprit, sont marqués par des conceptions de la personne diversifiées. On peut se demander à la suite de l'anthropologie américaine, si une théorie indienne des émotions ne vient pas modeler, en Asie du Sud, une expérience autre du Sujet.

Si l'interdit est universel sa répression peut s'organiser selon des modalités différentes. Se refusant à appliquer ici la distinction entre maladie physique et maladie mentale, les études présentées constatent, toutes, qu'en Asie du Sud, la possession démoniaque exprime des désordres variés, que les tenants de l'analyse freudienne nomment hystérie, et qui reçoit des thérapeutes locaux des appellations diverses. En effet, il ne s'agit pas d'enfermer le malade et son symptôme dans un diagnostic mais plutôt de l'inviter à fréquenter un sanctuaire religieux, dont le dispositif symbolique contribue à l'efficacité de la cure.

En Inde, la prise en charge de l'affliction devient une préoccupation collective car la famille du malade n'hésite pas à entreprendre un long voyage pour se rendre dans un lieu de pèlerinage réputé, la tombe d'un saint musulman, ou le temple d'une déesse hindoue. Les patients et leurs familles campent dans les prémisses du sanctuaire où les accueillent diverses catégories d'officiants qui les soumettent au rythme particulier de la circambulation, les invitant à parcourir différents itinéraires qui vont exprimer peu à peu la traversée résolue de leurs angoisses. En effet, c'est la reconnaissance de la possession démoniaque, comme source de conflits et sa résolution par la possession divine, qui permet déjà au sujet d'être enfin possédé par le saint, ou la déesse, qui le délivrera de son mal et fera de lui un dévot, souvent capable de prendre en charge l'autre .

Dans d'autres cas, le guérisseur peut libérer le patient de sa culpabilité en produisant, sous hypnose, une seconde personnalité qui a déjà assouvi les désirs les plus sombres du consultant. Dans ce cas, la représentation imagée de la faute ou de la transgression tient lieu de réparation morale.

Le modèle explicatif du thérapeute indigène varie selon le groupe social d'appartenance de ce dernier; par exemple, le praticien traditionnel hindou, de haut statut, s'appuie sur les concepts de la médecine ayurvédique qu'il articule aux critères de la psychiatrie occidentale, considérant que la maladie mentale est une perte de conscience. A l'inverse, le thérapeute chrétien pratique l'hypnose et élabore une théorie où des éléments de morale chrétienne se mèlent au mesmérisme et traduisent l'opposition du normal et du pathologique.

Les sanctuaires musulmans qui sont souvent des hauts lieux du soufisme évoquent, bien sûr, d'autres courants spirituels avec lesquels ils ont fusionné, telle l'idéologie indienne du renoncement qui transparaît dans l'idéal du saint et qui s'exprime, encore plus clairement, dans les étapes obligées de la quête spirituelle des chamanes ou des médiums.

Comme le renonçant, le chamane doit se retirer en forêt et quitter un certain nombre de ses attachements au monde. De même, le médium hindou, fondateur d'un sanctuaire thérapeutique, ou officiant d'un temple consacré à la Déesse, a souvent obtenu ses pouvoirs au terme d'une crise spirituelle. La relation duelle qu'il établit avec chacun de ses patients, tient compte de leur histoire, même si les suggestions qu'il leur propose ressemblent, souvent, à de simples prescriptions rituelles. En effet, ce type de médium ou de prêtresse assument plusieurs identités dans la mesure où, dans certains cas, l'inversion sexuelle marque chez eux la prise de conscience distancée de leurs angoisses passées. Les rites qu'ils célèbrent à l'intention de leurs clients leur permettent donc d'assumer plusieurs identités possibles au cours de l'exorcisme, et de conjurer ainsi les démons qui, eux aussi, changent de forme et de nom.

Toutefois, dans d'autres cas, le chamane loin d'établir cette relation duelle avec son patient, propose à ce dernier un horizon symbolique façonné par l'histoire locale.

Si les femmes sont, en Inde, davantage victimes de possession démoniaque que les hommes, c'est sans doute parce que les transes leur fournissent le moyen d'exprimer des revendications impossibles à formuler dans le contexte familial. C'est en ce sens que la société exprime l'idée que les femmes sont les patientes privilégiées des cultes thérapeutiques tandis que les hommes, souvent aux prises avec l'autorité paternelle, fréquentent avec assiduité des guérisseurs et des chamanes. Les thérapeutes locaux parviennent à décharger les patients de leurs angoisses en les délivrant de la culpabilité de leurs fautes, en s'appuyant également sur l'entourage des malades qui, souvent, prennent part à la cure.

Si la question de la spécificité de l'Oedipe indien reste bien sûr ouverte, notons au passage, le caractère possessif de la mère indienne qui s'exerce surtout sur les garçons jusqu'à un âge tardif, plusieurs des articles réunis dans ce volume soulignent combien la possession sert à exprimer des conflits psychologiques. D'autres concepts centraux dans la culture hindoue, telles les notions du pur et de l'impur, traduisent souvent des dégrés de malêtre: ainsi l'impureté apparaît-elle liée à l'expression de l'angoisse.

Certains temples et lieux de pélerinage ont la réputation de guérir ceux qui souffrent de possession démoniaque. Les pélerins et leurs familles ont toute confiance en l'efficacité symbolique de tels lieux qui, grâce à l'évocation du pouvoir d'un saint ou d'une déesse, rechargent le corps et l'esprit du pélerin d'une énergie nouvelle. Ainsi, le patient est délivré des démons qui l'assiègent pour être enfin possédé par le personnage divin dont le pouvoir curatif va l'apaiser. Les actes auxquels on soumet le patient, circambulation, flagellation, jeûne, bain glacé, silence, le soumettent à une forme d'autorité proche d'une autorité parentale et lui permettent d'accèder à une dimension universelle, celle du Soi, qui transcende l'individu prisonnier de son histoire personnelle et de ses symptômes.

Si toutes les contributions soulignent la nécessité de nommer le démon et de dépossèder le patient de son mal, les représentations conceptuelles de la maladie mentale diffèrent selon les cas: ainsi, pour les brahmanes du Kérala, la maladie mentale est une sorte de refuge pour ceux qui ne peuvent faire face à la réalité, tandis qu' au Karnataka, elle résulte souvent d'une transgression ou d'une faute. Toutefois, le manque, la perte, le vide qui attirent le Sujet vers son délire peuvent être comblés par l'image parentale et divine du dieu ou du saint. Soit, la cure implique une seconde naissance dans une sorte de lignée spirituelle, soit elle fait découvrir au patient une seconde personnalité enfouie au plus profond de lui-même. C'est pourquoi, en Asie du Sud comme au Viêtnam, la psychiatrie et la médecine moderne s'évertuent en vain à soulager les âmes. Si plusieurs des articles soulignent bien que les patients et leurs familles ont intériorisé certaines catégories nosologiques de la médecine occidentale, souvent présente sur le terrain, ils concluent aussi que cette dernière ne résout pas de manière satisfaisante le problème de l'étiologie qui est toujours ancré dans l'histoire du sujet.

Toutefois, si le chamane ou le médium sont, parfois, des intercesseurs privilégiés, ce n'est pas seulement parce qu'ils dépossèdent le patient de ses démons mais aussi, parce qu'ils sont partie prenante des enjeux politiques et idéologiques de la communauté. Dès lors, la question de l'identité du groupe, caste ou tribu, hindous, musulmans, confucianistes ou chrétiens, s'inscrit en filigrane dans toute demande individuelle, car au niveau étiologique il n'est pas rare que le mal soit attribué à l'Autre. L'hindou, qui se croit victime d'un sort jeté par son voisin musulman trouvera la paix en visitant la tombe d'un saint de l'Islam, car en se souciant des dieux de ses voisins, on abolit ainsi les différences que créent les frictions quotidiennes.

Les sanctuaires thérapeutiques, tout comme les petits temples ou officient médiums et chamanes sont des hauts lieux de tolérance où la famille du malade apprend à accepter le "désordre" qui l'accablait avant la visite au sanctuaire. La solidarité qui unit les patients et leurs familles s'exprime parfois par le truchement de la possession, puisque les patients de certains sanctuaires peuvent, sous l'emprise des transes, suggérer des remèdes aux maux qui accablent leurs voisins.

Celui qui part apaisé, sait pourtant qu'il lui faut revenir car l'expérience de la maladie, puis de la cure, lui ont fait découvrir que s'il attribuait parfois à ses voisins l'origine de son mal, il peut aussi leur être redevable.

Reste a savoir si les patients s'en retournent guéris, ou simplement apaisés pour un temps. Les auteurs des différentes contributions n'ont pas toujours la même appréciation de la valeur curative du traitement. Tous soulignent, néanmoins, l'importance de la possession du rite d'exorcisme qui neutralise la violence des trances provoquées par des esprits malveillants. La fréquentation assidue des lieux de pélérinage inscrit dans un processus diacronique et collectif les afflictions individuelles: dès lors, les anciens novices deviennent des initiés.

Si certains des auteurs de ce volume nous mettent en garde contre les dangers du psychologisme, la plupart s'accordent à souligner l'importance de la relation duelle (prêtre/possédé) qui joue sur les différents registres culturels et religieux. La cure permet de mettre à distance le malêtre, qui s'inscrit dans un registre cosmologique et renvoie, à travers de multiples formes de l'alterité, qui tour à tour assaillaient le patient, à l'histoire même du sujet. Le rituel permet ainsi une dépersonnalisation par le truchement d'une série d'identifications aux figures divines qui dépossèdent avant tout le devot de lui-même pour le rendre capable d'affronter sa propre vie.

Résumés français des articles

Et pourtant, ils tournent . . . religion, maladie et thérapeutique dans le Sud de l'Inde

J. ASSAYAG (Dir. Sciences Sociales, Institut Français de Pondichéry)

A partir du constat de l'absence d'une définition monotypique des catégories nosologiques et du caractère variable, dynamique et négocié des descriptions pathogéniques dans la culture populaire du Sud de l'Inde, l'observation du culte rendu à un saint musulman au Karnataka—intercesseur local d'Allah —montre comment maladie et infortune se confondent, religion et thérapeutique se chevauchent; par le moyen collectif notamment de la transe giratoire autour du divin défunt, cette décharge d'affects qui induit la possession et prépare à l'exorcisme. La circumambulation rituelle représente une initiation en communication avec le saint: l'évanouissement permet de se décharger des émotions ambivalentes et la rotation contribue à dépersonnaliser l'individu tout en lui permettant de structurer un comportement deviant auquel il confère une expression choréographique. Celle-ci traduit à la fois les angoisses profondes et la quête religieuse des possédés. Traitement "systémique" rendu efficace par l'organisation structurale et psycho-dynamique (stéréotypée) de ce type de complexe culturel, reliant Terre et Ciel, qui, en autorisant périodiquement la symbolisation des maux et des dissociations psychiques, facilite l'insertion des individus malades ou affligés dans la famille, le lignage, la communauté. Se gardant d'une interprétation en termes psychologiques, l'auteur préfère priviligier l'action rituelle et les transformations qu'elle est susceptible de provoquer chez les dévots. La dimension de l'alterité, telle qu'elle s'exprime dans le contenu religieux, n'est donc nullement réductible à la traduction des désordres par des termes thérapeutiques. En revanche, l'opposition spatiale du saint, enterré dans sa tombe, et duquel exhale le *baraka* , et des démons qui assiègent incessament le corps des possédés, est systématique. Ces deux dimensions—horizontale et terrestre d'un coté, verticale et celeste de l'autre, constituent l'architecure onirique du *dargāh.*

Tourner en rond sur le chemin droit au Nom du Père. Une étude de la transe de dépossession à Murugmalla

DR. FRANCK ROLLIER (Psychiatre et psychanalyste, Antibes)

A Murugmalla, (Karnataka), les possédés rentrent en transe autour du tombeau (*dargāh*) d'un Saint de l'Islam. Au-delà de la personne sociale, y-a-t-il une place pour un Sujet entre le moment de l'apparition des symptômes et de l'angoisse, leur reconnaissance comme Possession, l'invitation à la transe (*Ṭawāf*) et l'initiation religieuse comme fin de culte? L'auteur propose une approche psychanalytique du rituel et de sa fonction dans l'économie psychique des possédés, qui se reconnaissent comme telles, et acceptent d'entrer en trance. Les cas analysés correspondent aux pathologies neurotiques ou psychotiques, ou même psychosomatiques, qui, parfois, ont leur équivalent dans la nosologie locale des désordres. Devenu objet de jouissance de l'autre qui l'habite, le possédé est prié de tourner rond et il s'essaye à mettre au pas ses démons convoqués devant le tombeau du Père. Ainsi, le *dargāh* est une "porte ouverte" . . . sur l'univers symbolique, la transe une expérience de langage et c'est par la nomination que le malêtre trouvera un Sens, faisant transiter le Sujet de l'expérience de la faille . . . à la révèlation de la faute. Qu'advient-il alors de la dette des vivants envers les morts? Et, s'il y a guérision à Murugmalla, quel en est le prix?

Pour l'auteur, Murugmalla et d'autres lieux de même nature en Inde, fonctionnent comme un "centre" qui permet d'actualiser la situation oedipienne, avec toutes les dimensions d'identification, de séduction, d'aggressivité et de jouissance qu'elle comporte. Le culte a donc une fonction normative, car il propose un modèle autorisé de disfonctionnement.

Le sanctuaire thérapeutique des tombes de Jod Gomaz, Karnataka

Y.J. SHOBHA DEVI ET G.S.BIDARAKOPPA (Université de Dharwar, Karnataka)

Cette étude porte sur un des sanctuaires musulmans les plus populaires, le Jod Gomaz Dargah de Bijapur, au Karnataka. Deux tombes, celle du saint et de son disciple caractérisent ce *dargāh* qui, depuis le dix-huitième siècle, est un lieu de pélerinage soufi. Ici, les malades, qu'ils soient hindous ou musulmans, viennent chercher la guérison de leurs maux. La durée symbolique de la cure est de quarante jours durant lesquels les malades et leurs familles vivent dans l'enceinte du sanctuaire. L'attitude de la famille du malade contribue à la cure, car les parents multiplient les gestes symboliques efficaces destinés à soutenir le patient et à l'accompagner dans le processus de guérison. Les patients guéris reviennent périodiquement offrir leur dévotion à l'esprit du saint et prennent symboliquement en charge les nouveaux arrivés qu'ils ont à charge de nourrir.

La possession, surtout féminine, est au centre du rituel au cours duquel on demande au démon de quitter le corps de la personne qu'il assiège. A cette possession démoniaque s'opposent les transes inspirées par l'esprit du saint au cours desquelles, le ou la possédée suggèrent comment remèdier aux douleurs des autres clients du sanctuaire. Le concept de Hazari, "le souci de veiller sur autrui" rend les anciens malades solidaires des nouveaux et fait de ce rituel un culte thérapeutique.

Souffrir pour devenir Soi-même: approche comparative de la thérapie traditionnelle au Bengale et au Karnataka

MARINE CARRIN (Centre d'Anthropologie des Sociétés Rurales' CNRS, Toulouse)

Cette étude traite des conceptions de la maladie et de l'infortune et des réponses symboliques qu'elles suscitent dans deux régions de l'Inde, le Bengale et le Karnataka. Au Bengale, les hommes et les femmes, originaires des basses castes et des tribus, fréquentent un grand nombre de sanctuaires thérapeutiques villageois où des prêtres-devins gèrent les désordres qui, souvent, se manifestent sous la forme de la possession. Dans ce contexte où religion tribale et hindouisme se côtoient, les identités fragmentées des groupes permettent l'émergence de l'individu au prix d'une crise personnelle, qui souvent, révèle une quête spirituelle. En effet, cette crise se dénoue chez les femmes quand les possédées acquièrent des qualités viriles et deviennent prêtresses. Chez les hommes, des signes de féminité viennent ponctuer l'acquisition des pouvoirs spirituels.

Au Karnataka, il existe des cultes thérapeutiques traditionnels où des patientes, surtout féminines, projettent les tensions qui les agitent sur des figures mythiques, agents autorisés d'une possession sacrée et non polluante. Contrairement à la situation qui prévaut au Bengale, la cure ne transforme pas le patient en guérisseur mais invite celui-ci à fréquenter d'autres types de sanctuaires où officient les prêtres possédés par la Déesse, qui sont, soit des officiants ayant acquis leur charge de façon héréditaire, soit, au contraire des médiums ayant fondé des sanctuaires au terme d'une crise individuelle.

Dans les deux régions, la dévotion dont la Déesse (souvent Kali) est l'objet, vient rythmer les étapes de l'élection spirituelle. Toutefois, tandis qu' au Bengale la divinité se manifeste sous la forme d'un destin inexorable, elle doit au Karnataka partager son pouvoir avec les *bhûtas*, démons, proches des dieux. C'est dans cette région qu'on rencontre des cultes thérapeutiques dont les adeptes sont des femmes qui, au cours des rites, sont possédées par un *bhûta* féminin, qui symbolise la condition difficile des femmes dans la société matrilinéaire.

Chamanes dépossédés et contre-sorciers dans les villages d'Inde du Sud

Frédéric Bourdier (Université de Bordeaux et CNRS)

Au Tamilnadu, deux pratiques thérapeutiques, le chamanisme et la médecine de type occidental s'imposent au détriment d'autres systèmes médicaux; telle la médecine ayurvédique traditionnelle. Le chamane, guérisseur et "danseur possédé", souvent originaire des basses castes et des tribus, rend un culte aux déesses de village et entretient une relation privilégiée avec ses esprits tutélaires. Elu par les divinités de la forêt, ce guérisseur doit, comme le renonçant, pratiquer certaines formes d'ascèse avant de pouvoir recevoir son initiation. Toutefois, tandis que la médecine et la chirurgie moderne deviennent de plus en plus sophistiquées même en milieu rural, les malades s'en détournent au profit des guérisseurs traditionnels qui, mieux que les praticiens modernes, se penchent sur l'origine et la cause du malêtre et de l'infortune.

Le nombre des chamanes ne cesse de croître et les rivalités qu'ils entretiennent et qui s'expriment au cours des grandes fêtes traduisent, par le truchement de la possession, les tensions qui agitent leurs groupes religieux d'appartenance. L'auteur souligne qu'en cas d'échec dans la cure traditionnelle, les villageois critiquent d'avantage tel ou tel chaman particulier, qu'ils ne remettent en question le shamanisme. La même attitude s'observe vis à vis des médécins modernes qu'on remet en cause individuellement, en cas de diagnostic erroné. En revanche, les services de santé publics sont perçus comme un corps déshumanisé, pourvu d'acteurs sociaux et responsables.

Toutefois, la présence de la médecine moderne planifiée par le gouvernement a poussé les chamanes "dépossédés" à agir avec plus de rationalité et à administrer des remèdes, tandis que les médecins puisent inconsciemment dans le registre religieux des symboles d'efficacité destinés à répondre à la demande qui leur est adressée.

Thérapie "psycho-religieuse au Kérala: une forme d'intéraction entre discours scientifique et traditions locales.

Gilles Tarabout (CNRS-CEIAS, Paris)

L'étude est centrée sur l'analyse des pratiques de deux thérapeutes du Kérala, l'un est hindou, l'autre est chrétien. Leur discours à tous deux est celui de spécialistes du traitement des maladies mentales. Chacun développe cependant un modèle explicatif qui lui est spécifique: le thérapeute hindou, un brahmane de haut statut, s'appuie sur des concepts de la médecine ayurvédique qu'il articule à ceux de la psychiatrie occidentale; le thérapeute chrétien, un prêtre catholique, pratique l'hypnose et a élaboré sa propre théorie où se mêlent éléments empruntés à des traités occidentaux en psychologie, mesmérisme, ayurvéda et préoccupations de morale chrétienne. Ces deux spécialistes ont cependant en commun un même idéal de la santé mentale—et de la cure—en la faisant découler d'un vécu social harmonieux. Et tous deux font intervenir une action divine dans la guérison ("thérapie psycho-religieuse" qui est d'ailleurs une formule forgée par le prêtre).

Ce type d'intéraction entre discours renvoyant explicitement à la science occidentale et au système religieux traditionnel est très général au Kérala—rappelons que le niveau d'instruction est dans cet Etat élevé, et une importante diffusion de la presse écrite n'exclut pas pour autant un profond attachement à des valeurs et des pratiques "traditionnelles". Mais les deux spécialistes étudiés jouent également sur un autre registre, celui du quiproquo assumé entre leur propre logique et celle de leurs patients. Dans la mesure où l'idéal thérapeutique est dans les deux cas une réinsertion harmonieuse du malade dans son milieu d'origine, la notion de "prise de conscience", par le patient, de la "rationalité" développée par le spécialiste n'a aucune place. La plupart du temps, ceux qui viennent consulter avec leurs familles élaborent leurs troubles en termes de possession par des puissances divines ou par des mauvais morts: les thérapeutes rentrent entièrement dans cette logique, vis à vis de leurs clients, et procèdent à ce que ces derniers considèrent alors comme constituant des exorcismes. Les thérapeutes, eux-mêmes, ne sont d'ailleurs pas sans une certaine souplesse à ce sujet, et s'ils proclament qu'il s'agit le plus souvent d'une opération purement psychologique, ils admettent la possibilité d'une véritable possession, et donc d'un véritable exorcisme.

L'articulation entre modèle explicatif se réclamant de la psychologie occidentale et vision religieuse s'effectue ainsi selon deux modes simultanés: une tentative de synthèse conceptuelle, propre à chaque spécialiste mais dont le principe est très largement répandu dans la société locale; un double langage, qui permet de laisser intact les explications traditionnelles de la maladie et de l'infortune.

Lieux et souvenirs, un rituel d'exorcisme chez les Tharu de l'Ouest du Népal

GISÈLE KRAUSKOPFF (Laboratoire d'ethnologie et de sociologie comparative, Université de Nantaerre Paris-X et CNRS)

L'auteur s'attache à cerner une catégorie nosologique tharu, "la maladie" *dabāu*, qui donne lieu à des rituels d'exorcisme tout à fait spécifiques. L'état *dabāu* est provoqué par un choc initial marqué par une perte de conscience, suivi d'un désordre physique ou psychique qui donne lieu à divers symptômes. Au cours de la cure on rend un culte aux sept soeurs, déesses populaires qui vivent en forêt, contrôlent une armée d'esprits sauvages et se manifestent n'importe où. C'est au travers du discours de l'officiant principal, à savoir le contenu des récitatifs rituels et l'établissement de l'autel du sacrifice, qu'elle tente de dégager "l'horiżon symbolique" proprement tharu dans lequel le guérisseur développe son interprétation du désordre: l'environnement et plus particulièrement le milieu sauvage d'une part, certaines catégories anonymes de malemort (celles des inconnus qui ont de tout temps traversé les forêts du Terai) d'autre part, y tiennent la première place. L'auteur voit cependant dans le "paysage" ainsi déroulé, une toile en quelque sorte vide, où le guérisseur trace les troubles de chaque patient. Cette interprétation très formelle n'apparait dès lors que comme une première étape du traitement. Autour de questions partiellement sans réponse, l'auteur tente de dévoiler les autres éléments et acteurs qui concourent au rétablissement du patient, en insistant sur l'importance du travail du souvenir, de la mémoire sociale, et du rôle du "corps" villageois. Toutefois, l'auteur souligne que la compréhension du processus de guérisson ne peut être réduit à la seule analyse du rituel, dans la mesure où ce qui est signifiant pour la cure, peut survenir entre les différentes phases de l'exorcisme.

Rites thérapeutiques des médiums sampaniers et représentations de la personne à Hué (Viêt Nam)

DIDIER BERTRAND (Centre des équipes de Recherche en psycho-pathologie, Université de Toulouse le Mirail)

L'analyse porte ici sur l'étiologie des maladies à laquelle les médiums ont recours et les différents modes de prise en charge qu'ils pratiquent et qui soustendent les représentations de la personne. La perte d'âme, la possession par les esprits victimes de malemort, sont parmi les maux les plus difficiles à traiter. Au cours de la cure, les médiums font appel à différentes techniques thérapeutiques qui mettent en jeu des éléments appartenant à la culture chinoise, telle l'utilisation des idéogrammes qui possèdent une vertu magique pour les sampaniers illetrés. La cure combine l'exorcisme qui consiste à chasser les esprits malveillants, et l'adorcisme qui permet au médium de ramener et de fixer les âmes errantes. La légitimation des décisions thérapeutiques suppose la recherche d'un consensus social auquel le processus de dramatisation participe par une mise en scène rituelle: habits, transes, danse, musique, encens qui scandent les différentes étapes—purification, réconciliation et réintégration—au cours desquelles, les investissements corporels restent importants.

L'interprétation des troubles s'opère par une explication de la réalité que le médium articule au monde des divinités et des figures mythologiques dominé, dans ces rites, par une déesse viêtnamisée d'origine Cham.

Plusieurs dimensions se superposent et filent la trame des rites de cure: tandis que la fonction proprement curative de ces cérémonies se fonde sur la préparation "magique" des remèdes, le discours religieux—au cours duquel on s'adresse aux esprits—nous révèle la portée psycho-morale de ces rites qui visent également la réparation des fautes. La liturgie devient donc une thérapie collective au cours de laquelle les patients se justifient de leurs actes vis à vis des figures parentales et ancestrales.

Contributors

Jackie Assayag, anthropologist, is a research scholar at the Centre for Indian and South Asian Studies, Paris, and presently Head of the Department of Social Sciences at the French Institute, Pondicherry. He has done his fieldwork mainly in Karnataka, and has published two books: *The Wrath of the Beheaded Goddess: Traditions, Cults and Power in South India* (in French,1992); *A la confluence de deux rivières: Musulmans et Hindous en Asie du Sud,* Paris, EFEO, 1995. (Translation forthcoming, OUP). With G.Tarabout he is editing *Alterity and Identity: Christians and Muslims in South Asia* (1997). He is also the author of *Essais Fabuleux on French Orientalism* (forthcoming). He has published a large number of articles.

Didier Bertrand is assistant lecturer in intercultural psychology at the University of Toulouse II - le Mirail. His doctoral thesis (1992) dealt with the language learning, acculturation and psychological adjustment of Indo-Chinese refugees. He has since taught psychology at Huê and Phnom Penh, and is publishing several articles in cultural psychology based on Vietnamese and Cambodian material. At present he is studying the role of psychology in the Cambodian mental health system, and is also engaged in a WHO study of alcoholism in Cambodia.

Frédéric Bourdier is a researcher in Societies, Health and Development, a CNRS unit at the University of Bordeaux-II. After completing his Ph.D. on health systems and socio-cultural perceptions of disease in Tamilnadu, he has been staying 18 months in Cambodia, among the indigenous populations of the North East, dealing with indigenous views of land and environment. He is now in charge of a project in south India concerning sexual behavior and socio-epidemiological aspects of HIV/AIDS contagion. He recently wrote 'Therapeutic encounters in Southern India' in J.Benoist, *Soigner au pluriel*, Paris, Karthala, 1996, 'Health and Sickness in the village: An assessment of Health conditions in South India', 1995 and

'Management and social representation of the ecological setting among the Irula, *Cahiers d'Outre-mer*, Avril 1994, Bordeaux.

Marine Carrin, is a social anthropologist with the French National Center for Scientific Research (CNRS), and attached to the Center for Anthropology in Toulouse. She has done extensive research among the Santals of Bengal, Bihar and Orissa. Books: (in French): *The Flower and the Bone: Symbolism and Ritual in Santal Society*, Cahiers de l'Homme, XXVI, Paris, EHESS, 1986. (In English) *Inner Frontiers: Santal Responses to Acculturation*, Bergen: Chr. Michelsen Institute, and 'Children of the Goddess, Devotion and Priesthood in Bengal' (in French), Paris, CNRS, Maison des Sciences d l'Homme Editions. She has also published a large number of articles on the Santals. In preparation, *Ritual Discourse, content and argument in Santal society*. She is now concentrating on her material from Tulunadu and is publishing several articles on this region.

Gisèle Krauskopff, social anthropologist, is a research fellow with the CNRS and a member of the "Laboratoire d'ethnologie et de sociologie comparative" (Université de Nanterre-Paris X). Her previous researches on the Tharus of Dang (Western Nepal) are mainly ethno-historical in perspective, dealing with the relation between ritual and social order and the relation between the Tharus and the ancient Hindu kingdom of Dang (impact of Hindu political centralisation of the peculiar agrarian conditions in the Terai lowlands on the Tharu social structure). She is presently working on Tharu and other ethnic movements in Nepal. Her main publications include (in French): *Masters and possessed persons. Ritual and social order among the Tharus (Népal).* Editions du CNRS, Paris, 1989, and, with M. Lecomte-Tilouine: *Dasai as a celebration of power, A Royal festival in Nepal.* Paris, CNRS, Editions des Sciences de l'Homme, 1996. Emotions, mélodies saisonnières et rythmes de la nature. Recent articles include: La littérature orale des Tharu de Dang (Népal) *Purusartha* 18. *Traditions Orales dans le Monde Indien,* Paris, Ed. EHESS: 350-72.

Franck Rollier is a practicing psychiatrist and psychoanalyst at Antibes. His doctoral thesis in Psychiatry, at the Université de Paris -VI, dealt with *Murugmalla, Possession and Therapeutic Rituals in a Muslim Tomb of South India, An Ethnopsychiatric Study* (in French). He has since published several articles on the themes of his specialization.

Y.J. Shobha Devi and G.S. Bidarakoppa are lecturers in Social Work at Dharwar University, North Karnataka. They did the study of the Jod Gomaz together. This is their first international publication.

Gilles Tarabout is a social anthropologist with the CNRS, attached to the Centre for Indian and South Asian Studies (CEIAS), Paris. He also teaches at the National Institute of Oriental Languages and Civilizations, Paris. He studies the society, culture, and religion of Kerala, and his books include: *Sacrificing and giving to see: an anthropological approach of temple festivals in Kerala* (in French), Paris, EFEO, 1986, and, with D.Vidal and E. Meyer as co-editors: *Violence and Non-violence in India* (Paris, EHESS, 1993).With J.Assayag he is editing: *Alterity and Identity, Islam and Christianity in India*, Paris, EHESS, and *Studies on Possession in South Asia. Self, Territory and Borders* (Paris, EHESS). He is also the author of *The Invisible and the Tangible. Divine Images and Ritual in Hinduism*, Paris, Gallimard (in French, forthcoming).

Index